THE TEACHERS & WRITERS GUIDE TO
CLASSIC AMERICAN LITERATURE

The Teachers & Writers Guide to
Classic American Literature

❖ ❖ ❖ ❖ ❖

Edited by

Christopher Edgar

and Gary Lenhart

❖ ❖ ❖ ❖ ❖

Teachers & Writers Collaborative
in association with
The Library of America

The Teachers & Writers Guide to Classic American Literature

Library of Congress Cataloging-in-Publication Data

The teachers & writers guide to classic American literature / edited by
Christopher Edgar and Gary Lenhart.
   p. cm
   Includes bibliographic references.
   ISBN 0-915924-71-4 (pbk. alk. paper))
     1. American literature--Study and teaching. 2. Creative writing--study and teaching.
I. Edgar, Christopher, 1961-. II. Lenhart, Gary, 1947-.

   PS42 .N38 2001
   810.9'000071--dc21

                              2001026687

Teachers & Writers Collaborative
5 Union Square West
New York, NY 10003-3306

Cover and page design: Christopher Edgar

Printed by Philmark Lithographics, New York, N.Y.
First printing

Acknowledgments

Many thanks to Christina Davis for her insightful editing and moral support. Thanks to Cheryl Hurley of The Library of America for her help, advice, and support. Thanks also to Matthew Sharpe, Jordan Davis, Nina Cobb, and Nancy Larson Shapiro. And a special thanks to Louise Hamlin, Katy Lenhart, and Amy Gelber.

Teachers & Writers programs are made possible in part by grants from the New York City Department of Cultural Affairs and the National Endowment for the Arts, and with public funds from the New York State Council on the Arts, a State Agency. Teachers & Writers Collaborative is also grateful for support from the following foundations and corporations: AKC Fund, Axe-Houghton Foundation, The David and Minnie Berk Foundation, Bronx Borough President and City Council, The Bydale Foundation, The Cerimon Fund, The Saul Z. and Amy S. Cohen Family Foundation, Consolidated Edison, E.H.A. Foundation, The Janet Stone Jones Foundation, Low Wood Fund, Inc., Manhattan City Council Delegation, M & O Foundation, Morgan Stanley Dean Witter Foundation, NBC, New York Community Trust (Van Lier and Beth M. Uffner Funds), New York Times Company Foundation, Henry Nias Foundation, North Star Fund, The Open Society Institute, Queens Borough President and City Council, Joshua Ringel Memorial Fund, Maurice R. Robinson Fund, Rush Philanthropic Arts Foundation, St. Ann's School, The Scherman Foundation, and the Wendling Foundation. T&W's 30th-Anniversary Endowed Residencies are supported by Marvin Hoffman and Rosellen Brown, the New World Foundation, Steven Schrader, Alison Wylegala (in memory of Sergio Guerrero), John Gilman (in memory of June Baker), and anonymous donors.

Permissions

and Special Collections. Frederick Douglass, courtesy of the National Portrait Gallery. Nathaniel Hawthorne, courtesy of the National Portrait Gallery. Zora Neale Hurston, courtesy of the National Portrait Gallery. Photograph copyright © Estate of Carl Van Vechten. Gravure and Compilation copyright © Eakins Press Foundation. Herman Melville, courtesy of the Berkshire Athenaeum. Edward R. Murrow, courtesy of Bettmann/Corbis. Lorine Niedecker, courtesy of Jonathan Williams. Eugene O'Neill, courtesy of the National Portrait Gallery. Photograph copyright © Estate of Carl Van Vechten. Gravure and Compilation copyright © Eakins Press Foundation. Edgar Allen Poe, courtesy of Brown University Library. Anne Porter, courtesy of The Parrish Art Museum. Fairfield Porter (American, 1907–1975). Anne, 1965. Oil on canvas, 47 x 38 in. The Parrish Art Museum, Southampton, N.Y. Gift of the Estate of Fairfield Porter, 1980. (10.186). Gertrude Stein, courtesy of The Metropolitan Museum of Art, Bequest of Gertrude Stein, 1947. (47.106). Photograph © 1996 The Metropolitan Museum of Art. Wallace Stevens, courtesy of Bettmann/Corbis. Henry David Thoreau, courtesy of the National Portrait Gallery. Jean Toomer, courtesy of Bettmann/Corbis. Walt Whitman, courtesy of the National Portrait Gallery. William Carlos Williams, courtesy of New Directions Publishing Corporation. Special thanks to the George Adams Gallery for use of Leslie Dill's painting *Poem Hands* (1995). Private Collection. Photo courtesy of George Adams Gallery, New York.

"January Morning" by William Carlos Williams, from *Collected Poems: 1909–1939, Volume 1*, copyright © 1938 by New Directions Publishing Corp. Reprinted by permission of New Directions Publishing Corp. "Thirteen Ways of Looking at a Blackbird" from *The Collected Poems of Wallace Stevens*, copyright 1954 by Wallace Stevens. Used by permission of Alfred A. Knopf, a division of Random House, Inc. "In Childhood," "Getting Up Early," "Looking at the Sky," "A Child at the Circus," and "Four Poems in One" by Anne Porter. Copyright 1994 by Anne Porter. From *An Altogether Different Language: Poems 1934–1994*, Zoland Books, Cambridge, Massachusetts. Used by permission of the author. "My Life by Water" from *The Granite Pail* by Lorine Niedecker. Used by permission of Jonathan Greene of Gnomon Press. "At the Fishhouses" from *The Complete Poems: 1927–1979* by Elizabeth Bishop. Copyright © 1979, 1983 by Alice Helen Methfessel. Reprinted by permission of Farrar, Straus and Giroux, LLC. The following essays appeared in previous Teachers & Writers publications: "Poets to Come" by Bill Zavatsky, in *The Teachers & Writers Guide to Walt Whitman* (revised for this current volume); "Language Is Power" by Lorenzo Thomas, in *The Teachers & Writers Guide to Frederick Douglass*; "Teaching James Baldwin" by Phillip Lopate, "*Cane* in the Classroom" by Julie Patton, and "Square Toes and Icy Arms" by Catherine Barnett, in *Sing the Sun Up: Creative Writing Ideas from African American Literature*; "'Stretchers,' Hairballs, and Whoopin' in the Fog" by Yvonne Murphy, in *Classics in the Classroom*; and "The Blackbird Is Flying, the Children Must Be Writing" by Sam Swope, in *The Alphabet of the Trees*.

Table of Contents

Introduction

What is American literature? What distinguishes it from English literature, or literature written in English in other former British colonies? In "The American Scholar," Emerson called for a literature emerging from the particularities of the new nation. Writers and scholars have been debating ever since just what those "particularities" consist of. In his 1855 preface to *Leaves of Grass*, Walt Whitman vaunted an indigenous literature based on the triumph of the common person over the vestiges of European feudalism. Writers as disparate as Mark Twain, William Carlos Williams, H. L. Mencken, Langston Hughes, and Margaret Walker have responded to Whitman's call. Other writers, such as Nathaniel Hawthorne, Henry Adams, Henry James, and Ezra Pound, have been less sanguine about America's contribution to culture and have warned of the dangers of democracy, particularly in regard to aesthetics. In practice, it may even be deceptive to assign individual writers to one side or the other of this divide. By the time he wrote *Democratic Vistas* (1871), Whitman himself was so sobered by the "piled embroider'd shoddy gaud and fraud" (*Poetry and Prose* [New York: The Library of America, 1982], p. 954) of the Gilded Age that he described democracy as still very much in an embryonic stage, with its "fruition ... altogether in the future" (p. 956). Still he proclaimed that the achievements of a democratic literature would eventually surpass the achievements of "any haut-ton coteries in all the records of the world" (p. 944).

In his *Studies in Classic American Literature* (1913), D. H. Lawrence offered an important outsider perspective on American literature, raging against the contradictions and inconsistencies that exist side by side in the greatest American books (e.g., Poe's tales, Hawthorne's *The Scarlet Letter* and *The Blithedale Romance*, Melville's *Moby-Dick*). It's difficult to tell whether Lawrence was bothered most by those authors unaware of these discrepancies, or by those pragmatists such as Emerson and Whitman who acknowledged their own contradictions with a shrug and good-natured "So what?" In the same spirit, I admit my own ambivalence to any hard and fast definition of American literature, but am confident that any definition must make room for the writers and poets discussed here.

There is a bias in the selection of American writers discussed in this book: included are those whose stories, poems, plays, and essays lend themselves most readily to use in teaching creative writing. The mission of Teachers & Writers Collaborative has always been at once pragmatic and inspirational: pragmatic, because as teachers our enthusiasms are tempered by the response of the students before us at the moment; inspirational, because we agree with Emerson that schools "can only highly serve us when they aim not to drill, but to create; when they gather from far every ray of various genius to their hospitable halls, and by the concentrated fires, set the hearts of their youth on flame" ("The American Scholar," *Essays and Lectures* [New York: The Library of America, 1983], p.59).

It goes without saying that the teachers who wrote the essays included here found that certain writers—some long dead—really spoke to their students. And not surprisingly, these teachers of writing were themselves fired by their subjects. Jordan Clary presents a poem by Stephen Crane to teenagers because the poem moved her powerfully when she was a teen. Clary also discovers to her own surprise that the poems of Emily Dickinson hold special appeal for men in prison. Lorenzo Thomas finds in Frederick Douglass an awareness that resonates thunderously 150 years later. As Bob Blaisdell burrows his way through a professional editorial assignment, he finds more and more in Henry David Thoreau that would be useful to his students. Kristin Prevallet discovers that the dispatches of World War II can inspire highly diverse students in New York City to explore their responses to the nightmare of contemporary conflicts.

All the American poets and writers covered in this book are included in the valuable Library of America series, a non-profit publishing venture that has been issuing comprehensive, authoritative editions of American writing since 1982, some 129 titles to date. Most writers published in the series have one or more volumes devoted to their work, and many others are represented in anthologies of poetry and journalism. Basing our book on these editions allows a convenient uniformity of primary texts, so you needn't rustle through a haphazard group of editions searching for that passage of Gertrude Stein or those lines from Henry James.

It may be inevitable that certain American writers are missing whom you would like to see included. We regret that Benjamin Franklin, Francis Parkman, Willa Cather, and W. E. B. Du Bois, to name a few, were left out, but none of our contributors used those authors directly to teach creative writing.

Assembling this book has been a pleasure. Some of these books I and my colleagues at Teachers & Writers had never read before, many we recalled fondly from our own school days. The problem with canonical texts is that having read them in school, we sometimes assume we have finished with them. Editing this book provided a reminder that these books continue to be read because they can be read over and over without exhausting their riches. To paraphrase a plaque long popular in roadside gift shops, "The older we get, the better these books seem."

—*Gary Lenhart*

[The first immigrants] saw birds with rusty breasts and called them robins. Thus, from the start, an America of which they could have had no inkling drove the first settlers upon their past. They retreated for warmth and reassurance to something previously familiar. But at a cost. For what they saw were not robins. They were thrushes only vaguely resembling the rosy, daintier English bird. Larger, stronger, and in the evening of a wilder, lovelier song, actually here was something the newcomers had never in their lives before encountered.

—William Carlos Williams, "The American Background"

Stephen Crane

Emily Dickinson

Walt Whitman

Jordan Clary

Three Voices

Teaching Stephen Crane, Emily Dickinson, and Walt Whitman

MOST OF MY TEACHING EXPERIENCES have been with shifting populations: students in continuation schools or court-probated day schools, or adults in prison. A given student may attend only one class or may come regularly for years. Because of this, I have had to design lessons that are short and can be read and responded to within a single session and at the same time accommodate the long-term student who wants to study an author or genre more in-depth. With a large folder full of poetry and lesson plans with me, I can usually respond to whatever a particular class needs. I try to present each group with a wide range, including both contemporary and classical literature, translations from other countries, and both formal and free verse. Three American authors I have used with differing results are Stephen Crane, Emily Dickinson, and Walt Whitman.

Stephen Crane

When I began working with teenagers, some of the initial poems I introduced to them were selections from Stephen Crane's *The Black Riders.* One of these was "In the Desert":

> In the desert
> I saw a creature, naked, bestial,
> Who, squatting upon the ground,
> Held his heart in his hands,
> And ate of it.
> I said, "Is it good, friend?"
> "It is bitter—bitter," he answered;
> "But I like it
> "Because it is bitter,
> "And because it is my heart."

I chose "In the Desert" because it is a poem with which I had personal experience. I first read the poem as a high school sophomore. My English teacher, Mrs. Mullins, was not like the other teachers at Jackson High. Young, beautiful and free-spirited, she was married to an artist and prone to leave books lying around her classroom that were supposed to be too mature for young readers. "In the Desert" was my first encounter with free verse. The poem's raw anguish struck a chord in me and I copied it down in my notebook. In fact, I learned the poem by heart and wrote it out from memory many times. With the passage of time I forgot who the author was. Then one day in graduate school I chanced across the Index of First Lines and decided to look up the poem's author. I was surprised to find it was Stephen Crane.

Since I thought that "In the Desert" has a certain angst that adolescents might respond to, I decided to try it with high school students. At the time, I was working in a continuation school in Susanville, California, a rural area in the north-eastern part of the state.

I tried to make my classes at the continuation school refuges as much as possible. I wanted the students to explore their ideas. It wasn't always easy. After I introduced Stephen Crane to them and read "In the Desert," I asked them to write down what they thought was the central metaphor of his work. They wrote pain, anger, bad weather, and death. Usually when I introduce a poem I pass out a typed copy so the students can follow along. This time, however, I deliberately wanted them to just listen. After the first reading, which had been followed by some discussion and their comments along the lines of "gross," or "I don't get it," I read through the poem a second time and had them just listen once more. As I read through the poem line by line, I paused to give them time to respond to each line by writing one of their own. When we finished I asked for three or four volunteers and we read the poem back line by line in a sort of round robin. After that, each student read aloud his or her entire poem. I also asked them to read their poems backwards from the last line to the first, an exercise I learned from a Nevada poet, Shawn Griffin. I've found that this helps beginning writers to become closer listeners. The resulting poems were quite imitative, yet they had much of the flavor of Crane's style:

> Dry, sandy, filled with cacti—
> an animal with darting, red eyes and a
> black, coarse coat.
> Protruding fangs.
> There was an awful mess. He looked

at his heart with pride as he
held it.
He knew how much hatred
he had thought for others.
"So wrong," he muttered.
"But it's me. I want it like that.
Because it's who I am."

—*Jamie Purvis*

A hot, arid place
with red and blue all about.
He dined on raw emotion,
wondering what he would do with his life.
He devours affection,
curious about the taste of love.
I asked it of him.
He said, "Love is sweet at first,
but it can go sour.
Still, it is divine,
for it is what you want it to be."

—*Rob Brocksen*

I asked my conscience if it's good to feel this pain.
I replied, "It sucks."
But I am content,
Because it sucks
And because it is my pain.

—*Cary Harrison*

I was especially intrigued by Cary's response. Cary had been at the school for only a few months. He used to sit at his desk hunched into his jacket staring at his hands, his mind far away from the classroom. The writing he did do was scrawled in great, loping letters across the page, each phrase bleeding into the next. It was often incoherent. This poem was something of a breakthrough for him as it was the first piece he ever completed, and although it was short, it adequately followed the assignment.

The next step was to have the students move beyond imitating Crane and write poems that were truly their own. It was still early in the year and most of the students were somewhat wary of poetry.

"How long should it be?" they asked.

"As long or as short as it needs to be," I told them. I have found the mention of brevity has the opposite effect, that it inspires students to write long, rambling pieces.

The poems the students at the continuation school wrote dealt with alienation and pain. There is a lot of heartache in kids whose entire lives are controlled by "the system." They live in foster homes or with broken, drug-addicted parents. Many expressed feelings such as these, from Danny Cressi:

The brick wall rises
infinite
between me
and myself.

Another student, Rick Baker, lived about fifty miles away in Ravendale, a town whose population fluctuates somewhere around 150. Before I became a writer-in-residence, I had sometimes substituted at the two-room schoolhouse for grades K–8 in Ravendale, and I had known Rick as an eighth grader in that school. There is a certain surreal quality to little high desert communities. The people are wary. They come in from ranches and trailers wedged into rocky ravines off dirt roads. Few of the homes have electricity; the school gets its electricity from a generator. The average attendance for most students is once or twice a week and they regard the teachers with suspicion.

When I encountered Rick again at the continuation school he described his hometown with phrases such as "sizzling serenity," "flat shadows." The wind was a "concert of chaos." Rick preferred to write short, descriptive paragraphs rather than poems. "Go for it," I told him. Later, I would go back over his writing with him and point out to him what I thought were the strongest parts. The following is an excerpt from a long, descriptive piece Rick wrote following the Stephen Crane exercise:

Shadows from the corners of sleep. Tweaked. Get wired. No food. Lots of drink. Tires screech as the big green Ford tears down the dusty dirt road.

Someone strikes a match. Watches for aliens. Gazing from the window of the two-story farm house at the motionless star. They swear it's moving.

Gather rock. Flat rock. Flat rock.

Tongue and teeth. The punishment of Ravendale.

Emily Dickinson

There is no way to work in a prison and not feel as if your blood has turned to concertina wire in your veins. There are sounds unique to prison: the creak of heavy doors sliding open, the jarring clang of them slamming shut, the beeps of scanners as you slide your ID under a laser. You are issued keys that look like dinosaur teeth that you have to loop over your belt, a cold reminder of where you are. There is a tenseness, a violence and hatred in the air. As I drove home after a night of teaching at the prison, watching the moon shining over the sage and bitter brush of the high desert, I couldn't stop thinking about the men inside, about the revolving, colorless world, the 80,000 watt bulbs that circle all night long from the tower, the yard, and the lethal electric fence surrounding it all.

The creative writing classes I taught were through the Arts-in-Corrections program, which also offered classes in music, visual arts, and drama. The instructors were not state-paid employees but independent contractors. At least one of my classes always took place on the high-security yard, where most of the men were doing anywhere from several years to life. Because of this, there was a constancy to my classes. Many of the men told me that the arts programs literally saved them. It was the one place they could escape the tension of the yard and for a short time explore their creative urges. Very few wrote about prison life. Most turned to memories and imagination, to anything that took them away from those gray walls.

One week a young man joined the class who remembered reading Emily Dickinson in school. He couldn't remember her poems, but something about her style stayed with him and he asked me if I would bring in some of her poems. The following week, the man who made the request wasn't there and I never saw him again, but I had a packet of Dickinson's poems, including several of her well-known poems, such as:

#1732

My life closed twice before its close—
It yet remains to see
If Immortality unveil
A third event to me

So huge, so hopeless to conceive
As these that twice befell.
Parting is all we know of heaven,
And all we need of hell.

The packet also included some lesser known, more esoteric pieces, such as:

#1158

Best Witchcraft is Geometry
To the magician's mind—
His ordinary acts are feats
To thinking of mankind.

I was surprised by the number of men for whom Dickinson's rich inner world especially resonated. I had thought they would find her too prim. Was it the works' slightly witchy, magical qualities? The uneven cadence? Her quirky use of punctuation and capitalization? Her internal musings? Whatever it was, reading Dickinson seemed to have a liberating influence on the men's poetry, and more than one told me their experience of her bordered on the mystical. Her reclusive life and the smallness of her physical world only added to her enigma.

One of my favorite classes was a writing class I taught on the A yard. I taught this class on and off for three years. The same core group of men attended from the beginning, and are, I believe, still attending as other instructors keep the writing workshop going. During my time with them, we were able to spend several weeks or months on a particular body of writing; besides Dickinson, we also studied Marianne Moore and Walt Whitman.

The following two poems from the class are by Lou Gary, and were published in the journal *Razor Wire, 1998* (Shawn Griffin, editor). Mr. Gary is one of the most brilliant men I have ever met. He was also an exception to the general prison population in that he was highly educated and well-read, not only in literature but in physics, natural science and many other subjects. I worked with him for several years and watched his work evolve in many ways. As well as poetry, he wrote fine short stories and personal essays. During the three-hour class each week, we read and discussed favorite selections. Some of the students were only interested in the reading. Others worked on their own stories or poems. I tried to allow time every week to read student work and discuss it with the class. One day Lou brought in drafts of these two poems, an experiment in rhythm and cadence with a single sentence:

SWM

SWM, 40, seeks partner who can recite Jerry Garcia's "Ashes to Ashes" in the 70s, 80s, and 90s version, and can talk into the night of Sweet Magnolia, weaving stories of the London performance at the Rainbow Theater with stories of Sturgies where the thunder of Harleys mixed with the sighs of

delight of the blood-red sunset in the Big Sky over fields of unharvested
alfalfa ripe on the stalk swaying in the gentle breath of the full moon illuminating the eyes of lovers, where Jerry's crisp guitar rings among the stars and
comets and meteors, the intergalactic harmony carried by the convergence of
our bodies with the fates, to be answered by the roar of Deadheads demand-
ing "Jerry" lost in the cosmos of disorder, no longer touching our soul, leaving us to find our way to that cool, sweet nirvana where we just might get
some sleep before daylight.

Gray Goose

Even though it was three a.m. and
it was my first corrections bus ride,
I still could see the interstate road signs, so when
the guy next to me asked if we were near East L.A.,
I could tell him we weren't and wouldn't be,
but that didn't stop him from asking every five minutes
even when we were barreling up the Grapevine
at seventy-five em pee aitch
with the driver giggling maniacally as the backwash
from the bus made Jell-O of Subaru hatchbacks piloted
by weary nomads heading for their dream vacations in Yosemite
not seeing the 100 behemoths clear-cutting
the very cords of the essence of primordial life
with bright yellow munchers wheeled by seventy-foot Firestones
which I pointed out to the East L.A. man by asking him
why they were so yellow, because who would want
to swipe a seven-story machine that you could see from space,
or maybe they were that color because they came from Hertz,
but he said you're loco, man, and asked the guy across the aisle
if the pass we were flying through at eighty-five
was anywhere near his cousin's house because
he wanted to leave a message for his old lady not to visit
him this week, but the other guy's gaze was lost in
the rising sun splashing burnished reds and saffron yellows
across the pitted and barred windows through which
the now-gone woods passed,
and I noticed the pitting was from the inside, which made sense
as the officer in the back with the birdshot-loaded gun
certainly didn't have any bird-like targets among the stumps of
redwoods.

(*"Gray Goose"* is a euphemism for the bus used to transport inmates from county
jail to state prison.)

When revising this essay, I decided to write to Lou and ask him what he remembered about our study of Emily Dickinson and, specifically, writing "SWM" and "Gray Goose." I sent him a draft of this essay and asked him for any comments he thought might be useful. He responded with:

> I had some notes, but they got tossed during the last lockdown ("too much stuff"). I do remember, though, what struck me about Dickinson: the element of wit. That humor was present with such concepts as immortality and expansiveness (or at least the very big). It impressed both my ear and eye. I can see why prisoners might be touched, not only because of her near-imprisonment in her father's house, but also because of the terseness and simplicity of her writing. Concise and soft-spoken words echo readily from concrete walls.
>
> I thought the unusual metrical variations to be freeing, especially after reading Shakespeare's sonnets. (We had recently spent several months covering Shakespeare—not only the sonnets, but *Hamlet*, *Othello*, and *A Midsummer-Night's Dream*.) I realized I could use the cadence of my familial tongue, impressed by the gutturals outside of English, as a poetic form.
>
> I remember trying to write the briefest possible form: poems with only one word in each line. Then trying to write poems where the words form a physical shape on the page. Then turning terseness to verbosity, but maintaining some kind of rhythm.

Walt Whitman

I approach Walt Whitman in much the same way I used to read the Bible, then later the *I Ching*. I open up *Leaves of Grass* and read a verse at random. But with the *Bible* I always seem to land on pages of begets or admonishments to dash my little ones against the rocks. With the *I Ching*, I feel that the random approach is cheating and I will only let myself do it once or twice a year—I really should be casting coins and drawing hexagrams. However, I feel that with *Leaves of Grass* I can open up the book once or ten times and always find some interesting thought to get me through the day. Sometimes I mark the date in the margins with a note as to what was happening when I came across a particular verse. For instance, I can look back and note that one November a few years back, when my father had a major heart attack, I opened to "And I will not make a poem nor the least part of a poem but has reference to the soul" ("Starting from Paumanok," Section 12). I have my husband's name penciled in next to Section 48 of *Song of Myself* and during a recent bout with depression I turned to a segment of "Birds of Passage," which begins :

"Whoever you are, I fear you are walking the walk of dreams." I think Whitman is very much like life itself: there's always a lesson to be learned if you can remain open to it.

Walt Whitman has been accessible and inspiring to both my teenage and adult students. His poetry is rich and varied, full of vivid moments that seem frozen in time. As an exercise with beginning students, to get them to pay attention to detail, I have them choose a particular scene, preferably of a place they know well, and describe it using as many details from personal experience as they can. To get them started I use selections from *Song of Myself*, such as these four lines from Part 9:

> The big doors of the country barn stand open and ready,
> The dried grass of the harvest-time loads the slow-drawn wagon,
> The clear light plays on the brown gray and green intertinged,
> The armfuls are pack'd to the sagging mow.

This exercise has worked equally well with urban and rural students. The results are often radically different from one another. These two were both written in the same class:

> Bullets shatter the night
> A homeless man shivers in the street
> A wife is beaten. She feels it is her fault.
> A twelve-year-old boy is jumped on. Five hours after flashing his colors he is shanked on the street.
> A girl is killed in a drive-by. Her dad was the target.
> Gang graffiti is plastered on every park wall and street.
>
> *—Corwin Berry*

and

> Trees sway in the brisk morning breeze
> as deer scurry down the mountain toward the valley floor.
> Smoke bellows from chimneys as the temperature drops.
>
> *—Jake Reaves*

Teenagers are often especially moved by the exuberance of Whitman's poetry, by its profusion and spontaneity, but adult students are more inclined to respond to his introspection. Adults respond to Whitman's visionary spirit. Reading Whitman for the first time is like discovering a mythology that was always inside us but which we didn't have words for.

Age tends to temper many of us. The questions we ask as we move through life may change; or if they don't, they take on new dimensions. Whitman both challenges and comforts this questioning:

> I have said that the soul is not more than the body,
> And I have said that the body is not more than the soul,
> And nothing, not God, is greater to one than one's self is,
> And whoever walks a furlong without sympathy walks to his own
> funeral drest in his shroud . . . .
>
> And I say to mankind, Be not curious about God,
> For I who am curious about each am not curious about God,
> (No array of terms can say how much I am at peace about God and
> about death.)

(Song of Myself, Section 48)

Whitman is a poet of both street corners and empty places, which is one reason that his influence affects so many diverse writers. One former student of mine who loved Whitman was August Bleed. I met August while teaching in prison. Although he had little formal education, words and images flowed from him seemingly without effort. While "inside," he began a rigorous self-education program that included readings of classics such as Shakespeare, Blake, and Old Norse poetry. He also taught himself French, and began translating poems from the French. August has now been released from prison and gone on to make a new life for himself. He continues to write and has developed a small following. Several small presses have published his work. Understandably, he does not want to be regarded as a "prison poet," although he does acknowledge that it was in prison where he first began to seriously develop as a writer. The following two poems by August were written, as he put it, ". . . At a time I happened to be reading *Leaves of Grass* for the first time, so one could say I was 'under the influence' of Whitman":

> I was once siamese with this world.
> I bear the scars of separation still.
>
> My bloody roots are exposed.
> The leaves of my fingertips wilt.
> The moist grave of my eyes close.
>
> My ego grows like a tapeworm
> Devouring every blade of grass
> Every blue sky
> From my mind

You said to me:
Don't let your singular flesh
Prevent you from growing fur
An eye where an ear was
Let your fingers flower

I'm not even sure it was flesh I wanted
Or god,
A state of mind
That might
Cause the seasonless prairie of my soul to sprout
And nurture the fragile roots of my life.

I want a ladder of compost and gardens
To the tiny planets that were once my life.

Words from Whitman

The sky was a torrential moan;
Wet syllables flailing my skull.
I'd been listening to the earth speak
In that same indignant tone for three days.
All the while, cars crept past,
Kept fading into the horizon.

Council Bluff is as far from anywhere
As a place could hope to be.
From the highway I wasn't sure it existed,
But the spotted yellow line
Warned me of its imminent arrival.
I may already have missed it.

The tarot reader, a thousand miles away, said, over coffee, it would
come to this:
That place in the road where you lose your mind
Or move on—
"There must be a bumper that keeps me from falling off the edge."

Jesus had it easy.
They just
Nailed him
To another
World.

August and I continue to correspond. When I asked him about these two poems, he wrote back, "The poems are, necessarily, nothing like

Whitman. But his experience as a gay visionary and vagabond resonates with my own mythology and I like to think that his ghost possessed my brain for a too brief and timeless moment, hence the title."

American poetry is part of our collective past, and it holds a unique place in the world of literature. Crane, Dickinson and Whitman were poets of the new world and their words echo the American spirit from their places in history. Crane is working-class and worldly. His poems from *The Black Riders* are ironic, often harsh. Dickinson, although less worldly than Crane, uses words no less harsh in her probings and keen insights into the workings of the human consciousness. Walt Whitman's words seem to swell up from the very earth herself. The diversity of these voices and the sometimes outlaw quality of their work speaks to so many individuals in different ways. The students I worked with came from a cross-section of culture, economics, and education, yet there was a quality in each of these poets that appealed to them all.

Bibliography

Crane, Stephen, *Prose and Poetry*. New York: The Library of America, 1984.

Dickinson, Emily. *The Complete Poems of Emily Dickinson*. Edited by Thomas H. Johnson. New York: Little, Brown and Company, 1960.

Razor Wire, 1988. Edited by Shawn Griffin.

Whitman, Walt. *Poetry and Prose*. New York: The Library of America, 1982.

Frederick Douglass

Lorenzo Thomas

Knowledge Is Power

Frederick Douglass and the Roots of Literacy

Narrative of the Life of Frederick Douglass, an American Slave, Written by Himself (1845) is a classic of American literature. It is also a work of writing that should not be known only in anthologized excerpts. Like the nineteenth-century platform speeches it is based on, Douglass' argument is meant to occupy an entire evening, engaging the reader in a symphonic swirl of logic and incident, pathos and polemic. One has to read the whole book, cover to cover, carry it around in a pocket. Misplace the slender paperback under a stack of household bills and find it again.

Poet Robert Creeley put it nicely: "Usage coheres value. Tradition is an aspect of what anyone is now thinking—not what someone once thought." Douglass' *Narrative* is a classic text because it speaks powerfully to each new reader, and has done so since 1845. In recent years I have included it as a required text in my Freshman Composition course. I use the cheapest Signet paperback edition, a straight reprinting of the original text. Because the college bookstore will not buy copies back, my students, packing or unpacking for their sophomore year, will find it again.

My students are usually amazed when, for the first time, they read Douglass' story. The *Narrative* is a well-made little book filled with eloquently recalled anecdotes, vivid perhaps because they were relatively recent in the life of the twenty-eight-year-old author, and stunning to the reader because of the horrific events they record. Following amazement is outrage. While my students see the plantation brutalities as atrocities, it is chapter 6 that really touches home. In it, Douglass describes how a kindly mistress begins to teach him to read, only to have the lessons abruptly terminated by Master Hugh Auld because "it was unlawful, as well as unsafe, to teach a slave to read," even (or, perhaps, especially) a bright eight-year-old like Frederick.

Perceptive readers, of course, soon realize how the author has manipulated our feelings. This four-page chapter is almost equally divided between the aborted reading lessons and a grim description of the merciless corporeal punishment suffered by the slave girls next door at the hand of the demented Mrs. Hamilton. Douglass presents the two incidents with almost no transition, thereby forcing us to recognize an equation of different forms of cruelty. Those of us who are, indeed, *reading* his book know which treatment will have the more crippling effect.

Finally, college students marvel that a man sentenced to illiteracy, a man who literally stole his education, can send them to the dictionary on every other page and startle them with the beautiful logic of his phrasing.

This last reaction is the reason that I assign the book. Indeed, the appetite for knowledge is the subject of this book. Asian-American and Hispanic students, who have no reason to cultivate a present-day guilt or resentment about "the legacy of slavery," gain as much as anyone from reading Douglass' *Narrative* because the work is a narrative of self-discovery. Compared to that theme, the author's graphic account of "the gross fraud, wrong, and inhumanity of slavery" is secondary.

The three incidents that seem to be the most crucial in this book appear in chapters 6, 7, and 10, and all involve *actions* that lead young Frederick toward self-determination and, in his case, literal self-mastery. The end of the reading lessons in chapter 6 leads to a determination to learn and the acquisition of a schoolbook in chapter 7. Chapter 10, however, involves a violent confrontation with a cruel slave overseer that masks the more interesting confrontation of African traditional lore and American plantation reality.

When denied reading lessons, Douglass says, "I understood the pathway from slavery to freedom." But it was obtaining a copy of Caleb Bingham's *Columbian Orator* at age twelve that really opened this pathway to Douglass. "Seldom has a single book more profoundly shaped the life of a writer and orator," notes biographer William S. McFeely. A genuine Connecticut yankee, Caleb Bingham (1757–1817) was a pioneering figure in public education for girls and the establishment of public libraries. *The Columbian Orator,* Bingham's 1797 anthology of sermons, Fourth of July speeches, Socratic dialogues, and other orations, was a popular and standard schoolbook intended by the author to "inspire the pupil with the *ardor of eloquence,* and the *love of virtue.*" Reading the book, Douglass was most impressed by a piece called "Dialogue between a Master and Slave," and by another he recalled as "one of [Richard Brinsley] Sheridan's mighty speeches," but which was likely Bingham's excerpt from an oration by the Irish nationalist Arthur O'Connor.

In "Dialogue between a Master and Slave," Douglass found the words that would become true in his own life: "It is impossible to make one, who has felt the value of freedom, acquiesce in being a slave." The dialogue runs only three pages, but it is an impressive early anti-slavery statement. The piece that follows must have been difficult reading for young Frederick and it is doubtful that he had any grasp of its context, but the impact of the selection on his imagination can be seen throughout the pages of the *Narrative*.

In the Irish parliament on May 4, 1795, member Arthur O'Connor—in a few years to become a political prisoner—rose in favor of a bill extending civil rights to Catholics. England, he thundered, could not have "so soon forgotten the lesson they so recently learned from America, which should serve as a lasting example to nations, against employing force to subdue the spirit of a people, determined to be free!" For O'Connor, the results of the American and French revolutions were indelible. In order for despotic governments to "effect a counter revolution in the European mind," he said, "they must abolish every trace of the mariner's compass; they must consign every book to the flames; they must obliterate every vestige of the invention of the press." It is easy to see why Bingham included this excerpt in *The Columbian Orator*. His young reader in Baltimore knew as little about Ireland as about the destinations of the ships on Chesapeake Bay, but there can be no doubt that the words in the book Frederick Douglass held in his hands struck him as true.

At the same time that Southern states were imposing ever more strict prohibitions against the instruction of slaves, Bingham's anthology found an unlikely reader who took the old New England professor's lessons very seriously. "If he could say words," writes McFeely, "say them correctly, say them beautifully—Frederick could act; he could matter in the world." As the twenty-year-old Frederick learned "the art of using my mallet and irons" in Baltimore shipyards, so he mastered language. The shipyards taught him the real (and misappropriated) value of his skilled labor and, by implication, of his clandestine letters. Douglass would conclude, in writing the *Narrative*, "to make a contented slave, it is necessary to make a thoughtless one." Literacy is both a state of awareness and a mechanism—a *mistery* in the sense of a common craft which, of course, can be accomplished with varying degrees of excellence depending on the worker's dedication to the task.

Reading Caleb Bingham's textbook helped Douglass learn to speak in the patterns of public eloquence; and the truth of what he had to say encouraged him to—literally—"reduce to writing" what he expressed so powerfully on the anti-slavery lyceum platform. Douglass admitted his inadequate writing skills when he began his public speaking career in 1842. "Yet three years later," notes historian Benjamin Quarles, "this unschooled person had penned his autobiography. Such an achievement furnished an object lesson; it hinted at the infinite potentialities of man in whatever station of life. . . ."

Douglass' achievement supports my belief that effective writing depends simply upon one's confidence in transcribing the words one already knows how to speak. There are some grammatical rules, of course, and also some issues of propriety—or, better, appropriateness. Writing is a mechanical process; but the sense of what is or is not appropriate is based on our personal awareness. What we call education is really the patient assembling of an inventory of ways of speaking. Facility in writing is the practiced ability to transcribe one's own way(s) of speaking with accuracy. Asking students to tape record and transcribe oral history interviews is one effective approach to achieving this facility; a systematic search through the *Oxford English Dictionary* for the etymology of words often carelessly used is another. Once we can hear our own voices—and those of other people—we can also learn how to multiply our options for speaking. The value of a work such as Douglass' *Narrative* is that it is a self-defining model and record of the process—just as the word <u>neologism</u> is itself a *neologism*.

"The power of literacy," notes Eric J. Sundquist, "stood in contrast to the folk culture of slavery in Douglass' view less for any inherent reason than because literacy was a weapon of resistance . . . forbidden to slaves." Nevertheless, Douglass' text suggests that there was an active culture of resistance even among slaves unable to achieve literacy. Douglass is careful to provide a footnote saying that certain superstitions belonged to "the more ignorant slaves." But when one Sandy Jenkins gives Frederick a protective talisman—an herbal root for which Jenkins claims magic potency— the Narrative teasingly acknowledges the possibility that there may be more than one pathway to knowledge, if not to freedom. The root is intended to prevent Frederick from being whipped and, in the fight that follows with his overseer, he defends himself. "The truth was," he writes, "that he had not whipped me at all."

This incident in chapter 10—Frederick's bloody fight with the sadistic Mr. Covey—always creates a problem in my classroom. Bright college students don't believe in the efficacy of Sandy Jenkins's African prescription for softening a slave-breaker's "<u>obdurate</u> heart." Historian Sterling Stuckey has demonstrated that African systems of knowledge (extending to artisanship and farming techniques that helped enrich the plantation owners) existed in the American slave population. As late as the 1930s, in fact, folklorist Newbell Niles Puckett found informants who identified snakeroot as one of the ingredients for avoiding a whipping. Nevertheless, students are skeptical about the notion that Sandy Jenkins's root enables Frederick to physically defeat Covey.

Once in a while, though, a clever student will wrestle with my Afrocentric interpretation of the magic root passage. "I'm just a construction grunt," wrote Michael Menendez,

> manually wrestling a living from the sweat of my brow and the strength of my back, but even I know there is no such thing as magic. Or is there? I dove back into the text in search of an answer to the mystical powers of the root.
>
> The magic root was the catalyst Douglass needed to break the chains which locked his whole being into slavery. Yes, most definitely, there are magic roots—pencils, typewriters, and anything else that causes us to rise up through misery and despair.

No one today, not even New Age folks, will believe in the actual magic of a root; we prefer to place our trust in psychology, technology, and practical explanations. In his song "Superstition," Stevie Wonder used the double-voiced coding of African American irony as cleverly as Frederick Douglass ever did. "When you believe in things you don't understand," he sings, "then you suffer." But it was not enough that Frederick Douglass understand the system of slavery; he had also to learn how to create, in himself, the power of self-definition that would enable him to defeat the system that bound him.

My purpose in assigning Douglass' *Narrative* is explicitly stated in another book I sometimes use in the same course, for the same purpose. "A book is a loaded gun," writes Ray Bradbury in *Fahrenheit 451*. "Who knows who might be the target of the well-read man?" Among Bradbury's characters are a fellowship of wanderers who have memorized the classics in a future age when, going the antebellum South one better, the state has declared it a crime for any citizen to own books. The totalitarian state has, in effect, forced literate people to recreate an oral tradition for safeguarding ideas; and has reduced those that Matthew Arnold termed "the true apostles of equality" to fugitives. "They weren't at all certain," Bradbury writes, "that the things they carried in their heads might make every future dawn glow with a purer light, they were sure of nothing save that the books were on file behind their quiet eyes."

"What to the American slave," asked Frederick Douglass in an 1857 speech, "is your Fourth of July?" He challenged his Rochester, New York, audience to confront the gulf between the nation's creed and its practice of slavery. Echoing the 137th Psalm, Douglass intoned, "To drag a man in fetters into the grand illuminated temple of liberty, and call upon him to join you in joyous anthems, were inhuman mockery and sacriligious irony." But Douglass knew that slavery was maintained by more than iron fetters. In chapter 11 of the *Narrative* he recalls that the only way to attain "contentment in slavery" required accepting his master's requirement of "setting aside my intellectual nature." "But in spite of him," writes Douglass, "and even in spite of myself, I continued to think, and to think about the injustice of my enslavement, and the means of escape."

It is clear that for Douglass "the means of escape" is to be understood in both a literal and a metaphoric sense. For poet Robert Hayden, Douglass' living monument is his ability to make us see that freedom is not an abstraction to be worried by linguists, <u>obfuscated</u> by philosophers, or fetishized in "the gaudy mumbo jumbo of politicians." The meaning of freedom, and freedom itself, must be found in the liberation of the mind, in "the lives grown out of his life, the lives / fleshing his dream of the beautiful, needful thing." As with Ray Bradbury's living books, this idea of freedom is an activity that we practice in our own lives.

For me, *Narrative of the Life of Frederick Douglass, an American Slave* is an extraordinarily efficient textbook, one that would have fit neatly into Bingham's *Columbian Orator*. As it is, Douglass' book gives to students the same gift that Bingham gave to him. That gift, that ability to whet the appetite for knowledge, is precious. Our humanness depends on our determination to always find it again.

Bibliography

Bingham, Caleb. *The Columbian Orator: Containing a Variety of Original and Selected Pieces; Together with Rules Calculated to Improve Youth and Others in the Ornamental and Useful Art of Eloquence.* Boston: Bingham and West, 1797.

Bradbury, Ray. *Fahrenheit 451.* New York: Ballantine, 1980.

Creeley, Robert. "To Define." In *Postmodern American Poetry* edited by Paul Hoover. New York: Norton, 1994.

Douglass, Frederick. *Autobiographies.* New York: The Library of America, 1994.

———. *Narrative of the Life of Frederick Douglass, an American Slave, Written by Himself. 1845.* New York: Signet-New American Library, 1968.

Gates, Henry Louis, Jr. *The Signifying Monkey: A Theory of African-American Literary Criticism.* New York: Oxford University Press, 1988.

Hayden, Robert. "Frederick Douglass." In *Collected Poems.* Edited by Frederick Glaysher. New York and London: Liveright, 1985.

McFeely, William S. *Frederick Douglass.* New York: Norton, 1991.

Puckett, Newbell Niles. *Folk Beliefs of the Southern Negro.* Chapel Hill: University of North Carolina Press, 1926.

Quarles, Benjamin. "Introduction." *Narrative of the Life of Frederick Douglass, an American Slave, Written by Himself.* Cambridge, Mass.: Harvard University Press, 1988.

Simpson, Lewis P. *The Fable of the Southern Writer.* Baton Rouge and London: Louisiana State University Press, 1994.

Stuckey, Sterling. *Going through the Storm: The Influence of African American History.* New York: Oxford University Press, 1994.

Sundquist, Eric J. *To Wake the Nations: Race in the Making of American Literature.* Cambridge, Mass.: Harvard University Press, 1993.

Nathaniel Hawthorne

Penny Harter

Behind the Masks

Nathaniel Hawthorne's *Tales* and *The Scarlet Letter*

TRADITIONALLY, students are introduced to the work of Nathaniel Hawthorne through his classic novel *The Scarlet Letter*, and through assorted tales anthologized in American Literature textbooks. They read about the plight of Hester Prynne and discuss its relationship to Puritanism in early New England society. But in order for students to best appreciate Hawthorne's narratives, they must first understand the two competing philosophies of nineteenth-century American culture, Transcendentalism and Romanticism.

Transcendentalism, as expressed by Hawthorne's friends Ralph Waldo Emerson and Henry David Thoreau, is an optimistic belief in human intuition. Not only did Transcendentalists believe that individuals could have a personal, first-hand relationship with God, they also believed that God, mankind, and the entire natural world shared a universal soul. The "oversoul," as Emerson called it, meant that no aspect of the natural world was insignificant; all was imbued with spirit and worthy of reverence. Some of these Transcendentalist ideas were inherited from European Romanticism, possibly originating in the works of English poets such as William Wordsworth. Even more than the English Romantics, however, the Transcendentalists put greater emphasis on learning from nature, and on exploring one's own inner spiritual world.

Other American writers—notably Hawthorne and Herman Melville—opposed the optimistic doctrines of Transcendentalism. Their works explored the darker aspects of Romanticism: a fascination with the tragic aspects of life and a recognition of both good and evil in nature and human experience. Hawthorne and Melville were also influenced by the Calvinist belief in original sin that had come to America with the Puritans.

Hawthorne was born in 1804 in Salem, Massachusetts, the town where a hundred years earlier men and women had been accused and executed as "witches." One of his ancestors was John Hathorne, active in prosecuting and condemning witches during the Salem witch trials. Nathaniel Hawthorne felt the guilt of this in his own life, seeing such evil as being perpetuated through later generations. After he graduated from Bowdoin College in 1825, he returned home to live a solitary life, devoting the next twelve years to learning the craft of writing. Either by accident or by choice, he explored again and again the theme of isolation, creating characters who are imprisoned by their own hearts.

My eleventh grade students and I approach Hawthorne's writing by examining how certain common themes are revealed in his fiction through the imagery and use of symbolism. One age-old theme in literature is the difference between appearance and reality. We discuss how characters' external appearances often conceal their true personalities or roles. (This is especially true in fairy tales, e.g., the beast is really a noble youth under a curse, etc.). I point out that Hawthorne uses this same theme of the contrast between appearance and reality in a number of his tales, and that his body of work is essentially of one piece, especially with respect to his focus on the concealed dark sides of his characters. "Dr. Heidegger's Experiment" and "The Minister's Black Veil" are two stories that emphasize the theme in three ways: physically, emotionally, and symbolically.

"Dr. Heidegger's Experiment"

In "Dr. Heidegger's Experiment" (1837), three elderly men and an elderly woman, all withered and unattractive to themselves and to one another, drink some water from the Fountain of Youth. For a brief and fevered time, their lives are transformed:

> But, the next moment, the exhilarating gush of young life shot through their veins. They were now in the happy prime of youth. Age, with its miserable train of cares and sorrows and diseases, was remembered only as the troubles of a dream, from which they had joyously awakened. The fresh gloss of the soul, so early lost, and without which the world's successive scenes had been but a gallery of faded pictures, again threw its enchantment over all their prospects. They felt like new-created beings in a new-created universe.
> "We are young! We are young!" they cried, exultingly. (*Tales and Sketches*, p. 477)

Hawthorne then goes on to raise the question of whether they actually *do* look younger—or only imagine that they do—for the haunted mirror on the wall, which was reputed to reflect "the spirit of all the doctor's deceased patients . . . whenever he looked thitherward," fleetingly seems to show something quite different. The reality and appearance do not match:

> Yet, by a strange deception, owing to the duskiness of the chamber, and the antique dresses which they still wore, the tall mirror is said to have reflected the figures of the three old, gray, withered grand-sires, ridiculously contending for the skinny ugliness of a shrivelled grand-dam. (*Tales and Sketches*, p. 478)

And Dr. Heidegger has learned a lesson from watching the characters' ludicrous behavior during his experiment. He states, ". . . if the fountain [of the Water of Youth] gushed at my very doorstop, I would not stoop to bathe my lips in it—no, though its delirium were for years instead of moments" (*Tales and Sketches*, p. 479).

This story also embodies another of Hawthorne's favorite themes, the inevitable negative results of human tampering with the natural order of things. The Romantics rebelled against the effects of the Industrial Revolution with its increased reliance on emerging technology and scientific research. Hawthorne revisits this theme in several other of his tales, including "The Birthmark" (*Tales and Sketches*, p. 764) and "Rappaccini's Daughter" (*Tales and Sketches*, p. 975).

Some good writing ideas emerge from "Dr. Heidegger's Experiment." The most obvious is for students to try writing stories in which an elderly character discovers a means to achieve youth again. They can explore what happens to the character as a result, perhaps writing in third person, perhaps in first. In addition, possibilities for exploring a desire for magical transformation might include fantasy, horror, or science fiction stories. The transformation, real or imagined, need not be from age to youth. Here are some other writing ideas based on transformation:

• 1) Write a story in which a character drastically changes physical appearance. The change can be reversible, or not. It could be from beauty to ugliness, male to female, human to animal, or the reverses of these. Include in your story how and why the change occurred. What is the effect of this transformation on the character(s) involved?

• 2) If you have ever acted in a play, write a first-hand account of how it felt to take on another persona, how the experience of playing a character changed you, and how enduring that transformation felt.

• 3) Horror stories often revolve around what I call "the betrayal of the familiar." Take a familiar and ordinary-appearing character (as Stephen King often does) and slowly reveal the hidden evil that motivates him or her. Be sure to give the reasons for this character's isolation within the prison of his or her own heart: Remember, good villains are believable, which means they can't be all bad. Create a little sympathy for your villain.

"The Minister's Black Veil"

"The Minister's Black Veil" (1836–37), one of Hawthorne's most enigmatic tales, prefigures many of the themes in *The Scarlet Letter*. In this story, the town's beloved minister suddenly begins to wear a black veil over his face, and does not take it off or allow others to remove it, even on his deathbed.

Before we read this story, I invite students to discuss the effects on a person's well-being of keeping a guilty secret. We look at what guilt can drive people to do—both in fiction and in life. I remind them of Edgar Allan Poe's "The Tell-tale Heart," in which the criminal is driven so crazy that in the end he gives himself away.

Next, we discuss masks and veils. We talk about what purposes a physical or emotional mask or veil might serve, and what such a mask or veil might conceal or reveal. Then the students read Hawthorne's story about a minister whose wearing of a black veil over his face both disturbs and frightens his congregation, fueling rumors about the reason for his unusual behavior. Slowly, as he does in *The Scarlet Letter*, Hawthorne reveals the unsettling effects of the veil both on the good people of the village and on the minister himself.

> There was the black veil, swathed round Mr. Hooper's forehead, and concealing every feature above his placid mouth, on which, at times, they could perceive the glimmering of a melancholy smile. But that piece of crape, to their imagination, seemed to hang down before his heart, the symbol of a fearful secret between him and them. Were the veil but cast aside, they might speak freely of it, but not till then. (*Tales and Sketches*, p. 377)

> It grieved him, to the very depth of his kind heart, to observe how the children fled from his approach, breaking up their merriest sports, while his melancholy figure was yet afar off. Their instinctive dread caused him to feel, more strongly than aught else, that a preternatural horror was interwoven with the threads of the black crape. In truth, his own antipathy to the veil was known to be so great, that he never willingly passed before a mirror, nor stooped to drink at a still fountain, lest, in its peaceful bosom, he should be affrighted by himself. (*Tales and Sketches*, p. 380)

Hawthorne also hints at the secret sin that may have caused the minister to adopt the practice of wearing the veil. The minister attends the funeral of a young lady of the parish:

> As he stooped, the veil hung straight down from his forehead, so that, if her eye-lids had not been closed forever, the dead maiden might have seen his face. Could Mr. Hooper be fearful of her glance, that he so hastily caught back the black veil? A person, who watched the interview between the dead and living, scrupled not to affirm that, at the instant when the clergyman's features were disclosed, the corpse had slightly shuddered, rustling the shroud and muslin cap, though the countenance retain the composure of death. (*Tales and Sketches*, p. 375)

And as the mourners follow the coffin to the graveyard, one remarks to another, "I had a fancy . . . that the minister and the maiden's spirit were walking hand in hand" (*Tales and Sketches*, p. 376).

A discrepancy between appearance and reality occurs here again, along with the aforementioned theme of "the betrayal of the familiar"— in this case a beloved and well-known pastor whose congregation feels betrayed by his mysterious behavior. In addition, in "The Minister's Black Veil" the reader observes the power of secret guilt in a character's life, repeating the theme of the mixture of good and evil in all human beings.

After further discussing the story, I encourage the students to write a poem or story reacting to the idea of a person wearing a physical mask or veil to conceal some physical, mental, or spiritual flaw. I ask them to consider the following questions as they write: What is the effect of the mask/veil on others around the character? Has the character chosen to wear the mask/veil, or has it been forced upon him or her? Is it ever taken off? If so, by whom? Under what circumstances?

There are a number of rich short fiction possibilities evolving from the symbolism of masks. For instance, students could try a story about a clown who never takes off his mask, or about a masquerade party, as in Poe's "The Masque of the Red Death," or about an alien forced to disguise itself while among us.

The Scarlet Letter

I usually teach these stories in the order above, using "The Minister's Black Veil" to segue into *The Scarlet Letter.* In Hawthorne's most famous novel, all of the major characters wear masks of some sort and are not what they seem to be. Hester's embroidered A masks a sincere purity of character, which she later demonstrates in her acceptance of her guilt and her blameless work among the poor and sick. Dimmesdale's minister's robes mask his guilt, although his behavior reveals it to the reader. Chillingworth's guise as a helpful doctor to Dimmesdale masks his intent to inflict revenge upon the man. And Pearl, the little elf-child dressed in scarlet, is not a real child at all until she cries on the scaffold. Until then, she is more a sprite, an otherworldly symbol both for the lovers' joy and for their guilty secret. Not one of the main characters is really as the Puritan community around them perceives him or her to be.

After students have read the novel, we further discuss the Hawthornian themes of the discrepancy between reality and appearance, the keeping of guilty secrets, and the masking of hidden sin, as they apply to this work. We also talk about which characters the students empathize with, and why. I ask them for writing ideas and offer my own. The list below is a combination of their ideas and mine. Of course, we talk about the thematic ideas, sharing our experiences, observations, and speculations, before we begin writing.

Scarlet Letter *Writing Ideas*

• 1. *Guilt*: From your own experience or observation, write a brief personal essay, poem, or story about how guilt can affect an individual's behavior.

• 2. *Secrets*: Keeping a secret over a long period influences the person who keeps it. Hester has two secrets: the identity of Pearl's father and the identity of her former husband. Chillingworth has his secrets, too: his own identity and his plans for Dimmesdale. And, of course, Dimmesdale has his own tortured secret of fatherhood and "sin."

From your own experience or observation, write a brief personal essay, story, or poem about how keeping a secret can affect someone's behavior. Perhaps a main character keeps a secret that ultimately destroys her or him. You can even "become" Dimmesdale or Hester, perhaps in a dramatic monologue or persona poem.

• 3. *Revenge*: Write a brief personal essay, story, or poem about how the need for revenge can dominate a person's thoughts and behavior. Base the piece on your experience or observation of someone plotting revenge on another for a real or imagined hurt. Include how this revenge harms the person who feels it, as well as the intended victim (if it *does* harm the victim). Remember, your characters may be of any age or sex. A child can plot revenge. So can a dying man.

The following poem by Doug Nally describes what he thinks Chillingworth is feeling, and what his secret plans for revenge have done to him:

The Burning Ember

A man stands staring across the way.
His eyes are telling what he cannot say.

His pupils enlarging—I feel drawn in
To his strange story shrouded in sin.

For years he travelled thinking hope lay ahead.
He returned to find hardship and betrayal instead.

A shell has developed around his soul, grown tired,
Caught in a life-long deceit that this sin has inspired.

Now all days are the same. He has but one drive:
To destroy those who wronged him, yet leave them alive.

But this anger unvented has wrought him inhuman;
Blinded by evil ambition, thinking like no man.

A shadow of a man. His heart, once whole,
Glows like an evil ember inside a frozen soul.

Doug has not only described Chillingworth, he has also imaginatively entered into the man's state of mind—and managed to do so in rhymed couplets as well.

• 4. *Nature symbolism*: Hawthorne uses nature symbolism to reinforce the drama in the novel. The rose grows by the prison door. The meteor draws a lurid and gigantic *A* in the night sky. Nature reflects and amplifies what is going on in the lives of the characters. Write a poem or story in which you create a mood using symbols from nature that parallel what the characters are feeling. Think about how Hawthorne presents Pearl's perception of the forest in the following excerpt from the end of chapter XVIII:

> The great black forest—stern as it showed itself to those who brought the guilt and troubles of the world into its bosom—became the playmate of the lonely infant, as well as it knew how. Sombre as it was, it put on the kindest of its moods to welcome her. It offered her the partridge-berries, the growth of the preceding autumn, but ripening only in the spring, and now red as drops of blood upon the withered leaves. These Pearl gathered, and was pleased with their wild flavor. The small denizens of the wilderness hardly

took pains to move out of her path. . . . A pigeon, alone on a low branch, allowed Pearl to come beneath, and uttered a sound as much of greeting as alarm. . . . A wolf, it is said,—but here the tale has surely lapsed into the improbable,—came up, and smelt of Pearl's robe, and offered his savage head to be patted by her hand. The truth seems to be, however, that the mother-forest, and these wild things which it nourished, all recognized a kindred wildness in the human child. (*Collected Novels*, pp. 294–295)

In the following poem, Sharon Burd describes the parallel she sees between Pearl and the brook. Pearl is "free and wild" in Sharon's poem, but she is still bound to her mother and the village. The brook also flows free and wild but is "bound to the earth forever."

Pearl

Babbling brook,
low mournful sounds
issue from your bed.

A small child plays
by your side
in a patch of sunlight.

She notices your sadness
and questions you why
your song is so sad.

Is it perhaps because
she is free and wild
while you must stay—

While you must stay
bound to the rocks,
bound to the earth forever.

• 5. *Place*: In a personal essay, poem, or story, explore the bond between person and place, such as the bond Hester has with the village or Pearl has with the forest. Write about a place with which you feel a bond, explaining why. Or write about a character who feels compelled to remain in a place or continually revisit it, one who is bound to a certain location, for either good or ill.

Sage Morris-Greene responded to this idea by writing about her love of the desert landscape behind her childhood backyard:

Lucky me! My place of peace is where I grew up—not my home, but the land all around it. Always I have felt more calm in nature, but especially in the desert canyons and cliffs behind my backyard. When I was old enough, I realized that there was nothing to keep me from going back there, that the three-foot-high cement wall was not really a barrier, but a stepping stone, a stepping stone into the magical wilderness that would take me away from any and all problems. Sometimes it was just the longing for wild animals and plants, for exploring, for getting lost to find my way back again, for seeing how far I could go out into the rocky primitive world before my nerve gave out and I came back home. Or else my joy was so great that the only way I could think to express it was to fly over the cement wall, swinging on tree branches, free-climbing up the steep cliff walls, or dangling my legs over the edge of hundred-foot drops, spitting and throwing rocks over the edge.

I wasn't always alone on these escapades, escaping real world stuff until the disappearing sunlight made me trudge back with sand in my shoes and new rocks in my pockets for my collection of the plain and ordinary stones of the world. I, of course, saw each of these rocks as unique and special, though now I know most of them were just smooth pebbles. When I went out into my desert world, the world of nomadic scavenging for parts of washing machines and old cans to be used in forts, sometimes I would be accompanied on my journey by my guys, the regular two or three, or even sometimes four when one of them had a friend.

And there were the stragglers, few and far between, tagging along with us. Of course they were welcomed and would revel in the fun that could be had attacking old barns and chasing snakes through the grass. Or sitting in a cavern, feeling the cool breezes blow, though only those who could really keep up would accompany us to the cliffs. The next day, however, they would be too late to join us; we would have already left, and we would be specks, blue and green and red, off atop the far mesas, and the mothers would sigh, relieved that we had left their child out of our games.

Sunsets, breezes, sounds, laughter—all of these things can be found in almost any place one goes to. But the places in our hearts that we never forget, those that bring to mind the place where we really were connected to the earth and the air, can't be duplicated. We remain connected to those places ever after; our memories hold true. To this day, certain scented breezes, the sounds of birds in the high-desert area that I live in now, and the sight of bands of children running off toward excitement and adventure, remind me of that place where I spent my summers, my days, my afternoons; I am forever connected to the warm and living earth where my feet are still planted, and my head is in clouds of dreams that still surround my life.

Sage has managed to re-create the strong bond she has with a place that continues to embody for her a sense of childhood freedom and all the imaginative possibilities that went with it. Her piece reminds me of the freedom Pearl felt in the woods, and the "kindred wildness" the forest recognized and reciprocated, separate from the real world with its "any and all problems."

• 6. *Otherworldly influences*: Pearl seems not of this world, almost an elf or sprite, made of new elements. Write a story or poem in which being around an otherworldly child (even an alien) influences several adults. The child's personality may be whatever you choose to make it, good or ill.

• 7. *Dramatic monologues*: Choose any moment in the narrative and try writing a dramatic monologue that shows what you think Hester, Dimmesdale, or Chillingworth might say. What are their thoughts about what has happened? Their memories? Joys and regrets? Fears?

• 8. *Personal symbols*: Hester is forced to wear the scarlet *A* as a symbol of her shame. Later, it becomes a symbol of her mercy. Write a poem or story about the changing role of a symbol in a person's life. This symbol could be a ring, an article of clothing, a doll, a teddy-bear, a photograph, a place, a person, a car—anything that rises from your memory or your imagination.

In the following poem, Kim Phillips writes about how she perceives her face to be a symbol of her soul.

My Scarlet Letter

This face I wear is my scarlet letter.
It is not purple,
nor is it sewn on with gold thread,
but it reflects my wrongdoings.

Everyone knows my face (they think).
But even I do not know my own face
for it changes every day
and bears my mistakes and triumphs.

When I have done wrong
people stare at my face questioningly.
I have no answer.

It is my "A," the mirror to my soul
and wears my feelings
upon its character.

Kim writes about how her face shifts, "for it changes every day / and bears my mistakes and triumphs." This idea can lead to a class discussion on the changing nature of symbols, both from the point of view of the observer and over time.

Further exploring with my students how Hawthorne uses symbolism, specifically nature symbolism, I try to select passages that show the forest as Hawthorne reveals it to be for the lovers—both a desolate and gloomy place and a place of truth. (Earlier, the class discussed the symbolism of the forest versus the town. We imagined what the forest must have been to the native peoples when the Puritans first arrived, and how and why it took on the semblance of evil to the Puritans.) Toward the end of chapter XVII, "The Pastor and His Parishioner," Hester reveals to Dimmesdale that Chillingworth is her husband. The following two paragraphs show the contrasting moods Hawthorne creates using imagery of the natural world:

> They sat down again, side by side, and hand clasped in hand, on the mossy trunk of the fallen tree. Life had never brought them a gloomier hour; it was the point whither their pathway had so long been tending, and darkening ever, as it stole along;—and yet it inclosed a charm that made them linger upon it, and claim another, and another, and, after all, another moment. The forest was obscure around them, and creaked with a blast that was passing through it. The boughs were tossing heavily above their heads; while one solemn old tree groaned dolefully to another, as if telling the sad story of the pair that sat beneath, or constrained to forbode evil to come. (*Collected Novels*, p. 286)

But then, when Dimmesdale says to Hester, "Advise me what to do" (*Collected Novels*, p. 287), her response shows her wider vision, and hope:

> "Is the world, then, so narrow? . . . Doth the universe lie within the compass of yonder town, which only a little time ago was but a leaf-strewn desert, as lonely as this around us? Whither leads yonder forest-track? Backward to the settlement, thou sayest! Yes; but onward, too. Deeper it goes, and deeper, into the wilderness, less plainly to be seen at every step; until, some few miles hence, the yellow leaves will show no vestige of the white man's tread. There thou art free! So brief a journey would bring thee from a world where thou hast been most wretched, to one where thou mayest still be happy! Is there not shade enough in all this boundless forest to hide thy heart from the gaze of Roger Chillingworth?" (*Collected Novels*, pp. 287–8)

Hester continues to encourage Dimmesdale until he tells her that he does not have the courage to "venture into the wide, strange, difficult world, alone!" to which she replies that he will not go alone. At this point, I ask the students to imagine how the story might end. (Note that Hawthorne used this very idea when he rewrote the Circe episode of *The Odyssey* and supplied it with a variant ending in "Circe's Palace" [*Tales and Sketches*, pp. 1382–1408].) Will the two run off into the forest? Take to the sea? Or will the web of guilt and revenge close around them? And what will happen to Pearl? After we discuss various possible endings and whether they seem believable or not, the students write endings, trying to emulate Hawthorne's style. We share these aloud, and later enjoy comparing them to the actual conclusion of the novel.

In asking students to write their own pieces that explore the social, emotional, moral, and spiritual issues that Hawthorne raises in his fiction, we help them to see the relevance of his work to their own lives. We come to better understand how great literature can be both a window into that wider world Hester speaks of, and a mirror in which we see more and more of ourselves.

Bibliography

Hawthorne, Nathaniel. *Tales and Sketches*. New York: The Library of America, 1982.

———. *Collected Novels*. New York: The Library of America, 1983.

Poe, Edgar Allan. *Poetry & Tales*. New York: The Library of America, 1984.

Julie Moulds Rybicki

Finishing Hawthorne's Stories

NATHANIEL HAWTHORNE'S NOTEBOOKS were first published by his widow, in censored form, in 1866 and 1868. Amazingly, a notebook presumed lost surfaced in the papers of a certain Barbara S. Mouffle in 1976. Ms. Mouffle, through extensive detective work, realized the old journal, long owned by her relatives, was written by Hawthorne.

Hawthorne's Lost Notebook (1835–1841) is replete with tantalizing story ideas: mystical fireflies and rising corpses, haunted songbirds, and cloud funerals. I was fascinated by the hundreds of story ideas—most of which Hawthorne never followed up on—that he noted down during these six years. Many are spooky, morbid or gruesome, and thus have a natural appeal to adolescents.

What can *Hawthorne's Lost Notebook* teach students? Most importantly, Hawthorne's ideas can get students out of the factual thinking mode and into the kind of imaginative anarchy that leads to fine stories and poems. By using Hawthorne's story starters, students also learn that stories do not usually come out whole and perfect, as finished masterpieces. In fact, most begin as fragments, starting from something small like an observation or an idea. Young writers reading the polished prose in Hawthorne's *Young Goodman Brown* or *The Maypole of Marymount* learn that Hawthorne went through the same process they do: he started with an idea, then drafted, revised, and polished his pieces before he sent them out for publication.

One way to show students this process is to take a story-starter idea from *Hawthorne's Lost Notebook* and let them see how Hawthorne developed it into a published story. For instance, Story Starter #25 (the swallowed snake—see Appendix A) becomes "Egotism; or, The Bosom-Serpent," in Hawthorne's early collection *Mosses from an Old Manse*. (See Appendix B for other stories likely begun from ideas in *Hawthorne's Lost Notebook*.) Or you might have students write a short piece using a Hawthorne story seed *before* they read the published story that came from it. The variety of results can be amazing; a single story starter, used by all the students in a class, can produce twenty-some very different tales! Some student examples I collected are showcased in Appendix C.

Another way to have students learn from Hawthorne's writing process is to have them create their own story-starter notebooks. Below is one possible way to schedule this. For a week, have students jot down story-starter ideas about scenes or any odd images or characters that cross their minds. Suggest that they keep their story ideas brief at first—the goal is to collect enough story premises so that no students ever say, "But I don't have anything to write about." You might start out by giving them a few ideas of your own, perhaps two or three each day. Keep your own notebook and share the story ideas with the class. Frequently, one interesting idea, when discussed, will spark many others.

After a week or so, you and your students can pick an idea and develop a story from it. You can select topics in various ways:

1. Everyone can choose his or her favorite ideas to develop.

2. Students can exchange journals and write pieces using each other's ideas.

3. Each student can pick his or her favorite two ideas. From those, you can make a master list from which everyone can choose.

Whichever method you use, have students then go through the following steps: opulent, uncritical first drafts, in which they let their ideas tumble onto the page; more exacting revision; group editing; solo polishing.

Finally, publish the completed stories and poems in a small volume. A little public glory is always gratifying to kids (and adults). Have a reading and/or book party. Have students submit their pieces to the school literary journal, or start your own journal or website.

Appendix A:
Story Ideas from Hawthorne's *Lost Notebook*

Hawthorne's quotations are in italics, with my suggestions, if any, underneath. The page number and the year the quote appeared in the *Notebook* are in parentheses. The thematic headings are my own.

The Dead (and the Unborn)

1. *All the dead that had ever been drowned in a certain lake [begin] to arise* (p. 78, 1838). The perfect premise for a scary story!

2. *In a corner of the burial ground,…are the most ancient stones remaining in the burial-ground;—moss-grown, deeply sunken. . . . "An aged man at nineteen years," saith the grave stone* (p. 69, 1838). How would a nineteen-year-old become an aged man—by a natural or supernatural event?

3. *Dialogues of the unborn like dialogues of the dead* . . . (p. 85, 1839). Write a conversation between two or more dead people. If unborn children could communicate, what would they say?

4. *John Ziska, a leader of the Hussites, ordered his skin to be made (after death) into a drum-covering* (p. 20, 1835–6). Would the man's spirit remain inside the drum? How would that spirit manifest itself?

5. *A lady's dead lover might be supposed to speak in the bird's voice. A bird in Cuba calling "Sophie" in the woods—being its single note* (p. 64, 1837–8).

6. *A tomb-stone maker* . . . *used to cut cherubs on the top of the tombstones, and had the art of carving the cherub's face in the likeness of the deceased* (p. 79, 1838).

More Spooky and Strange Situations

7. *The chimney of an old house: it might be fancied that witches, on their broomsticks, have often flown forth through it, on their midnight excursions* (p. 12, 1835).

8. *In an old house a mysterious knocking might be heard, on the wall, where had formerly been an old doorway, now bricked up* (p. 14, 1835).

9. *To have one event operate in several places,* . . . *for example, if a man's head were to be cut off in the town, men's heads to drop off in several other towns* (p. 19, 1835–6). What if some strange event in your town—a murder, an unusual birth, a celestial event—seemed to be connected to similar events in nearby places?

10. *The scene of story or sketch to be laid within the light of a street-lantern; the time, when the lamp is near going out; and the catastrophe to be simultaneous with the last flickering gleam* (p. 13, 1835).

11. *A satirical article might be made out of the idea of an imaginary museum, containing such articles as Aaron's rod, the petticoat of General Harrison* . . . *Perhaps it might be the museum of a deceased old man* (p. 26, 1835–6)
Make up another imaginary museum with a strange theme and detail its odd exhibits: a museum of light bulbs or broken windows, a museum of alarm clocks or celebrity shoes.

12. *A show of wax figures, consisting of murderers and their victims. . . . The showman is very careful to call his exhibition the STATUARY; he walks to and fro before the figures, talking of the history of the persons, the moral lessons to be drawn therefrom, and especially the excellence of the waxwork* (p. 75, 1838).

13. *An old volume in a large library—every one to be afraid to unclasp and open it, because it was said to be a book of magic* (p. 18, 1835).

14. *Cleaning an obscure old picture* (p. 64, 1837–8).

15. *Some very famous jewel, or other thing, much talked of all over the world. Some person to meet with it, and get possession of it, in some unexpected manner, amid homely circumstances* (p. 61, 1837–8). If an ordinary person stumbled across some great treasure, would it bring good or bad luck to its discoverer?

Whimsy and Innocence: Fireflies, Clouds, and Snowballs

16. *A person to catch fire-flies, and try to kindle his household fire with them* (p. 80, 1838). Describe a person who does magical things—someone who lights fires with fireflies whose arms can become oak branches.

17. *A cloud in the shape of an old woman, kneeling, with arms extended towards the moon &c.* (p. 62, 1837–8). Write a story in which the characters are clouds.

18. *When scattered clouds are resting on the bosoms of hills, it seems as if you might climb into the heavenly region,—earth being so intermixed with sky, and gradually transformed into it* (p. 83, 1838–9). What would happen if a character could walk into the sky?

19. *Moonlight is sculpture:—Sunset, and sunlight generally, Painting* (p. 82, 1838–9). Write story where the Sun is a painter, or the Moon is a sculptor.

20. *A poodle-dog, trained by Prof. Blumenbach at Gottingen, hatched hen's eggs, and took a motherly care of the chickens, attending on them and providing them food* (p. 24, 1835–6). Write the story of an unlikely mother/child relationship.

21. *Describe a boyish combat with snow-balls, and the victorious leader to have a statue of snow erected to him* (p. 31, 1836–7).

22. *Picture a child's (of four or five years old) reminiscence, at sunset, of a long sunny summer's day—his first awakening, his studies, his sports, his little fits of passion and grief—perhaps a whipping &c.* (p. 37, 1836–7).

Mirrors

23. *Make one's own reflection in a mirror the subject of a story* (p. 18, 1835). If your mirror image had a personality and a life of its own, how would it act? What would be behind the mirror?

24. *An old looking glass—somebody finds out the secret of making all the images that have been reflected in it pass back again across its surface* (p. 65, 1838).

Outer Beauty Versus Inner Decay

25. *A snake taken into a man's stomach; and nourished there from fifteen years to thirty-five—tormenting him most horribly* (p. 32, 1836–7).

26. *Gnomes, or other mischievous little fiends, to be represented as burrowing in the hollow teeth of some person who has subjected himself to their power* (p. 57, 1837).

27. *A man living a wicked life in one place, and simultaneously, a virtuous and religious one in another* (p. 58, 1837–8). Write a story where a character is leading two lives, one good and one dangerous. Will he or she get caught?

28. *A person, while awake and in the business of life, to think highly of another and place perfect confidence in him; but to be troubled with dreams, in which this seeming friend appears to act the part of a most deadly enemy. Finally it is discovered that the dream-character is the true one* (p. 81, 1838).

Points of View: Varying Perceptions of the Same Character

29. *To make a story out of a scarecrow—giving it queer attributes. From different points of view, it should appear to change sex, being an old man or woman, a gunner, a farmer, the Old Nick &c.* (p. 1, 1840). Take the same event (such as a scarecrow spirit appearing all over town) and write about it from the points of view of the different townspeople.

30. *To look at a beautiful girl, in her chamber or elsewhere, and picture all her lovers, in different situations, whose hearts are centered on her* (p. 65, 1838). Write a story in paragraphs, each of which features a different point of view—all centering on one character.

Writers and Madmen

31. *A person [is] writing a tale, and [finds] that it shapes itself against his intentions; that the characters act otherwise than he thought; that unforeseen events occur; and a catastrophe which he strives in vain to avert. It might shadow forth his own fate—he having made himself one of the personages.* (p. 19, 1835–6) Write a horror story in which the characters won't behave the way you want them to—they talk back to the author, and rebel.

32. *A letter, written a century or more ago, but which has never yet been unsealed* (p. 37, 1836–7).

33. *Story Titles: "The Frenzied Father," "The Maniac Mother," "The Crazy Child"* (p. 34, 1836–7).

34. *Thanksgiving at the Worcester Lunatic Asylum. A ball and dance of the inmates, in the evening—a furious lunatic dancing with the Principal's wife* (p. 81, 1838). Describe a fantastic ball or dance with unusual guests—bugs, birds, zombies, stars, etc.

Appendix B:
Some Lost Notebook Story Starters That Hawthorne (Quite Possibly) Developed into Published Stories

Twice-Told Tales:
"The Great Carbuncle" may have been developed from story starter 15 (treasure).
"The Prophetic Pictures" relates to ideas 14 and 24 (paintings/mirrors).
"Fancy's Show Box" relates to ideas 11 and 12 (museums).
"Howe's Masquerade" relates to idea 34 (costume ball).

Mosses from an Old Manse:
"A Select Party" relates to ideas 17 and 18 (clouds).
"Monsieur Du Miroir" relates to ideas 23 and 24 (mirrors).

"The Hall of Fantasy" relates to ideas 11 and 12 (museums).
"Feathertop" relates to idea 29 (scarecrow).
"Egotism; or the Bosom-Serpent" relates to idea 25 (swallowed serpent).
"A Virtuoso's Collection" relates to ideas 11 and 12 (museums).

The Snow-Image, and Other Twice-Told Tales:
"The Snow-Image" relates to idea 21 (playing in snow).
"Main Street" relates to ideas 11 and 12 (museums).
"Graves and Goblins" relates to ideas 2 and 6 (graveyards).

Appendix C:
Student Writing Samples

Following are some examples created using Hawthorne's story starters:

Story Starter 1: *All the Dead that had ever been drowned in a certain lake [begin] to arise.* When John Rybicki, a writer-in-residence who works for InsideOut, introduced this story idea to an eighth grade class at Pelham Magnet Middle School in Detroit, Chantell Tucker tackled this scary story starter using good sensory details:

Rachman Returns

Rachman from under the water returns with seaweed on him and everybody he touches turns into ice. His hands feel like rust. His eyes are brown with yellow veins in them and he talks like a gorilla. Only one kid in the entire world could stop him—a witch girl—and people thought she was crazy. He searched for this witch and finally found her. She put him back in the water and made him unfreeze the people.

Classmate Jean Marquicelle also included highly imagistic lines in her scary tale:

The drowned people in the river come back to life, kicking seaweed from their feet. Their bodies are decomposed and their bones look like sharp knives.

Story Idea 16: *A person to catch fire-flies, and try to kindle his household fire with them.* The following sample was written by fourth grader Kristina Ford, a student in Channing Todd's fourth grade class at Eagle Lake Elementary School (Edwardsburg, Michigan):

Cassie gets fireflies and puts them in little kids' bedrooms for night-lights. The fireflies form into dream catchers. When Cassie comes to a homeless child, she gets extra, to make covers made of fireflies. If she has extra fireflies, she dumps them in the river and the river shines like the sun. If Cassie put the fireflies upon unbloomed flowers, they make the flowers bloom. When the flowers bloom, they shine bright as diamonds. Cassie meets a man called Ronnie and he also collects fireflies. They find them together. They grow very fond of each other. One night, while collecting fireflies, they meet Mike, the Animal Man. . . .

Fourth grader Al Warner's fireflies act very differently, and also have a sense of humor:

One hundred million fireflies start exploding and make one hundred million people all over the world. Then the fireflies fly all over and make everyone nice to everyone else on the planet. There are also one hundred fireflies who make hundreds of rabbits, who start hopping around making hundreds of flowers. When the rabbits start making flowers, the flowers start spreading peace all over the earth. Then the fireflies start making thousands of dollars to give to the homeless. As soon as the people get all the money, everyone starts getting jobs. After the fireflies give all the homeless people money, houses begin to appear out of nowhere. When that's done, the fireflies make very funny jokes.

Story Starter 23: *Make one's own reflection in a mirror the subject of a story.* This topic was a popular pick in Brian Forcelle's senior English class at McBain Public High School (Michigan). Jennifer Pillsbury wrote of round, bespectacled Doug, a new homeowner eager to examine a malevolent mirror in his dark, cobwebbed attic:

Doug cautiously climbed up the creaking wooden steps to the attic with only a single candle to light his path. The only other source of light was a filthy round window on the opposite end of the attic. Then the narrow beam of light shone down on something that seemed completely out of place. A long mirror with a silver frame and intricate carvings depicting angels and demons was leaning against the wall. Strangely, it wasn't covered with a thick layer of dust and the silver frame still shone brightly despite its age.

As Doug approached the mirror, an eerie chill seemed to radiate out from it. It caused his skin to tingle, and he shuddered. Doug stared curiously at his reflection in the mirror, and for a moment, he thought he saw a sly grin spread across his reflection's face, but it vanished as quickly as it appeared. Then the surface of the mirror seemed to push forward slightly. Against his better judgment, Doug laid his fingers on the spot to examine it. The glass shifted beneath them. Ripples formed and moved outward from the bulging spot, disfiguring his reflection, which was once again smiling. Suddenly, an icy hand reached out from behind the glass and grabbed him by the wrist. . . . The last thing he heard was the cracking and shattering of glass as it crashed all around him.

Story Starter 25: *A snake taken into a man's stomach; and nourished there from fifteen years to thirty-five—tormenting him most horribly.* This idea inspired very different responses in two students. Pelham fifth grader Tanisha Pruitt wrote an innocent and haunting account of the swallowed snake:

> A woman went to a food place and ordered a number seven dinner. She did not know what this was, but she said she'd try it. People were laughing at her because she ate a live snake. The next day, she had a big snake living in her belly. Then she went to the bathroom, and went back to her room. The snake was gone for good. It had turned into a baby boy.

After writer Jonathan Johnson introduced Hawthorne's serpentine quote to his Interlochen Fine Arts Camp class, junior high student Lauren Pecarich re-imagined it. She wrote a snake charmer's song, sung to lure the snake out from the man's stomach.

Charmer's Song

The redness in feel and touch,
a sack of condensed heat
craving for a lost time
crouched beyond the devil's reach.
The forsaken hill, so green and lush
is covered with ashen faces
that scream out from death's line
the sharp intake of breath
like spectators at a football game.
The cravers sit and watch
as the snake falls out from white teeth
and the man stands up.

Story Starter 29: *To make a story out of a scarecrow—giving it queer attributes. From different points of view, it should appear to change sex, being an old man or woman, a gunner, a farmer, the Old Nick &c.* Pelham fifth grader Larry Smith chose to write on the scarecrow in an interestingly grotesque manner when the idea was presented in Chris Kusulas's fifth grade class:

> Scarecrow lives in the neighborhood. At night when Scarecrow wakes up, worms shoot out of his head. When people look up to the streetlights, they

see worms falling. In the morning, up in the sky, people see the worms chilling on the clouds.

Fellow fifth grader James Shamily wrote kindly about his scarecrow:

The scarecrow in my neighborhood is my friend. My mom said we had to get him and put him in our backyard for Halloween. I tried to tell her he was my friend, but she wouldn't listen. The scarecrow cried because the hot sun in the backyard was on him. He got mad, and my mom said he was a monster and she ran out the door. Then the scarecrow came home with me and we had some popcorn.

Bibliography

All above quotations (including some odd spellings and punctuation) were taken from *Hawthorne's Lost Notebook 1835–41: Facsimile from The Pierpont Morgan Library.* Transcript by Barbara S. Mouffle. Introduction by Hyatt H. Waggoner. University Park: Pennsylvania State University Press, 1978.

Related works include:

Hawthorne, Nathaniel. *The American Notebooks by Nathaniel Hawthorne.* Based upon the original manuscripts in the Pierpont Morgan Library and edited by Randall Stewart. New Haven: Yale University Press, 1932.
———. *Passages from the American Note-Books of Nathaniel Hawthorne.* Two volumes, edited by Sophia Hawthorne. Boston: Ticknor and Fields, 1868.
———. *Tales and Sketches.* New York: The Library of America, 1974.

Edgar Allan Poe

Bob Boone

Go with Poe

Teaching Edgar Allan Poe's Tales

WHEN I FOCUS on a single author in my creative writing classes, be it Gwendolyn Brooks, George Orwell, or Emily Dickinson, it is usually to teach a specific type of writing. But sometimes I'm seeking something much simpler: I just want to shake up the class. I want to introduce the students to writing that is so inspiring or outrageous or just plain different that they will be jarred loose from lethargy and feel the urge to get their ideas and feelings down on paper.

Last spring my writing classes were dying a not-so-slow death. My students frowned when they wrote and what they turned in was predictable and unimaginative. They were "going through the motions."

These are no ordinary kids. They are in a program called Young Chicago Authors (YCA), which gives talented high school writers from the city a chance to keep developing their talents. The students begin the program as sophomores. As well as attending weekly classes, they go to readings, perform community service, take trips, meet authors, and teach classes to younger kids in the schools. When they graduate, they receive $2,000 per year for college. The students come from all backgrounds. Most of the time, they are as dynamic as any students I have ever taught.

Most of the time.

After one dreary excuse for a class that spring, I decided to abandon my own prompts and finish by focusing on a single author. That week I met a group of YCA seniors to discuss college. I used the occasion to ask them whom they might like to read. "Let's do Poe," suggested Mollie. "I haven't read Poe since eighth grade." My first reaction was that Poe was too obvious. Anyone can read Poe and like him. But the more I thought about him, the more I liked the possibilities for various subjects and voices and themes. The students had read Poe before in English classes; now they would read him in a writing class.

Four days later, on a warm Saturday morning, I passed out copies of "The Tell-Tale Heart" to the fifteen students in my class and explained that, for each of the next three weeks, we would start a class by reading a

Poe story. When they wrote afterwards, they could respond to something in the Poe story or write whatever they wanted. Whatever they wanted to do, Poe would be there if they needed him.

Before we read "The Tell-Tale Heart" aloud, I asked the students to pay attention to Poe's images, to notice how he told the story, to let their senses be taken in, to look for things to borrow, and to be captured by the mood. "Make yourself available," I told them.

I nodded to a tall sophomore from Hyde Park named Chris, who lately had become our designated reader. As Chris read, the class smiled, laughed, groaned, winced, and gasped at this story, which almost all of them knew well. I found myself savoring Poe's language and the plot more than I ever had before.

I asked for a quick recall: Sounds? The beating of the heart. The squeaking floorboards. Sights? The bulging eye. Smells? The candle burning. I fired off several "What if" questions: "What if someone else had told the story?" "What if the murder took place right away?" "What if the author used only one-syllable words?" "What if the killer had another motive for killing his boss?" Next I passed out a few writing ideas:

• Write what happens after the tale ends and the narrator gives himself up.
• Write a police officer's account.
• Relate a true story in which you get even with someone.
• Describe a time you couldn't hide your guilt.
• Write an original story that begins with the first words of "The Tell-Tale Heart." ("True!—nervous—very, very dreadfully nervous I had been and am; but why *will* you say that I am mad?"[*Poetry and Tales*, p. 555])

I reminded the students that they could also write whatever came to mind. Their tales could be true or made up. They could be in prose or poetry. Whatever they did, I wanted them to use a strong narrative voice, to consider the connections between feelings and actions, and to create vivid settings. I wanted them to take it seriously, to feel this was more than an exercise, that what they scribbled down hurriedly could become something significant.

So they wandered off to write—some to the duct-taped couches, some to desks, some to the rugs, some to corners, some to the stairwell, some to the back porch, and a few to a café down the street. I made myself a cup of coffee and then walked through the YCA offices, which are actually the top floor of an old building in Wicker Park. Many of the kids were writing nonstop and barely noticing me. I decided to stroll through the neighborhood while they wrote.

Ninety minutes later, we were sitting in a circle on the floor ready to share. First I asked what they now thought of my plan to use Poe. "A great idea," beamed Mollie, whose idea it had been in the first place. The others appeared relaxed and pleased. Their notebooks and journals looked full.

Ben, a little guy with big hair, volunteered to read his story, an account of what happens after the cops arrive:

> The irritating smiles vanished from the faces of the officers, doing much to relieve the horror that had overcome me. The old man's heart continued to beat, but noticeably quieter than before. The men stared at me blankly for a moment. I slid down into my chair, as the nervousness that had been surging through my veins was replaced by an onslaught of quiet serenity. The men stood, and moved towards me. Their voices grew harsh as they interrogated me. I revealed to them—and I admit that I did so with a certain amount of pleasure and pride—my flawless plan.
>
> Their eyes grew wide as I described what I had done with the dismembered body. The youngest of the officers pulled a pair of handcuffs from his belt, and fastened them around my wrists. They asked me where I had put the crowbar that I used to pry up the floorboards, and after I told them, the officer who had handcuffed me went to get it.
>
> One of the remaining officers grabbed me by the collar and thrust his face up close to mine. With a great deal of anger and a small amount of fear in his voice, he questioned my motive. Ha! What did he know? He never had to endure the stares of the old man's vulture eye. Thinking of that hideous eye immediately takes away any remorse that is building up inside my conscience.
>
> Of course the officer, lacking the aforementioned knowledge, had little insight into the cause of my actions, and therefore had no sympathy for me. He called me mad, and spat upon my face. Before my rage could get a firm hold on me, the younger officer returned with the crowbar. It took me a minute to identify the correct floorboards, but I did so, and the men went to work. As the boards were pried up, and the mutilated body was revealed, a look of disgust and sickness came over their faces. I begged them to open an eyelid on the severed head, so that they could see the reason behind my so-called crime. Oh, how I know that if only they had done my bidding, I would certainly have gained their sympathy. However, they did not do as I asked, and the officer who had previously said and done very little pulled out his baton and slammed it into my skull. Barely conscious, I watched a trail of blood trickle onto the ground as they dragged me outside so that I could be taken to the station. I am fairly certain that I fell unconscious at this point,

for the next thing I remember is waking up in this dark, dirty cell, locked up like the madman they had accused me of being.

Smiles and nods. The others were impressed that the story felt so "finished." Chris appreciated phrases such as "lacking the aforementioned knowledge" and the other Poeisms. Rebecca thought Ben did a good job keeping the narrator in character: Little things still made him mad. I thought Ben made a smart move by ending with the narrator still convinced he's sane.

Ben was one of the few students who had not lost interest in writing, so I was not surprised by his strong effort. Hyo was another story. Lately, she hadn't been writing anything at all. Today, however, she cheerfully offered to read her version of what the cops might have reported.

Did I realize he was mad? Oh, yes, from the start, I knew something was wrong with him. As soon as he opened the door, he started making these nervous smiles. At first, I just thought he was on some kind of antidepressants. He kept smiling without any reason. He couldn't walk straight and kept looking around the house the whole time my partner and I were there. So we couldn't just leave him there, we being police officers and all, we decided to stay a little longer with him since he looked very lonesome living in that gigantic mansion all alone, without the old man. My partner and I had warm hearts.

The second thing I noticed about his sick behavior was that as soon as we mentioned the shriek, he begged us to search the house. You know, we were there to ask him a few questions, not for investigating. My partner and I couldn't say no since our job was to serve the citizens. We searched everywhere, even all the closets in the house. Boy, were we exhausted.

Oscar pointed out that Hyo's cops do "cop-like things": They ask questions. They search. They draw obvious conclusions. They fear for the safety of the servant in the large mansion. Ben was amused by the phrase "Boy, were we exhausted!" ("It sounds like something people say after putting up a tent.")

Several students wrote true stories—mostly revenge pieces. Danny, who lately had been promising much and producing little, described a fight with his older brother Juan, who happens to be a graduate of Young Chicago Authors.

Lexe got even with her sister "for her stupid little tricks through the years":

I waited for what seemed like eternity until finally I heard my sister come out and climb into bed. Believing that I was sleeping, she said, "Good night,

Lexe." I said good night from the closet and watched through the shutters as she rolled over and closed her eyes. I counted off at least a minute in my head and then I slowly started to switch the closet light on and off. I heard my sister turn to my bed and stammer, "Le-e-x-e?"

Finally I couldn't hold it anymore. I started laughing hysterically because I knew I had gotten her, and I opened the closet door.

It's funny, though, every time I remind her of this incident she claims that she knew it was me and was just playing along—I highly doubt it.

I told Lexe and Danny that I admired their willingness to let us get a peek at their darker sides. Writers should be able to show some bad qualities. The others thought that Lexe had built suspense in a Poe-like way. ("I waited for what seemed like an eternity. . . .") Barth thought the last paragraph was important because it showed her sister's character. And "It gives Lexe a reason to scare her one more time."

Of the other true-story options, the "getting even" story found several takers. Oscar, perhaps our least angry student, described another student at his school "who thinks he is better than everyone else."

I don't doubt at all that it was he who wrote an anonymous article in the school paper saying that everyone in our school is so ugly that every time he looks around, he wants to throw up. All this person does is criticize other people.

I'm always close. I hear all the awful things he has to say. "Did you see what she did to her hair?" "Why is she wearing those ugly and old looking clothes?" "Why is it that everyone dresses so weird?"

I say to myself, "If I thought someone was weird, I would think it was you." The good thing is that no one knows that they are being talked about behind their backs.

What gets me even more mad is that he pretends to be a very nice friend and tells others how nice they look when in the reality, he has something bad to say. All I want to do is get up and tell him, "What's the problem? Why is everybody less of a person than you are?" But I don't. I'll keep it to myself until that one day when I get really mad.

Several students decided to start stories with Poe's first sentence. Here is Alex's:

True!—nervous—very, very dreadfully nervous I had been and am; but why *will* you say that I am mad? I tell you now, ever so carefully, of the sinful deed, which I, so very meticulously, carried through. It was at the corner pantry store, a place which over the years of my childhood I had wandered into from time to time. Usually I did so for trivial, meager tasks, food, candy, and other such meaningless childhood necessities.

It was through these adventures that I had become very well acquainted with the store's clerk, as we made a commonplace ritual of discussing our day to day affairs. I had even made a regular habit of purchasing a bag of chips and a can of coke every time I came into the store. It was on this particular day, however, that I had something very different in mind.

Why I even decided to do what I did, I know not, only that once my mind grabbed hold of the idea, I could not escape it. It soon became the very object of all my thoughts, and I began finding myself staying up for hours at night as my mind began to formulate my devilish plan. For weeks on end, I planned and schemed, and when that very day came, I was ready. As I approached the store, I made sure to do it with a certain swiftness, as not to attract unwanted attention.

Naturally, we wanted to know more about the "devilish plan," but he wasn't telling.

Anamaria wrote about a girl who must make a speech at graduation. "I like this character," Anamaria told us. "She does the kinds of things I would like to do, but I'm afraid to do."

I took a seat in the auditorium. How dreadfully nervous I was. My hands trembled as I accepted the diploma. When the principal introduced me, I took a deep breath. Here goes nothing. I hurried to the podium so quickly that I didn't see Michael, the star athlete, who had nothing better to do than trip me.

I lost it. I took off one of my highheeled sandals and aimed at his head. I scored. The students, the teachers, and the parents gasped. What did I do?

I calmly put on the sandal. I flipped my hair back with one manicured nail and stepped to the podium as if nothing had happened.

We all agreed that the "one manicured nail" was a marvelous detail.

At the start of the next week's class, I told the students that I was tremendously pleased about what had happened last week. "We're all awake again. Poe woke us up!" One of our college students, who types up the student work, popped in to say that she had enjoyed the Poe pieces more than anything she'd read in a long time. "You guys are all sick," she said with a friendly smile.

Chris started the next session off by reading "The Masque of the Red Death." It was a pleasure to hear—big words and all. The second paragraph has some beauties such as massy, sagacious, castellated, girdled, buffoons, and improvisatori. The class especially liked the phrase appliances of pleasure.

I then passed out a list of writing ideas, adding my usual, "But if you want to respond in your own way, find a quiet place and start writing. You can even go outside if you want. . . ." (It was 40 degrees and raining—a good old Chicago spring day.)

Here were the ideas:

- Write a story that takes place at a party or celebration.
- Write a story told by someone who likes to use big words.
- Write a modern day fable in which a group of arrogant people get what they deserve.
- Rewrite this story from Death's point of view.
- Write a folk tale that begins "The people from the island of Durf thought they had it all figured out."
- Begin a story with "I had to rip off his mask. I had to. I had to. What else could I do?"

Ninety minutes later, the kids seemed even more pleased with themselves than they had the week before. They were anxious to hear what the others had written.

Wayne offered to read first. He stood up and narrated in the voice of Death, but he told the story of a celebration:

> I am the specter, the uninvited guest of the next locale to which I shall claim my next guest, and lead him to the abode of which I belong. I am the unnoticed, the unreal, the cloaked taker of life. I have always been present to witness the fall of another human life.

Wayne was a big fellow, made bigger by the roller blades he was sporting that day. He was also the emcee at our poetry slam and was writing a play about a minister who loses faith. Loren asked if he could find some way to "sneak Death's speech" into the play. Wayne said he would think about it.

Chris read next. He had gathered up several ideas and words and started a poem:

> The phantasm was a terrible sight
> He sent to me a gruesome fright.
> I screamed and ran so I could see
> No more of him. This would not be.
> He came at me all grim and rude
> His cloak was black and blood-bedewed

Chris must have been the first high school student ever to use "blood-bedewed" in a piece of rhymed poetry, we all agreed.

The folk tale about the island of Durf also had some takers. Evonne, who had never tried anything like this before, came up with this:

> The people from the island of Durf thought they had it all figured out. They thought they could outsmart death by cheating him out of his plans. They don't know that death is very sagacious and and could never be beaten. The people from the island of Durf shouldn't have even thought they could run from him because now he's really out to get them. The people from the island of Durf made plans to leave the island before Scar Face could hit them. No one has ever known of a pestilence being so ugly and painful. Every life Scar Face touched, it terminated. The people who caught this disease almost instantly died. Their face would develop deep black scars while on other parts of their body their skin would be literally peeling off. This disease kills in three minutes. Every piece of skin is gone except the skin on your face which has the deep black scars. This is how death chose to take their lives.

Bill told Evonne how easy her writing made it for him to conjure up the action. The others liked her use of repetition. Evonne reminded us twice that this "is all new to me." Usually she writes poetry or true stories about people from her neighborhood, never fantasy.

Several kids had chosen the last option, the story about removing the mask. I asked them to read their first paragraphs since time was running out.

> REBECCA: I had to rip off the mask. I had to. I had to. What else could I do? Don't you ever wonder what death looks like? Think how incredibly awesome it would be to stare into the unmasked face of Death and truly know what you are up against. I had to do it. I knew that once I did, I would feel victorious and glorious.

> URSULA: I had to rip off the mask. I had to. I had to. What else could do? He looked so horrible in it—the blood dripping down his right cheek like tears. He was dreaming of Death. I had to save him.

> HYO: "I had to rip off the mask. I had to. I had to. What else could I do?" The words echo in the living room.
> "No you didn't have to rip off the mask!" scorns the mother.
> "No, I had to I had to!!!" cries Helen.
> "But why, Helen, why?" asks the mother.
> "Because his mask reminded me of the ghost I saw in the dream . . . it was horrifying. I was scared, Mommy," sobs Helen.

> MARCUS: I had to rip off his mask. I had to. I had to. What else could I do? I had to know who was the man behind the red mask. So I waved my hand in front of his face to make sure he was completely knocked out. I tugged and

tugged, but the mask wouldn't come loose. As I was giving my final yank, a black-gloved hand reached up and grabbed my forearm.

Applause. The class left laughing.

For the next and last session, we descended into the catacombs with "The Cask of Amontillado." The kids listened carefully as Chris read slowly and deeply. I was sure that this story with its ingenious plot, heavy language, and gloomy setting would get this group off and writing. I didn't even hand out prompts. My only recommendation was that "You might write a story that that takes place underground."

When we reconvened, Loren volunteered her piece, which happened to be a description of a recent dream:

> I'm in some old house. No one can see me. I'm just observing. The lights are off, and there's no light switch to flick. Three characters from the soap opera Passions are here—Tabitha, the witch; Charity, whose destiny is to destroy all evil; and Kay, who wants Charity's boyfriend, Miguel.
>
> Tabitha is on one side of a vent whispering something to Charity, who is listening on the other side. Charity tries to make out what's being said. Kay is standing next to Charity asking what she hears. Charity doesn't answer. Tabitha whispers a chant to Charity, and suddenly a mist comes from Charity's body and travels through the vent to Tabitha. Kay tries to grab Charity but her hands go straight through her. On the other side of the vent Tabitha collects the mist in a jar.

Everyone liked the mist, especially Rebecca. "Loren made something that couldn't happen seem so real. I love 'collects the mist in a jar'!"

Alex was one of several students who wrote stories taking place underground.

> Slowly, I opened my eyes and my dim surroundings came into view. I had been sleeping but somehow I had little recollection as to how I got where I was or how long I had been asleep. I ran my fingers over my face, suddenly feeling a terrible headache. A sliver of light crept through a tall window near the ceiling. The wall was constructed of a crude brick and bore no decorations. The only piece of furniture I could see was the worn bed which I found myself lying on. The bed itself was made of wood and covered with filthy rags. I moved myself to a sitting position, and as I did, I saw an old wooden door across from me.
>
> I ran my hand over my face, still feeling somewhat drowsy. Drawn by curiosity I managed to get up so that I could look through the keyhole. I found myself looking at what appeared to be part of a hallway. A small torch hung upon the stone walls of the hallway, but other than that, it was completely empty. I frowned and made my way down to the bed.

I walked up to the door examining it momentarily. It had no handle and looked almost as if it wasn't a door at all. I pushed on it slightly but to no effect. I mumbled to myself and pushed again, this time much harder. The door creaked as if about to break but still didn't budge. I kicked at it and then cursed violently as if the pain ringed through my foot. Quickly I went to the opposite side of the room and then ran at the door full speed.

And that's where Alex stopped. "I'll have to decide what happens next," he said. I told Alex I liked the way he started in the middle of the action. Somehow, he just has to work in the background, and he should have a great time figuring that out.

Luis also started an "underground story" that was similarly filled with fear and gloom. Like Alex, he started in the middle.

The storm still raged on. But it was quiet in the cathedral except for the silent whisper of the bishop and the loud clash of thunder that echoed from every corner of the enormous structure. The black angel had already claimed the lives of half of our men, women, and children. Hundreds upon thousands of people fled the country for fear of the black angel. However he did not spare any lives. So the people were often killed on their way to freedom. And others like myself hid in the cathedral and spent the last of our days in silent prayer. The black angel was very swift and silent like a panther on the prowl. The only defense against the angel was prayer. It has been seven months since we locked ourselves in the cathedral. And on my knees I am not sure if I can pray to the shrines or the walls. These walls are so cold. We have no food either. The black angel breathes on my neck. These walls are so cold.

Muhadji's underground paper includes this short, telling paragraph:

That's when I decided to make a window. I knew our world had significantly changed since three years before. It was hard being bossed around. The conditions were horrible. We paced back and forth and nearly wore out the floor. The children were diseased by now. There wasn't any food left. Bodies lay limp. The flesh looked eaten through. And sunlight we hadn't seen.

These kids always liked to read aloud, but today, hearing Poe read aloud, they were reading their own work with a special delight. It was as if they wanted the audience to imagine, as clearly as they, the scenes playing out in their minds.

Ben wrote a story about someone named Gomer. "I wanted to rant a little," he told us. "And I've always liked revenge as a motive."

Gomer might think I have forgotten, but he's wrong, wrong, wrong. In fact, I remember it like it was yesterday. We had been in my basement playing darts. I had finished throwing my darts and I was going to the board to collect them when the bastard yelled, "Joe, watch out!" I turned around in time to see the grin fade from his face as one of his darts hit me dead in the eye. The pain was indescribable.

That was two years ago. I have to wear an eye patch now and I have no depth perception. I had gotten over these inconveniences, however, and the time had come for me to get revenge. Gomer was my cousin. He was the youngest of my cousins, and the only one of them that would ever hang out with me. His family finally came to visit mine, and I was ready for him.

After going through the boring, yet apparently necessary process of greeting the rest of his family, I invited him down to the basement to play Nintendo. I offered him some Coke and he happily accepted. I made no mention of my eye patch.

I went to the bathroom, and upon my return, I saw that my glass of Coke was now half empty while his own remained untouched. Damn that bastard! "You're drinking my Coke," I said sharply.

"Sorry, Gomer, you can have mine, I haven't drunk out of it yet."

"No," I hissed. "You will drink your Coke."

"That's okay, I'm not really thirsty anymore."

"I'LL SHOW YOU NOT THIRSTY ANYMORE!" I screamed as I whipped out the 9mm pistol I had concealed in the pouch of my sweatshirt. Joe stared at me in horror, as I held the gun to his head. "DRINK IT!" I shouted.

"What the hell?!" he started nervously. "Joe what's the big deal? It's just a Coke. . . ."

"NO," I replied, "It's Coke with a heavy dose of arsenic in it. Now drink!"

"I'll tell you one thing about Poe," Rebecca blurted out. "He certainly shows us us how to rant and rave. We all seem to like that voice."

"I love it," said Ben. "It's not me, but it sort of is. It's fun to shout every once and a while."

Ben was right. It is fun to shout. It's fun to tell tall tales. It's fun to be jealous, and to create gory and frightening scenes. It's fun to reveal our darker sides. When the kids left that day to begin the summer vacation, I was convinced that Poe had done for my class what I had wanted him to do. For three weeks the students had written passionately. They had tried on new forms and reintroduced themselves to old ones. They had experimented in different voices. Most of all, they had rediscovered the enormous satisfaction of losing themselves in a piece of writing.

Bibliography

Poe, Edgar Allan. *Poetry and Tales*. New York: The Library of America, 1984.

Henry David Thoreau

Thoreau, the Writing Coach

If you have ever done any work with these finest tools, the imagination and fancy and reason, it is a new creation, independent of the world, and a possession forever. You have laid up something against a rainy day. You have to that extent cleared the wilderness.

—Henry David Thoreau, Journal, May 1, 1857[1]

All that a man has to say or do that can possibly concern mankind, is in some shape or other to tell the story of his love,—to sing; and, if he is fortunate and keeps alive, he will be forever in love.

—Henry David Thoreau, Journal, May 6, 1854[2]

IT IS UNFORTUNATE that Thoreau never delivered a lecture or wrote an essay about writing. In his letters and journals as well as in *Walden* and *A Week on the Concord and Merrimack Rivers*, Thoreau occasionally talks about his modus operandi and even gives others and himself some advice. But Thoreau's ideas about writing are most abundantly clear in his journals. He began to keep his first journal in 1837 at the suggestion of his friend and mentor Ralph Waldo Emerson. By the end of Thoreau's life, his journals ran to some seven thousand pages.

If there could only be one statement Thoreau made that typifies what he did as a writer, it is the following:

Let me suggest a theme for you: to state to yourself precisely and completely what that walk over the mountains amounted to for you,—returning to this essay again and again, until you are satisfied that all that was important in your experience is in it.[3]

The key (or difficulty) for teachers is to get students to identify the experiences that are important to them. We cannot teach experience, but we can encourage students to assess their own, and Thoreau's journals offer an inspiring example to follow. Thoreau's week-long trip with his brother, for instance, about a hundred pages long in his journal, became *A Week on the Concord and Merrimack Rivers*, an immense and wild 500-page grab bag of his journal entries, essays, literary criticism, and poetry. "All that was important in [Thoreau's] experience is in it."

A description from "Sunday":

Having reached a retired part of the river where it spread out to sixty rods in width, we pitched our tent on the east side, in Tyngsboro, just above some patches of the beach plum, which was now nearly ripe, where the sloping bank was a sufficient pillow, and with the bustle of sailors making the land, we transferred such stores as were required from boat to tent, and hung a lantern to the tent-pole, and so our house was ready. With a buffalo [skin] spread on the grass, and a blanket for our covering, our bed was soon made. A fire crackled merrily before the entrance, so near that we could tend it without stepping abroad, and when we had supped, we put out the blaze, and closed the door, and with the semblance of domestic comfort, sat up to read the gazetter, to learn our latitude and longitude, and write the journal of the voyage, or listened to the wind and the rippling of the river till sleep overtook me. There we lay under an oak on the bank of the stream, near to some farmer's corn-field, getting sleep, and forgetting where we were; a great blessing, that we are obliged to forget our enterprises every twelve hours. Minks, muskrats, meadow-mice, wood-chucks, squirrels, skunks, rabbits, foxes, and weasles [sic], all inhabit near, but keep very close while you are there. The river sucking and eddying away all night down toward the marts and the seaboard, a great work and freshet, and no small enterprise to reflect on.[4]

A reflection from "Thursday":

We can never safely exceed the actual facts in our narratives. Of pure invention, such as in our narratives, there is no instance. To write a true work of fiction even, is only to take leisure and liberty to describe some things more exactly as they are. A true account of the actual is the rarest poetry, for common sense always takes a hasty and superficial view. Though I am not much acquainted with the works of Goethe, I should say that it was one of his chief excellencies as a writer, that he is satisfied with giving an exact description of things as they appear to him, and their effect upon him. Most travelers have not self-respect enough to do this simply, and make objects and events stand around them as the center, but still imagine more favorable positions and relations than the actual ones, and so we get no valuable report from them at all. In his *Italian Travels* Goethe jogs along at a snail's pace, but always mindful that the earth is beneath and the heavens are above him. His Italy is not merely the fatherland of lazzaroni and virtuosi, and scene of splendid ruins, but a solid turf-clad soil, daily shined on by the sun, and nightly by the moon. Even the few showers are faithfully recorded. He speaks as an unconcerned spectator, whose object is faithfully to describe what he sees, and that, for the most part, in the order in which he sees it. Even his reflections do not interfere with his descriptions. In one place he speaks of himself as giving so glowing and so truthful a description of an old tower to the peasants who had gathered around him, that they who had been born and brought up in the neighborhood must needs look over their shoulders, "that," to use his own words, "they might behold with their eyes, what I had praised to their ears"—"and I added nothing, not even the ivy which for centuries had decorated the walls." It would thus be possible for inferior minds to produce invaluable books, if this moderation were not the evidence of superiority; for the wise are not so much wiser than others as respecters of their own wisdom. Some, poor in spirit, record plaintively only what has happened to them; but others how they have happened to the universe, and the judgment which they have awarded to circumstances.[5]

* * *

Thoreau worried that his range was very narrow ("I believe I have but one text and one sermon"[6]), but he also believed in spontaneous walks in new directions: "It is wise to write on many subjects, to try many themes, that so [sic] you may find the right and inspiring one . . . You must try a thousand themes before you find the right one, as nature makes a thousand acorns to get one oak."[7] (Thoreau had not one but two mighty oaks, Nature and Civil Disobedience.) Sometimes his declarations on the writing process sound a bit like pep talks:

> The more you have thought and written on a given theme, the more you can still write. Thought breeds thought. It grows under your hands.[8]

> Don't suppose that you can tell it precisely the first dozen times you try, but at 'em again, especially where, after a sufficient pause, you suspect that you are touching the heart or summit of the matter, reiterate your blows there, and account for the mountain to yourself. Not that the story need be long, but it will take a long while to make it short.[9]

Does this mean that we, as writing teachers, have a little Socrates—and a little Knute Rockne—in us? Perhaps so. Our knowledge of something allows us to make exponential progressions in our thinking and writing about it. This is one reason we read books together and share our writing—so that thought will breed thought.

> Write often, write upon a thousand themes, rather than long at a time, not trying to turn too many feeble somersets in the air,—and so come down upon your head at last. Antaeus-like, be not long absent from the ground.[10]

One criticism you could make of Thoreau's civil disobedience essays is that he doesn't stay on the ground. He takes long, angry, sustained flights as he bravely (and persuasively) scolds his fellow citizens. But those very extended expressions of anger and rage at society are intermixed (or undercut) in his journals, which document his own day-to-day trials and his cool but loving observations on, for instance, muskrats and autumnal tints. I believe that even Thoreau would agree that his journals more truly reflect his thoughts and experiences than his most declamatory essays: "I trust you realize what an exaggerator I am,—that I lay myself out to exaggerate whenever I have an opportunity,—pile Pelion upon Ossa, to reach heaven so. Expect no trivial truth from me, unless I am on the witness-stand."[11] I would argue that his journals were his "witness stand."

By the time Thoreau stopped keeping journals—in 1861, a few months before he died—he had written more than two million words in them. He saw the consistency of personality and how the unconscious revelation through our journals of who we are is truer than any series of deliberate and conscious revelations.

> How simple is the natural connection of events. We complain greatly of the want of flow and sequence in books, but if the journalist [that is, journal-keeper] only move himself from Boston to New York, and speak as before, there is link enough. And so there would be, if he were as careless of connection and order when he stayed at home, and let the incessant progress which his life makes be the apology for abruptness. Do I not travel as far away from my old resorts, though I stay here at home, as though I were on board the steamboat? Is not my life riveted together? Has not it sequence? Do not my breathings follow each other naturally?[12]

My first pedagogical success with journals occurred when I was teaching community college students in Manhattan. I was naïve, new to New York City, and didn't restrict the journal's topics to the obviously very narrow ones of classroom projects: reading, writing, research. From my students' two pages a week, I learned more about everyday life in Manhattan, Brooklyn, Queens, and the Bronx—and the experiences of recent immigrants—than I had gleaned from the many books of journalism and history I was then reading. One of my favorite students, who wrote essays entitled "Me Versus Me" and "My First Gun," went AWOL after the spring semester break. I was surprised and delighted when he returned. To make up for the month of missed classes, Asan, an ex-graffiti artist from the Bronx and self-styled entrepreneur, handed me thirty-odd pages of handwritten binder paper.

"Wow," I said.

He nodded.

"Your journals?" I asked.

"Yeah.—That's enough, you think?"

Several students fell behind on their journals; a few of them, when they finally got them in, pretended they had been keeping them all along. ("I been doing them, I just keep forgetting to bring them in.") A few, including Asan, managed in what must have been one or two sittings to recreate their life week by week.[13] I found a couple of these after-the-fact journals to be extraordinary, even if they were practically fictional recreations. Asan's was the best, a dramatized explanation of where he had been those several weeks: in or on his way to the hospital. The doctors never told him if he had pneumonia or bronchitis (after a week of tests, tuberculosis and AIDS had been ruled out), but while he was lying in bed, his friends ("the Gods") and girlfriend ("my Earth") visited. On at least two occasions the Gods and he smoked marijuana together (he knew this was unwise), and on a few other occasions he made love with Earth. (This required blocking the door with furniture.)

Although assigning open-topic journals seemed to me one of the best ways to encourage my students to write, I became frustrated when I realized the students weren't doing their reading. So after one semester, I steered the direction of their journals back to the limited topics that had a more direct classroom relevance and applicability (such as reading assignments, prospective themes, directed observations), thus giving up a lot of my enjoyment in reading about their lives.

Did Thoreau ever feel frustrated by his devotion to journal-keeping? Did he ever feel it was merely escapism? His journals were his truest friend and confidant, so much so that a rebuke from a human friend made him ruefully reflect:

> I have got to that pass with my friend that our words do not pass with each other for what they are worth. We speak in vain; there is no one to hear. He finds fault with me that I walk alone, when I pine for want of a companion; that I commit my thoughts to a diary even on my walks, instead of seeking to share them generously with a friend; curses my practice even. Awful it is to contemplate, I pray that, if I am the cold intellectual skeptic whom he rebukes, his curse may take effect, and wither and dry up those sources of my life, and my journal no longer yield me pleasure nor life.[14]

No, Thoreau never gave up on his journals, and most of his friendships soured after a time of exposure.

* * *

Last year, after reading twenty volumes of Thoreau's work before editing a book of his quotations, it was impossible for me not to try to put into practice in my teaching what he said and did about writing. I teach at

Kingsborough Community College in Brooklyn, and nature—though it exists nearly everywhere, even in New York City—was a topic I shied away from trying to get my students to write about.[15] (I am, however, interested in cities as natural human habitats and I love the "publicness" of New York.) We read, in a second-semester English class, not *Walden* (whose subtitle is *Or Life in the Woods*), but *Sidewalk* (whose subtitle could be *Or Life of the Down-and-Out Entrepreneurs in the City*), a sociological study by Mitchell Duneier about the sidewalk book vendors on Sixth Avenue in Greenwich Village. I decided to ask my students to go to a public spot in New York City and to just sit there, doing nothing for an hour but taking notes on what they saw, heard, smelled, touched, and tasted.

Kijana Kilkenney, a student from Brooklyn, made the best of a very cold hour in Harlem:

> It is Friday, March 17th, 2000. It is a frigid cold night. It's a strange night, because this time of season is usually comfortable. It's generally in the lower forties at night. This night is freezing. . . .
>
> I was supposed to meet my cousin at 125th and St. Nick in Harlem. I left my house at 12:45 A.M. to meet him. I took the D train to the stop and reached there roughly about 1:30.
>
> It is very cold outside. There is no sign of my cousin. I'm standing in front of a 24-hour bodega by the pay phones. This is where I told them to meet me. I never thought this would be my spot of observation, but after standing here for a long period of time, I'm noticing everything.
>
> This location isn't much different than any other junction in New York City. Train station, corner store, chain restaurants, and pay phones.
>
> My back is to the stores on 125th. I'm facing north up St. Nick. I often look left and right to see it. They are coming from the west or east. The wind is really severe at this point. There is a McDonald's behind me (which is closed). There is a Popeye's diagonally across the street, which is open. I see people going in and out. I begin to contemplate whether I should go in to stay warm, but I choose to stay outside hoping they'll come soon. Across the street and to the left of me is M & G's, a soul food restaurant that has been there for decades. It's closed now, but the lights on the sign are still flashing.
>
> I can't help but notice that I'm seeing the same faces walk by me during my wait. People are walking in and out of the bodega. Some have even stayed in there so long that I forget that they went in.
>
> I try the pay phone, but it's not working. It took my quarter, so I moved to the next. Since my cousin and the rest of the people were coming from upstate, I knew it would be a long-distance call. I put in a quarter knowing that it would be the least amount of money I needed. The phone told me I needed to deposit fifty cents or something along those lines. Thinking all I needed to add is another quarter, that's what I did. The phone kept my

money. I hung it up, turned the coin return knob, and nothing happened. "You have to put in fifty cents." This was a woman's voice coming from the phone. It was a real live voice. "Excuse me," I said, surprised, and wondering how someone got on the other end of the phone. "You need to put in fifty cents," she repeated.

"Okay," I said, still stunned that I was talking to someone without calling the operator.

There is a double-parked car on the corner of St. Nicholas. Its hazard lights are blinking, and if I'm not mistaken it's been there since I got here. Cabs wait on the other side of St. Nick for any passengers. There are about four cabs waiting. Still no sign of my cousin.

About three guys walk into the corner store. One has on a tan parka with jeans, another with all black. No one is really talking because the cold air really makes it hard to speak. Several cabs stop in front of me and passengers get out and enter the store.

This corner store (which isn't exactly on the corner) seems to be a hot spot for those who want a late-night snack or beer. Several people walk out with brown paper bags twisted around a bottle.

The kid with glasses steps out and sees an attractive girl who seems to have no other plans but to get home. "Where you going?" said the boy with glasses. "To the train," said the girl in a tone hoping she's not asked any more questions. Of course he walks with her around the corner to the station.

Sick, cold, and tired of standing outside, I decide to go back downstairs. The station is long and cold. It has orange colored tiles. There are two exits/entrances, one on 127th and the other on 125th, where I am. I'm standing behind the booth by the new vending machines for MetroCards.

This guy approaches me showing me his MetroCard and saying something I can't understand. "I'm not getting on," I say.

"I'm trying to help you get on."

"Nah," I replied.

He nodded his head as if saying, "You fucking liar."

I'm not really in the mood to talk to anyone unless I'm getting answers for why I'm still fucking here. He walks away and comes back to me about five minutes later.

"The world is crazy. All these images." He's speaking to me because I'm the only one here.

"What?" I said, wishing he would leave me alone.

"All these images, you know what I'm saying, fam?"

"Yeah," I say, not really knowing what the hell he's talking about, but I know of the images that are out here.

"All these things got people falling into fashion wearing all these labels."

"Right," I said. Now I'm zoning him out, but he's still talking. He has on a charcoal color coat with writing across the chest, but I can't read the words. His head is covered with a knit hat. He has a short but long enough beard so that you can't see the skin. He looks like it's way past his bedtime. Either his eyes are low and red from smoke, or he's just tired, or both. His head is to the side, almost touching his shoulder. Every once in a while his words chime into my head. "Know what I'm saying, fam?"

I'm looking at the station walls and the steps. The walls have photographs of Harlem from the 1920s through the '50s.

"I'm not saying it's a black and white thing. For all I know you could be half white."

"Right," is all I could say.

"You have to know what you're dealing with. I dabble in it, but I have an understanding of what I'm getting into. You have to know a little something about everything."

He begins to walk away. I'm guessing maybe he saw that I have some brains in my head and he was satisfied with that.

"One last thing, fam." ("Fam" is short for "family.") "You were born and raised here?"

"No," I say.

"Where are you from?"

"I was born in Guyana."

"When did you come here?"

"I came here about '86, '87."

"About fourteen years ago," he said.

"Yeah."

"So would you say there's any difference from then to now?" he asks me with a look on his face as if this was the final question and the one that really matters.

"I'd say if anything it changed for the worse. It got worse."

"All right, that's it. I just wanted to see where your head was at on that."

He's walking away and turns around. "I hope your girl ain't stand you up."

I just nod my head.

"Never that, right?" he tells me as he walks to the turnstile.

"You're still here?" A question from a guy walking towards him with a blue parka on.

"Yeah, I'm waiting for you," the guy said who I was just talking to.

"You went to Speed?"

"No, but I'm going to . . ." He says a name, but I can't hear it.

I look at my watch, and it is 2:15 A.M. In all I've been here for forty-five minutes. I decide to go back upstairs one more time for a while before I leave for good. I walk up the steps and stand right back in the same spot as before. I see the same faces continuously walk back and forth. The kid with the glasses is with one other kid.

"Use this phone," says the kid with glasses, pointing at the phones by where I'm standing.

"They don't work," said the newcomer as he was crossing the street to get to the other phones.

At this point I'm done. I didn't expect this to be my spot or location for observation, but I ended up being here for so long I had to observe everything. I'm too tired to ride the train all the way back to Brooklyn, so I decide to walk to my grandmother's house in the neighborhood. I begin to walk down 125th to Amsterdam. I'm still looking back and forth to see if for some strange reason they arrive an hour later.

I make a left on Amsterdam and cross LaSalle and make a right between the buildings. I enter her building and ring the bell several times. There is no answer. I would've called first, but my grandmother turns her ringer off in the night. My last chance was hope she didn't tonight. I walked down 123rd to Amsterdam and used the phone. It was my last quarter. It was either this or the train.

"Hello," said a surprisingly not-so-tired voice.

"Hi, Ona. I'm sorry to be calling so late, but I was supposed to see Kahlil over an hour ago, but he never showed up."

"Where are you?"

"Right downstairs."

"Okay, ring the bell. I'll buzz you in."

Once I arrived to her floor I noticed she had on a nightgown.

On a night where I planned to observe pretty women, I observe cabs, stores, beer drinkers.

A week later, following Thoreau's lead, I asked my students to return to the same spot, but at a different hour or day of the week, and to spend another hour taking notes. Thoreau the journal-keeper continually returned to the same spot—sometimes on purpose, sometimes not. This precipitated some discoveries of dramatic changes in Nature:

Ah, the pickerel of Walden! When I see them lying on the ice, or in the well which the fisherman cuts in the ice, making a little hole to admit the water, I am always surprised by their rare beauty, as if they were fabulous fishes, they are so foreign to the streets, even to the woods, foreign as Arabia to our Concord life. They possess a quite dazzling and transcendent beauty which separates them by a wide interval from the cadaverous cod and haddock whose fame is trumpeted in our streets. They are not green like the pines, nor gray like the stones, nor blue like they sky; but they have, to my eyes, if possible, yet rarer colors, like flowers and precious stones, as if they were the pearls, the animalized nuclei or crystals of the Walden water. They, of course, are Walden all over and all through; are themselves small Waldens in the animal kingdom, Waldenses. It is surprising that they are caught here,—

that in this deep and capacious spring, far beneath the rattling teams and chaises and tinkling sleighs that travel the Walden road, this great gold and emerald fish swims. I never chanced to see its kind in any market; it would be the cynosure of all eyes there. Easily, with a few convulsive quirks, they give up their watery ghosts, like a mortal translated before his time to the thin air of heaven.[16]

I asked my students to do what Thoreau suggests: "If you are describing any occurrence, or a man, make two or more distinct reports at different times. Though you may think you have said all, you will to-morrow remember a whole new class of facts which perhaps interested most of all at the time, but did not present themselves to be reported."[17] But I could not have anticipated the excitement that my students' follow-ups generated in me as I read. How can life, apparently so mundane, even as we record it, be so exciting when we return to it?

Here are selections (about fifty percent of the total) from John Sosa's two visits to a bookstore café in the Village:

[Day One] *11:37* A female, about 45 years old, thin, and has salt and pepper hair [she is hereafter referred to as "s/p"]; sits to the left of me. . . . *11:39* Another female, with auburn curly hair, whose age I think is mid-forties, approaches and sits at the table with s/p. . . . S/p and Curly start talking to each other immediately. . . . *11:43* I notice the cashier putting on lipstick. Curly and s/p are still talking. I manage to overhear s/p say, "Yes, Suzie needs to be more cautious, she doesn't think things out beforehand." . . . *11:44* Curly got up and went to the counter. Curly and the cashier are talking to each other. Cashier said, "Last night I got home at 1:30 . . ." I couldn't hear the rest of the conversation. Half a minute later, the cashier helps another customer. *11:45* S/p takes out a small bottle of Aleve. S/p is sorting through the pills. . . . S/p eating some type of pastry with a cherry filling. Curly comes back with a bagel and some type of small coffee. . . . *11:52* S/p is wearing light blue jeans and a pink shirt. S/p gets up and goes to the window. S/p takes a quick glance at me, then looks out the window to Broadway. I am paranoid and think that she realizes that I am noticing her a bit too much. She might think I am some kind of psycho and sic the police after me. I consciously make an effort to make more observations out of the corner of my eye. Curly has disappeared somewhere, I didn't notice when she left. Curly left her coat here, so she will be back. *11:54* S/p comes back to her table for a sec, then goes to the magazine section. I didn't look to see if s/p really did go to the magazine section. I did not want to alarm s/p any more than I might already have. When s/p walked by me, I noticed the scent of the perfume she was wearing. The scent of the perfume is very soft and delicate, a light scent, not overpowering. Usually when I smell a woman's perfume I get a soapy taste in my mouth, but not this time. I like the scent of this perfume a lot. *11:55* S/p did go to the magazine section. She came back with a big magazine named *W*. S/p also tied up her shoulder-length hair into a ponytail. *11:58* Curly reappeared, and now is sitting at the table with s/p. . . . *11:59* A couple start talking to s/p. They are speaking softly. I can't make out exactly what is being said. I can tell introductions are being made by the "nice to meet you" handshakes. The male and s/p appear to be the only two who know each other. The conversation between them is natural and swift. . . . S/p talks and male listens. S/p: "Let's find another, so you two can sit down." Male: "No, that's o.k. We're not staying long." S/p comes to my table, "May I take this chair?" "Yes, of course," I respond. *12:04* The couple take their coats off and get comfortable. S/p speaks to the female, "He's an honest man, not too many people are honest." Woman: "Yes, he's an honest man, but I can't be waiting any more." S/p: "Of course you shouldn't wait. You deserve better than . . ." I couldn't hear anymore of their conversation. . . . *12:07* I turned my head to see the cashier looking at me. Either she likes me, or is curious as to what I'm doing. . . . *12:19* After the couple leave, s/p and Curly start speaking to each other in hushed tones, making sure no one can hear them. The music right now is kind of sixties. It's a bit noisier. Not as quiet or calm as when I first walked in. People are moving around more. *12:20* Time to go to work.

[Day Two] *1:49* I am back at the bookstore sitting in a corner, where a man with a lap top computer was sitting before. I prefer the view I get here. I am able to see more. I also don't have that feeling that something is going on behind me. More people are here than the last time I was here. But it doesn't feel busy. Everyone here is settled at his or her table. . . . *1:58* I am sitting with a woman, who looks to be in her early twenties. She was sitting at this table when I first got here. I asked her, "Is anyone sitting here?" She said, "No." Then she moved some of her stuff on the table to make room for me. She picks up her cell phone as if she is going to use it, then puts it down. Under a magazine she is reading is *The New York Times*. . . . The same cashier who took my order last week is working today. I ordered a large mocha this time, once again to fit in. . . . Right now the cashier is looking at a magazine at the counter. She looks up every now and then to check for customers. . . . *2:24* Curly [from last time] is here. She sits with a woman. She doesn't seem to see me or recognize me, which is good. I prefer to stay unnoticed. I wonder where s/p is. . . . *2:31* The bookstore employee cleaning the tables comes to my table. He starts wiping the table, but not too close to intrude upon my writing or the woman's reading. With the other hand he picks up the woman's tray. It looks discarded. The woman immediately says: "No, not yet." Employee: "You still want it?" Woman: "Yes, I just covered it." Now the employee asks, referring to *The New York Times*, "This yours?" Woman: "Yes." Employee now referring to two magazines that were next to me: "This yours?" I reply, "No." I hand him the magazines. Employee to woman (about another magazine): "This yours?" Woman: "That you can take." *2:34* Cell phone rings. It belongs to the woman sitting with me. "Hello?—You didn't go today.—What do you mean where am I?—In the city.—Okay.—I don't know.—Yeah, okay.—Bye-bye." . . . *2:38* Something a friend told me once comes to mind: "If you sit in a place long enough something is bound to happen." After the woman I was sitting with leaves I look at the two magazines she was reading, *PC Privacy* and *Lap Top*. . . . Kind of cool since I am a computer science major. . . . *2:48* Curly finished her coffee and is now putting on her coat. I don't know when she got it, but all of a sudden she has a big, fake potted plant. Curly did not have that when she came in. . . .

The students' final projects involved reading about and talking to residents of the neighborhoods surrounding the sites they wrote about: Marine Park, Crown Heights, College Point, Roosevelt Island, Brighton Beach, the East Village. In other words, my students did research. I wanted them to have their own experiences through which to filter the research, rather than the other way around. I wanted my students to see and know the place, to be informed writers, to be Thoreaus rather than retailers of processed impressions and information.

> If you make the least correct observation of nature this year, you will have occasion to repeat it with illustrations the next, and the season and life itself is prolonged.[18]

> Thoughts accidentally thrown together become a frame in which more may be developed and exhibited. Perhaps this is the main value of a habit of writing, of keeping a journal,—that so we remember our best hours and stimulate ourselves. . . . Having by chance recorded a few disconnected thoughts and then brought them into juxtaposition, they suggest a whole new field in which it was possible to labor and to think. Thought begat thought.[19]

(Again, those begetting thoughts!)

> It is surprising how any reminiscence of a different season of the year affects us. When I meet with any such in my Journal, it affects me as poetry, and I appreciate that other season and that particular phenomenon more than at the time. The world so seen is all one spring, and full of beauty. You only need to make a faithful record of an average summer day's experience and summer mood, and read it in the winter, and it will carry you back to more than that summer day alone could show.[20]

Walter Harding, Thoreau's excellent biographer, wondered how Thoreau could have possibly conceived of his massive, life-long journal as his main work.[21] But it *was* his main work, and Thoreau, in an inclusive, Boswellian way, thought that a work of accumulated details rather than a predetermined focus or thesis was more biographically and artistically revealing and true:

> I do not know but thoughts written down thus in a journal might be printed in the same form with greater advantage than if the related ones were brought together into separate essays. They are now allied to life, and are seen by the reader not to be far-fetched.[22]

> Never endeavor consciously to supply the tone which you think proper for certain sentences. It is as if a man whose mind was at ease should supply the tones and gestures for a man in distress who found only the words; as when one makes a speech and another behind him makes gestures.[23]

> We should not endeavor coolly to analyze our thoughts, but, keeping the pen even and parallel with the current, make an accurate transcript of them. Impulse is, after all, the best linguist, and for his logic, if not comfortable to Aristotle, it cannot fail to be most convincing.[24]

> As for style of writing, if one has anything to say, it drops from him simply and directly, as a stone falls to the ground.[25]

This series of quotations from Thoreau makes me think how foolish we are to always insist that our students plumb their journals for the "real" essay, story, or poem. We can learn and see as much or more from our students' journals in their "raw" state. As it is, I see that the writers often edit out of their essays the best, liveliest, most direct material from their reading-response journals, because for one reason or another they come to believe the journal's informality is less than acceptable.

One might argue that *Walden* provides an excellent counter-example to Thoreau's own promotion of a journal's quality of seeming "allied to life," impulsive, and not "far-fetched." Yet as purposeful as *Walden* seems, it is still an original creation, forged out of the material in Thoreau's journals, knocked together in a dramatic and sturdy way. *Walden* may not be the whole (or even best) of Thoreau, but it is clearly just what he wanted to say, at the time. Without *Walden*'s existence, would Thoreau have become one of American literature's All-Stars? I doubt it. Would he have continued to write his journals had he not made a name for himself with that book? Yes, because he needed the journals. For most readers, *Walden* and the civil disobedience essays are the entry and last stop. This is too bad, I believe, for the journals reveal a much stranger, much more likable and greater man:

> Time never passes so quickly and unaccountably as when I am engaged in composition, i.e., in writing down my thoughts. Clocks seem to have been put forward.[26]

My Journal should be the record of my love. I would write in it only of the things I love, my affection for any aspect of the world, what I love to think of.[27]

A journal, a book that shall contain a record of all your joy, your ecstasy.[28]

I would fain keep a journal which should contain those thoughts and impressions which I am most liable to forget that I have had; which would have in one sense the greatest remoteness, in another, the greatest nearness to me.[29]

A journal is a record of experiences and growth, not a preserve of things well done and said.[30]

In a journal it is important in a few words to describe the weather, or character of the day, as it affects our feelings. That which was so important at the time cannot be unimportant to remember.[31]

Finally, Thoreau—like Franz Kafka, another devoted journal-keeper—believed that you cannot trick the journal; the least touches of self-consciousness and pretension eventually show themselves as the smudgy handlings of the author while the real deal is what shows through the undirected but artful details:

> Of all strange and unaccountable things this journalizing is the strangest. It will allow nothing to be predicated of it; its good is not good, nor its bad bad. If I make a huge effort to expose my innermost and richest wares to light, my counter seems cluttered with the meanest homemade stuffs; but after months or years I may discover the wealth of India, and whatever rarity is brought overland from Cathay, in that confused heap, and what perhaps seemed a festoon of dried apple or pumpkin will prove a string of Brazilian diamonds, or pearls from Coromandel.[32]

I would urge any teacher who is interested in cultivating students' imaginative writing, and who is not bound by test preparations, to try an assignment that gets students off campus. Have them write about what they see and hear and smell and touch. Have them return there and write again, and some time later in the classroom or at home reflect on what they experienced. I guarantee you that you will have in your hands coherent, compelling, original "essays" of experience that reflect their interests and intelligence more truly than any prescribed analysis of literature or social issues.

Bibliography

Thoreau, Henry David. *A Week on the Concord and Merrimack Rivers. Walden. The Maine Woods. Cape Cod.* New York: The Library of America, 1985.

————. *A Week on the Concord and Merrimack Rivers*. Orleans, Massachusetts: Parnassus Imprints, 1987.

————. *Familiar Letters*. Multiple volumes. Boston: Houghton Mifflin, "Manuscript Edition," 1906.

————. *Journal*. Mulitple volumes. Boston: Houghton Mifflin, "Manuscript Edition," 1906.

Notes

1. Henry David Thoreau, *Journal* (Boston: Houghton Mifflin, "Manuscript Edition," 1906), Volume IX, p. 350. All the following quotations from Thoreau's *Journal* and letters are from the 1906 edition, unless otherwise noted.

2. *Journal*, Volume VI, p. 237.

3. Thoreau. *Familiar Letters* (Boston: Houghton Mifflin, "Manuscript Edition," 1906), Volume 6 [Nov 16, 1857], p. 320.

4. Henry David Thoreau, *A Week on the Concord and Merrimack Rivers* (Orleans, Mass.: Parnassus Imprints, 1987), pp. 138–9.

5. Ibid., pp. 408–409.

6. *Familiar Letters*, p. 67 [April 4, 1843].

7. *Journal*, Vol. II, p. 457 [Sept. 4, 1851].

8. *Journal*, Vol. XIII, p. 145 [Feb. 13, 1860].

9. *Familiar Letters*, p. 320 [Nov. 16, 1857].

10. *Journal*, Vol. III, p. 107 [Nov. 12, 1851].

11. *Familiar Letters*, p. 220 [April 10, 1853].

12. *Journal*, Vol. I. p. 341 [March 20, 1842].

13. James Boswell was, like Thoreau, a steady journal-keeper, and sometimes recreated his journal in terrific detail from memoranda.

14. *Journal*, Vol. III, p. 390 [April 4, 1852].

15. For excellent tips, see Matthew Sharpe, "Urban Nature Writing," in *The Alphabet of Trees: A Guide to Nature Writing* edited by Christian McEwen and Mark Statman (New York: Teachers & Writers Collaborative, 2000).

16. Henry David Thoreau, *Walden* (New York: Dover, 1995), pp. 183–4.

17. *Journal*, Vol. IX, p. 300 [March 24, 1857].

18. *Journal*, Vol. V, p. 100 [April 7, 1853].

19. *Journal*, Vol. III, p. 217 [Jan. 22, 1852].

20. *Journal*, Vol. V, p. 454 [Oct. 26, 1853].

21. "How he ever thought it could be published when he had great difficulty in getting his short essays published, we do not know," writes Walter Harding in the introduction to his good *Selections from the Journals* (New York: Dover, 1995), p. v.

22. *Journal*, Vol. III, p. 239 [Jan. 27, 1852].

23. *Journal*, Vol. III, p. 213 [Jan. 21, 1852].

24. *Journal*, Vol. II, p. 35 [March 7, 1838]. On the other hand: "Unfortunately many things have been omitted which should have been recorded in our journal, for though we made it a rule to set down all our experiences therein, yet such a resolution is very hard to keep, for the important experience rarely allows us to remember such obligations, and so indifferent things get recorded, while that is frequently neglected. It is not easy to write in a journal what interests us at any time, because to write it is not what interests us." *A Week on the Concord and Merrimack Rivers* (Orleans, Mass.: Parnassus Imprints, 1987), p. 415.

25. *Familiar Letters*, p. 312 [August 18, 1857].

26. *Journal*, Vol. X, p. 263 [Jan. 27, 1858].

27. *Journal*, Vol. II, p. 101 [Nov. 16, 1850].

28. *Journal*, Vol. IV, p. 223 [July 13, 1852].

29. *Journal*, Vol. II, p. 143 [Jan.–Feb. 1851].

30. *Journal*, Vol. VIII, p. 134 [Jan. 24, 1856].

31. *Journal*, Vol. VII, p. 171 [Feb. 4, 1855].

32. *Journal*, Vol. I, p. 182 [Jan. 29, 1841].

Herman Melville

Ange Mlinko

Reading Melville's Sentences

Teaching *Billy Budd*, *Benito Cereno*, and "Bartleby, the Scrivener"

IN THE 1850S, when Herman Melville wrote some of his greatest works ("Bartleby, the Scrivener" and *Benito Cereno*, among others), the United States was still a young country. The American Revolution was still fresh in the collective memory and "American Literature" was only just coming into being—as was the American, as opposed to English, language. Melville believed that the American Revolution had given birth to American literature, and was thus inseparable from it. With the Revolution in mind, he prophesied that the conflict between authority and human rights could never be resolved. ("In armies, navies, cities, or families, in nature herself, nothing more relaxes good order than misery" (p. 679).While the Revolution guaranteed freedom from tyranny and the Constitution guaranteed the pursuit of happiness, enshrining these concepts would prove problematic for those local tyrannies (most blatantly, slavery) that persisted after the British were defeated. For Melville, the United States, a government based on the overthrow of government, embodied a contradiction that would prove an eternal source of civic tension. Melville became one of the first great American writers because he made this tension the seed of his art.

When I first read Melville in high school, his work did make an impression on me—after all, the narrative of subversion ("I prefer not to," as Bartleby says) is the teen dream! But his prose stood in the way. His sentences were hard to read, even for a budding writer who loved words. Unlike the next great American stylist whose theme was rebellion—Jack Kerouac—Melville's prose does not aim to intoxicate; rather than the rushing floodwaters of liberation, it is the sturdy dam in the process of crumbling. Hence his sentences are really built, fitted like masonry. The challenge is to show students that this style is of a piece with Melville's focus in "Bartleby," *Benito Cereno*, and *Billy Budd*: the authority figure in crisis, not the rebel in glory. While using the proper language of authority, Melville's aim was to turn it on itself and expose its blindness. It is no accident that lawyers and courts figure prominently in all three works, and that all three involve a figure of authority coping with a "revolt from below."

What is the proper language of authority in Melville? High diction. Those who speak in high diction are the superiors in the social hierarchy, and by its use, maintain the *appearance of command* (as one may have a "command of the English language"). High diction in Melville's time was of course the language of British upper classes, characterized by Latinate vocabulary, complicated syntax, circumlocution, and strict impersonality of voice—qualities demonstrated by Bartleby's narrator:

> The nature of my avocations for the last thirty years has brought me into more than ordinary contact with what would seem an interesting and somewhat singular set of men, of whom as yet nothing that I know of has ever been written:—I mean the law-copyists or scriveners. (p. 635)

This sentence breaks a few rules of "good" sentences: it's wordy, vague, and too long. Why not say "my law practice" instead of "the nature of my avocations"? Why say "more than ordinary contact" rather than "close contact"? Isn't the description "interesting and somewhat singular" vague and even nonsensical? After all, how can one be "*somewhat* singular"? Here's another long sentence, from *Benito Cereno*:

> The more so, since with an untimely caprice of punctilio, rendered distressing by his cadaverous aspect, Don Benito, with Castilian bows, solemnly insisted upon his guest's preceding him up the ladder leading to the elevation; where, one on each side of the last step, sat for armorial supporters and sentries two of the ominous file. (p. 687)

Here, Latinate words are used where simpler Anglo-Saxon ones would be clearer (why say cadaverous when you could say deathly?). An undue abstraction makes the sentence vague ("insisted upon his guest's preceding him up the ladder to the elevation" could be simplified to "insisted that Captain Delano go first up the ladder to the poop deck"). There are too many subordinate clauses and commas, and the whole thing could be broken into at least two sentences.

High diction's intricate grammar reflects a hierarchical world view (reflected in, say, subordinate clauses!). Abstractions may serve as euphemisms (are *armorial supporters* armed guards?) and Latinate words (*punctilio*) have signified courtliness for at least two thousand years. Significantly, "Bartleby," *Benito Cereno*, and *Billy Budd* all involve "official" judgement and legal language; the forms the stories take bounce between eyewitness account, hearsay, and post-mortem. *Bartleby*'s narrator is a lawyer; a deposition contradicts the evidence of Captain Delano's eyes; *Billy Budd* is convicted by a court martial. Perhaps most importantly, we are conditioned to hear objectivity in the impersonal tones of high diction—and "objectivity," of course, is supposedly closer to Truth. It is the nature of high diction that it gives the benefit of the doubt to its user, who knows how to employ its loopholes and diversions. Those lower in social stature—the scriveners, sailors, and slaves—are always at a disadvantage. As Captain Vere explains to Billy Budd's drumhead court:

> Even could you explain to them [the ship's company]—which our official position forbids—they, long molded by arbitrary discipline, have not that kind of intelligent responsiveness that might qualify them to comprehend and discriminate. (p. 1416)

Melville himself knew both privilege and privation—as well as both "languages." He came from an upper class family, but his father lost their wealth. In 1841, barely into his twenties, Melville set out for the South Pacific as a common sailor. As he wrote in *Moby-Dick*, a "whaleship was my Yale College and my Harvard." Melville led this life for only four years, but the stories he accumulated would fuel his writing for the next forty-five. A good American, he believed that "all men are created equal"; this idea must have superseded his loyalty to his captain, for he took part in a mutiny. It may have taken on even greater resonance when he lived among the natives of the South Seas, whom he regarded sympathetically in an era when blatant racism prevailed.

Given his background, Melville was positioned to parrot authority's language practices. Given his experiences, he knew that much authority was flawed if not corrupt. Imbued with the ideals of American Independence, he saw ancient structures replicating themselves under the banner of Freedom. So when he struck back at these ancient structures, he did so in their native language, from the point of view of authorities all but blind and deaf. Like Bartleby's seeemingly polite "I prefer not to," Melville undermines hierarchy and authoritarianism through a creative use of language's technicalities and loopholes. In doing so, he sought to strengthen—to use the contemporary term—the rights of man.

*   *   *

Melville's prose rewards close study, and nothing encourages close study more than imitative exercises. Ask your students to describe an episode in high diction, using an impersonal voice and Latinate vocabulary. (A sampling from Melville includes *avocation, punctilio, plenipotentiary, valetudinarian*—have a good dictionary on hand.). What do they sense about the authority of the narrator they have become in this exercise? Do they feel more in command of their subject? Or do they feel like stuffed shirts?

Remind your students that this is simultaneously an exercise in breaking the rules of "good" writing, such as simplicity, clarity, and short sentence length. Discuss the implications of this. What do they think Melville would say about it? You might refer them to page 1365 in *Billy Budd*:

> In this matter of writing, resolve as one may to keep to the main road, some bypaths have an enticement not readily to be withstood. . . . At the least, we can promise ourselves that pleasure which is wickedly said to be in sinning, for a literary sin the divergence will be.

Another good Melvillian exercise (based on the murky circumstances of *Benito Cereno* and *Billy Budd*) is to have students write two or more accounts of the same "incident." First they can write the newspaper's version—which can tell only some of the truth, or be completely false. How did it, then, get to be published? Then have them create a different version or versions—perhaps a deposition or a song ballad—which tell a different story from the newspaper account. Encourage them to experiment with the possible discrepancies between the "official" story and the "inside story."

Students can also compare Melville's use of these themes and techniques with major twentieth-century modernists: in literature, James Joyce (*Ulysses*) and William Faulkner (*The Sound and the Fury*) experimented with multiple points of view; Marcel Proust (*Remembrance of Things Past*) explored how one's own perceptions of Truth change over time, and Vladimir Nabokov, in *Pale Fire*, juxtaposed a poem and the story of the poet's death recounted by an unreliable narrator. In film, this technique has been used over and over, in movies ranging from Akira Kurosawa's *Rashomon* to Oliver Stone's *JFK*.

Bibliography

Melville, Herman. *Pierre. Israel Potter. The Piazza Tales. The Confidence-Man. Uncollected Prose. Billy Budd.* New York: The Library of America, 1984.

Walt Whitman

Bill Zavatsky

Poets to Come

Teaching Whitman in High School

MY FIRST SUSTAINED READING of Walt Whitman took place in the fall of 1965 or the spring of 1966. It was his *Song of Myself*, a good chunk of which I read while sitting in a lobby at the New School for Social Research in New York, waiting for a jazz improvisation class to begin. After three years at a small college in Connecticut, I had "dropped out" and worked for a year. When I resumed my education after having transferred to Columbia, I felt myself at a new beginning. Whitman confirmed my adventure—the new life on which I had embarked as well as the stirrings of a real commitment to writing, especially to poetry. That afternoon, at the New School, Whitman's rolling line forever fused itself to the long-lined solos of the jazz artists that I most admired; and all I had to do was look around me to see that he was one of the great poets of New York.

But more than this, Whitman's work touched experiences in me that had long been buried, experiences the nature of which I can only call spiritual. Some years ago, when I started teaching his poems to my tenth- and twelfth-grade English classes, it was because he was one of those writers who confirmed a sensation that, up through my teens, I had now and again felt: the gift of seeing everything in my range of vision with a startling clarity, as if whatever I turned my gaze toward was bathed in the beam of a powerful searchlight, but not at the expense of surrounding objects, which retained their focus. Concomitant with this heightened sense of vision was the sensation of being connected to all that I saw, joined to it in a oneness that both dazzled me and left me with a feeling of inner joy. These states did not last very long, and they were so extraordinary that I was afraid to investigate them, even to mention them. (They seemed qualitatively *different* from the feelings of piety or devotion or exaltation that I experienced as a Roman Catholic boy.) The manifestation was not linked to creed or dogma, but showered down upon me when I least expected it—on a spectacularly clear fall day, or a summer afternoon as I walked down a tree-lined street, heading home from a baseball game. All I knew was that they "happened," that I was grateful for these visitations, and that I would remember the effect that they had had upon me.

Now every year I teach Whitman to my "Poets to Come," the future generation of writers that he addressed in his short poem of that name. I preface our reading of his work by describing the experiences that I have just related. There is a hunger in young people—"religious" or not—to discuss "heightened" transpersonal experiences. In doing so I never feel that I am forcing a belief system on my students. For example, as I gave my little personal introduction on the first day of our Whitman studies, two female seniors were madly scribbling notes to one another. With a frown, but really out of curiosity, I walked over to read what one of them had written: "I have these experiences *all the time!*" Her friend had responded enthusiastically in the affirmative. Indeed, adolescence brings with it the development of the ability to entertain abstract concepts of a sophisticated nature, making Whitman, the self-described "poet of the body and the soul," a perfect companion.

There are higher levels of spirituality in poetry than the writings of Whitman—the poems of William Blake or Hindu texts like the *Bhagavad-Gita*—but at present these seem out of my own teaching range despite my absorption in them. What Whitman seemed to have experienced, however, was far more profound than my own little moments of transport. What especially appealed to me was Whitman's directness, the sense that he was speaking from the heart of a great mystery in a language that I could understand. Neither I nor my students need to cut through a lot of cultural differences and symbol-systems to understand Whitman, and this is what I wanted to explore and to communicate to them: an apprehension of spiritual matters that was immediate. Not that everything in his work is transparent; the studies of what Whitman meant in *Song of Myself* are still tumbling off the presses. I simply wanted the excuse at least to touch on spiritual things, and Whitman supplied the occasion.

Of course, all poetry is spiritual to a greater or lesser extent. Whitman himself wrote:

> Much is said of what is spiritual, and of spirituality, in this, that, or the other—in objects, expressions.—For me, I see no object, no expression, no animal, no tree, no art, no book, but I see, from morning to night, and from night to morning, the spiritual.—Bodies are all spiritual.—All words are spiritual—nothing is more spiritual than words. (*An American Primer*, p. 1)

Elements of Whitman

After I tell the story of my youthful "experiences" and read aloud the passages from *Song of Myself* quoted in the first item of the following list, my classes and I use the chalkboard to make a grand list of the features that seem to be characteristic of Whitman's poems. (My seniors generally read *Song of Myself*, "The Sleepers," "Faces," and "I Sing the Body Electric" from the 1855 text of *Leaves of Grass*; my sophomores read the final edition of the *Song* and "Crossing Brooklyn Ferry.") Here's our list:

1. *Spirituality*: By which is meant an appeal to or manifestation of transcendence; an understanding that each individual is identical with the One. Everywhere in his work, but most notably in *Song of Myself*, Whitman refers to the central fact of his life, the spiritual experience which he evidently had sometime in the early 1850s, first memorialized in section 5 of *Song of Myself* *:

> I believe in you my soul . . . . the other I am must not abase itself to you,
> And you must not be abased to the other.
> . . .
> I mind how we lay in June, such a transparent summer morning;
> You settled your head athwart my hips and gently turned over upon me,
> And parted the shirt from my bosom-bone, and plunged your tongue to
>   my barestript heart,
> And reached till you felt my beard, and reached till you held my feet.
>
> Swiftly arose and spread around me the peace and joy and knowledge that
>   pass all the art and argument of the earth;
> And I know that the hand of God is the elderhand of my own,
> And I know that the spirit of God is the eldest brother of my own,
> And that all the men ever born are also my brothers . . . . and the women
>   my sisters and lovers,
> And that a kelson of the creation is love;
> And limitless are leaves stiff or drooping in the fields,
> And brown ants in the little wells beneath them,
> And mossy scabs of the wormfence, and heaped stones, and elder and
>   mullein and poke-weed. (ll. 73–74, 78–89)

And in section 7 he returns to it:

---

* The quotations throughout this essay are from the first (1855) edition of *Leaves of Grass*. Though the sections of the poem were not numbered in the first edition, the paperback Penguin edition (which I use with my students) gives line numbers and shows the numbered sections of the poem in brackets. I have followed it for ease of reference. The Library of America Whitman volume includes both the 1855 edition and the final "Deathbed Edition."

Has any one supposed it lucky to be born?
I hasten to inform him or her it is just as lucky to die, and I know it.

I pass death with the dying, and birth with the new-washed babe . . . and
    am not contained between my hat and boots,
And peruse manifold objects, no two alike, and every one good,
The earth good, and the stars good, and their adjuncts all good.

I am not an earth nor an adjunct of an earth,
I am the mate and companion of people, all just as immortal and fathom-
    less as myself;
They do not know how immortal, but I know. (ll. 122–129)

The erotic language of the first description is perfectly consistent
with the narratives of saints and mystics. Relative to the piercing of the
heart imagery in section 5 (see above), we read Saint Teresa's account of
being pierced with a spear by an angel. (See the J. M. Cohen translation
of *The Life of Saint Teresa of Ávila by Herself* [Penguin Books, pp.
210–11].) We likewise examine a reproduction of Bernini's famous sculpture based on this passage for a better understanding of what Whitman
may be suggesting. We also read selections from the poetry of Kabir,
Rumi, and St. John of the Cross, all of whom speak of God as their
"lover."

2. *Emphasis on the physical body*: That the body is good, clean, pure.
"Welcome is every organ and attribute of me, and of any man hearty and
clean,/ Not an inch nor a particle of an inch is vile, and none shall be less
familiar than the rest." (ll. 49–50)

3. *Celebration and Praise*: All of creation is good and worthy of praise.
Kenneth Koch and Kate Farrell mention that the *Song of Myself* is an
"exuberant inventory of the world (and so of Walt Whitman) in which he
congratulates and praises all the parts of life in great detail, and all for
just existing." (*Sleeping on the Wing*, p. 37)

4. *Love for All Things, Whether "Good" or "Evil"*—a repudiation of
duality, which is merely the misreading of a unified principle, since the
unenlightened human mind is incapable of grasping the One. Further-
more, the compassion that we find everywhere expressed in Whitman's
writing may be seen as a form of imagination, allowing us to feel what
others are feeling. (For this last idea see section 11, "Twenty-eight young
men bathe by the shore" [ll. 193–210].)

5. *Equality*: of all humans; also, there is more than a hint in Whitman
that the processes of nature exist on a par with human life. Section 32
begins, "I think I could turn and live awhile with the animals . . . they are

so placid and self contained,/ I stand and look at them sometimes half the day long." (ll. 684–685)

6. *Emphasis on the Present Tense*: Another technique that Whitman uses to generate the feeling of "eternity" and immediacy in many of his greatest poems is to keep to the present tense. In *Song of Myself* the present tense dominates the action.

7. *The Democracy of the List*: Whitman's lists "level" everything, thus making everything equal. This is to say that finally, in his lists, nothing takes precedence over another thing, and that despite the chronology, nothing comes first or last. The notion of the democratic—another key idea in Whitman's work—abides in such a conception.

8. *The Simultaneity of the List*: Chains of events happening at once result in a feeling of timelessness. The poet is thus godlike, standing at the center of time, able to see and feel all things at once. Also, the poet tends to disappear into his enumerations, a technique that increases the feeling of spirituality, of Oneness, calling to the detachment from ego. Simultaneity also creates a sense of movement, often of speed, in the text.

9. *Repetition*: A phenomenon of the list. It creates an incantatory feeling that approaches the rhythms of the prayer or chant, heightening the sense of the spiritual. A discussion of Whitman's use of rhetorical devices such as anaphora (the repetition of the same word or words at the *beginning* of a line), epistrophe (the repetition of the same word or words at the *end* of a line), symploce (the combination of anaphora and epistrophe), and syntactical parallelism can sharpen the students' understanding of Whitman's poetic technique. These devices literally "make" his meaning.

10. *Physical Description Alternating with Abstract Spiritual Musings*: Whitman gains a tremendous power in his work because he continually buttresses his spiritual insights with concrete particulars observed, and vice versa. Again, see part 5 of *Song of Myself*, which moves from the revelation of the summer morning to "the peace and joy and knowledge that pass all the art and argument of the earth" (l. 82) and back to physical details like "leaves stiff or drooping in the fields" (l. 87).

11. *Sexuality*: Whitman does not shy away from expressions of sexuality; this connects several of the above categories in our list—spirituality, equality, democracy, physical description, love, celebration, and, of course, eroticism.

12. *Fearless Use of the First-Person Pronoun*: Whitman never shies away from using the word "I." *Song of Myself* begins with it ("I celebrate myself") and virtually ends with it ("I stop somewhere waiting for you"). The constant use of the *I* is another element that creates the instantaneous intimacy of Whitman's voice.

13. *Intimacy of Address*: The voice of Whitman is warm, friendly, encouraging, animated by the excitement found in face-to-face conversation. He addresses the reader directly, creating a sense of closeness rare in poetry. (See Stephen Railton's excellent essay, "'As If I Were With You,'—The Performance of Whitman's Poetry," on Whitman's use of "you," in *The Cambridge Companion to Whitman* [pp. 7–26].)

14. *Individuality*: Despite the tendency of catalogue poetry to "dissolve" the author's identity, his or her individual personality persists by virtue of the literary choices made and style adopted. (The students and I were forced to acknowledge a paradoxical element here: to know that one is an individual and at the same time at one with the Whole.)

15. *Adoption of Personae*: Whitman is fond of wearing masks in his poetry. For example, he assumes a variety of identities in section 10 of the *Song*: hunter, seafarer, clamdigger, witness, protector of a runaway slave.

16. *The Immortality of the Soul*: "And to die is different from what any one supposed, and luckier." This line concludes and summarizes section 6, which begins with the famous opening, "A child said, What is the grass? fetching it to me with full hands." (6.1) The realization of individual death is transcended by the understanding that the soul is immortal.

17. *Natural Diction Spiced with "Poetic" Diction*: Whitman's sound—his choice of words—is very close to ours, very "modern." The "everydayness" of his vocabulary reflects the common sights and sounds that he celebrates. Whitman's language is also highly concrete and sensual, as if it could be grabbed and held before the eyes and felt with the hand. At the same time, we note that his use of certain words and expressions (sometimes from the French, especially in the poems after 1855) may be a bit off-putting: "venerealee" for one afflicted with venereal disease; "amies" for "female friends"; "chef-d'oeuvre" for "masterpiece"; "ambulanza" for "ambulance"; "eleves" for "students"; "bussing" for "kissing," etc.

18. *A Poet of the City*: Whitman was the first great poet to write of New York City, which connects to . . .

19. *The Poet as Reporter*: For many years Whitman worked as a newspaperman. He went out into the streets, using his eyes and ears to gather facts—sights, sounds, smells, textures—that create the fabric of his writing. This technique was to lay the foundation for everything that he would write. In short, observation—the merging of one's sensibility with one's surroundings—is another way of being-at-one with the "other." It is a form of meditation, and thus intersects many of these other categories. That Whitman stands as a witness to his times is a hallmark of his work.

20. *The Poet as Storyteller*: There are anecdotes and short narratives throughout Whitman's long poems, especially in *Song of Myself* and "The Sleepers," even though these poems are thought of as a non-narrative works. "[T]he subject was so large that anything, it seemed, could be part of it and could be included." (Koch and Farrell, *Sleeping on the Wing*, p. 37)

21. *"Participle-loving Whitman"*: Here is the first stanza of "The Sleepers" in which I have emphasized the present participles by placing them in italics:

I wander all night in my vision,
Stepping with light feet . . . . swiftly and noiselessly *stepping* and *stopping*,
Bending with open eyes over the shut eyes of sleepers;
Wandering and confused . . . . lost to myself . . . . ill-assorted . . . .
    contradictory,
Pausing and *gazing* and *bending* and *stopping*. (ll. 1–5)

The present participle stretches action by virtue of its elastic *-ing* ending. It suggests action in the process of completion, but not yet finished, and implies (like so many of Whitman's techniques) the eternal present and the Eternal. It is a technique that must be used carefully; otherwise it can succumb to the greeting-card effect of "soft" poetry. See Ezra Greenspan's enlightening article on Whitman's use of this part of speech in *The Cambridge Companion to Walt Whitman* (pp. 92–109).

22. *Frequent and Unusual Use of the Ellipsis*: Particularly odd in nineteenth-century poetry, this piece of punctuation is Whitman's hieroglyph for the drawn breath, the pause for thought, the opening-up of the poem into timelessness, the intrusion of the eternal into consciousness whenever we leave off speaking—that is, when the individual ego is adumbrated. At the end of a poem the ellipsis usually means something like, "I have nothing more to say." In Whitman it means something different: a unit of breath; little stars or planets rolling by. . . . (Whitman struck out the ellipses in editions of *Leaves of Grass* that appeared after 1855.)

23. *The Long Line*: Whitman's long lines contain or generate many of the above qualities. His line is a rolling wave, an oceanic motion, a planetary orbit, the process of drawing and exhaling breath as a focus in meditation. (The long line also testifies to Whitman's devotion to opera.)

The origin of Whitman's line in Biblical literature seems evident. Here is a passage from the Old Testament (which I have arranged into verse lines) that contains the seed of Whitman's major theme in *Song of Myself*:

Comfort ye, comfort ye my people, saith your God.
Speak ye comfortably to Jerusalem, and cry unto her, that her warfare
    is accomplished, that her iniquity is pardoned: for she hath
    received of the Lord's hand double for all her sins.
The voice of him that crieth in the wilderness,
Prepare ye the way of the Lord, make straight in the desert a highway
    for our God.
Every valley shall be exalted, and every mountain and hill shall be
    made low: and the crooked shall be made straight, and the rough
    places plain:
And the glory of the Lord shall be revealed, and all flesh shall see it
    together: for the mouth of the Lord hath spoken it.
The voice said, Cry. And he said, What shall I cry? All flesh is grass,
    and all the goodliness thereof is as the flower of the field:
The grass withereth, the flower fadeth: because the spirit of the Lord
    bloweth upon it: surely the people is grass.
The grass withereth, the flower fadeth: but the word of our God shall
    stand for ever. (Isaiah 40:1–8, King James Version)

The voice of God speaks through the mouth of the prophet, and Whitman himself for a time thought of his book as a "new Bible" for the American masses.

Grass recurs as a life-image throughout literature and mythology. The Oglala Sioux holy man Black Elk, at the beginning of his autobiography, says: "So many other men have lived and shall live that story [of an individual life], to be grass upon the hills" (*Black Elk Speaks*, p. 1; my interpolation in brackets). We grow, flourish, and die like blades of grass. Whitman's title suggests the leaves (pages) of a book, at once eternal and transitory. We can also imagine a book printed on blades of grass, each blade being the page of the book of eternity. Guy Davenport notes that "this one universal plant [is] absent only in the deserts of the poles," and that "the first paper was leaves of grass, papyrus" (*The Geography of the Imagination: Forty Essays* [San Francisco: North Point Press, 1981], p. 76). Hence Whitman's description of it as a "uniform hieroglyphic." Grass, tenacious and ubiquitous, is also a perfect symbol for democracy. (Again note that Whitman's image is ambiguous: the grass may need deciphering, but it is also universal, accessible to all.)

Naturally there is much more to be said on all these subjects, and there are plenty of insights attendant on a close reading of Whitman. My students and I arrived at these ideas in a class session of "brainstorming," and I offer them as points of departure for further discussion. Use them as best suits your purpose.

Techniques for Imitating Whitman

My students wrote imitations of Whitman using our list of 23 characteristics, trying to include in their poems as many of them as possible. If students had experienced "cosmic" moments that my personal introduction or Whitman's poetry reminded them of, or that Whitman's poems revived, I urged them to include these moments in their poems, and to present them as fully as possible. Here are some practical techniques for imitating Whitman.

• 1. Whitman's poems give the feeling of being *in* reality, so I took the students outside to a little community park in our neighborhood where all of us could sit and write. This exercise proved useful to students who found it difficult to identify with the spiritual aspect of Whitman's poetry; direct observation gave them images and events to "hang on to." Thus a "Whitman imitation" can also be a transcription of reality—a meditation on what passes before the eye and ear. These observations could be written down in prose, then later arranged into Whitmanic verse lines. (According to biographer Paul Zweig, Whitman ultimately found his poetic voice through years of writing prose—everything from newspaper articles to journal entries. His early poetry is mediocre, at best.) Here's a first draft of my foray into the garden:

> Small apartment buildings being built in the air around us.
> I watch the workers in yellow helmets and heavy-soled boots walk the
>   rooftops, banging and buzzing away, shouting and laughing.
> An airplane flies over. What am I thinking?
> Strands of cassette tape festoon a nearby tree.
> I sit on a bench in the garden planted with dozens of blossoming
>   flowers and shrubs,
> alive with immense bees that flash in and out of the Indian summer
>   sunlight, strong because of the clearness of the air.
> Small gnats attracted to skinny black trees attack my face as I write.
> I puff my cheeks and whoosh, they go spinning upwards!
> There is the shadow-work of these little trees to try to get down in
>   words, the twisted puppet patterns thrown on the white-washed
>   brick sides of adjacent brownstones.
> The shadows remind me of the black ink that unrolls from the tip of
>   my black pen, shiny in the sunlight.
> Tiny suns race up and down its barrel like meteorites!
>
> I look at the students as they write, ranged in odd or formal positions
>   around the circular garden, scribbling in our notebooks, and think
>   about making a list of what each of us is doing.

Are they sneaking looks at me, too, I wonder, as I note this down?
Alton creeps near some bushes, training his ever-ready camera on a
  black cat that has suddenly appeared.
Half of us are watching him and madly trying to write it down.
Alison sits on a rock, crosslegged, staring her eyes down at her pad,
  looking like Buddha.
My pen is moving along the page—I can't stop writing!

Other observations—drawn from reality, from memory, or from the imagination—can be interspersed with this "on-the-spot writing." This new material may be of a philosophical or cosmic nature, but should be balanced by the "minute particulars" captured for the pen by the eye and ear. The point is to let abstract ideas be generated and controlled by concrete images, and not the other way around: start with the skinny black tree in the garden that a thousand gnats are whirling around and *then* speak of the years that fly so quickly at Time's frozen face. Then move back to another concrete image—the splotchy, neon-like colors on the bow tie of the assistant principal, for example.

It would also be a good idea to use some of the rhetorical devices employed by Whitman that I mentioned in the ninth item of the list of qualities: anaphora, epistrophe, symploce, and syntactical parallelism. It's easy to find examples of these techniques in Whitman's poems.

• 2. If it isn't convenient to go outdoors, students can rely on remembered images. Writers can start with something that they know well—their trip to school in the morning, for example. I like Phillip Lopate's idea (expressed in the Ric Burns documentary, *New York*) that Whitman's long line can be likened to the long streets of New York City. What one would do, walking down them, Lopate says, is to make an inventory of what one sees and hears and smells. The walk or ride to school on a bus can become a catalogue of discovery rather than a boring waste of time. Students can write their trip from memory and then revise over a couple of days as they get to "re-see" their neighborhood.

• 3. Students can also "borrow" material from magazines and books if there is a danger of running out of steam. (News magazines and *National Geographic* are good sources of images, and headlines can be plucked at random from a couple of newspapers spread out on the table as one writes.) In fact, if your school has a library, it might be the ideal place to do this kind of writing, as long as students aren't too distracted by the temptation to do nothing but browse through books and periodicals.

Once students have achieved a Whitmanic *flow* in their work, this kind of poem can keep going and going. It can be stocked with anecdotes and little stories, as well as fleeting descriptions. It can be broken into sections that are more or less self-contained, or ones that spill over into the next section. Read another of the great poems in *Leaves of Grass*—"The Sleepers," a kind of miniature version of *Song of Myself*—for Whitman's use of these techniques.

Study the endings of Whitman's poems and you will note that they often simply trail off, or end rather abruptly, even arbitrarily; many of them might end anywhere. The impressions simply stop coming, or in some way cease, as if the poet decided to step out of the river of being that carried the images. This quality, too, is a mark of Whitman's work, or of the kind of poem that records a stretch of mental time in which anything might happen. Some critics have felt that Whitman's writing is a sort of stream-of-consciousness or free-association technique. Here too the spiritual is invoked: the feeling that one is centered in one's body and in no need of heading anywhere. One *is*, and whatever swims through the mind is registered, then let go of. That is how students might learn to think of this kind of writing: grab the image, get it down, then be ready for the next image. What unifies the perception of these images is the mind—and, in the largest sense, the Mind that watches over the whole universe, which *is* the universe.

Here is a good example of the kind of work produced by my students for their Whitman imitations. The writing idea here was to produce a "lost section" of the *Song of Myself*.

The Lost Stanza from Walt Whitman's *Song of Myself*

I feel what the salmon feels as he flips and flops through cold water streams.
I feel what the salmon's translucent pink scales feel like as they open and close, reaching for air,
And I too feel as the cold water stream does . . . as the reached-for air does.
I feel how it is to be a shiny black smooth rock in a child's hand.
I am the child who throws the rock and watches it skip three times over the surface of the water
Or how the water-skier feels as she skips three times over the surface of the water.
I feel the weight of the stocky businessman as he slides into a cab.
I feel the ripped maroon vinyl sinking below his Brooks Brothers trousers
And I know how his young wife feels as she sits at home watching the T.V.

I feel for the cameraman . . . I feel for the substitute teacher . . . I feel
   for the nurse.
I feel what the orphan feels as prospective parents come to pick the
   handsomest or the prettiest child.
I feel what the proud father feels when he witnesses his daughter's first
   kiss on their porchswing.
I feel what the girl without a prom date feels when she calls her out-
   of-town cousin Chuck.
I too feel how Chuck feels as his mature city cousin asks him to her
   prom.
I feel for the flower pinned to a dress . . . I feel for the cotton fibers . . . I
   feel for the dressmaker in the factory.
I am the glamorous starlet who feels the blinding spotlight on her
   face.
I feel as the spotlight feels when it plays upon her foundation and her
   crow's feet.
I feel as the oldest usher feels, having to walk up two flights of stairs.
I feel what the stairs feel when pricked by a woman's spike heel.
I feel the pain shooting into the woman's ankle as she trips.
I feel the cement under the cop who walks the beat.
I feel what his billyclub feels as he wraps his young and eager fingers
   tightly around it.
I am the convict . . . I am the prosecutor . . . I am the rejected jurist at
   home watching the case on the news.
I feel for the white sand beaches in the south of France . . . I feel for
   the black sand beaches in Hawaii.
I walk along the shorelines.
I feel what the sand feels as it lodges in my big toenail
And I feel as the nail feels when I pick the grains out.
I feel all . . . I am as all is.

   —*Liz Thompson*
   (In *Columbus: The Literary Magazine of Trinity School*, Winter 1991)

A Polemical Aside

I have before me three poetry textbooks used in high school and college.
Two of these texts, which incidentally feature substantial anthologies that
"fill out" the books, offer poems by Walt Whitman. The first book (532
pages) reprints six Whitman poems, none of which is longer than twenty-
four lines (the average poem is thirteen lines long): "Beat! Beat! Drums!";
"Cavalry Crossing a Ford"; "I Saw in Louisiana a Live-Oak Growing";
"A Noiseless Patient Spider"; "O Captain! My Captain!"; and "The Run-

ner." An additional snippet, ten lines from *Song of Myself*, introduces the book's anthology section. In all, the book contains 89 lines of Whitman's poetry.

The other anthology—564 pages—does much better: "Out of the Cradle Endlessly Rocking," certainly one of Whitman's greatest poems (183 lines); "When I Heard the Learn'd Astronomer"; "Cavalry Crossing a Ford"; "When Lilacs Last in the Dooryard Bloom'd," the Lincoln elegy that is far superior to "O Captain! My Captain!" (and a poem of 206 lines); "A Noiseless Patient Spider"; and "The Dalliance of the Eagles." Average: 70.6 lines per poem, though the four short poems here are ten lines or fewer. At least we are given a sense of Whitman's *heft* as a poet in the longer works.

For comparison I went to a widely used poetry text currently in its seventh edition. It contained five poems by Whitman—"A Noiseless Patient Spider," "Come Up from the Fields Father," "Had I the Choice," "There Was a Child Went Forth" (the "heavyweight" here, at thirty-nine lines), and "When I Heard the Learn'd Astronomer." Total: 103 lines of Whitman; average poem: 20.6 lines.

It doesn't take a statistical genius to see that, if indeed Whitman is one of our nation's major poets (and he is), and if he is one of the great poets of the world (a universally acknowledged fact), we are being short-changed in the quantity (not to mention the quality) of his work that is being offered to our students. A quick tally shows *what* of Whitman gets anthologized—poems ten lines or fewer that don't pack much of a punch or don't contain much of Whitman's philosophy. They are imagistic sketches, not even vignettes, and in them the poet simply does not have the opportunity to do what he does best—stretch out and soar. Of "O Captain! My Captain!," perhaps the most anthologized Whitman poem, biographer Justin Kaplan has reported:

> Sometimes [Whitman] regretted ever having written it. ("It's My Captain again; always My Captain," he exclaimed when the Harper publishing house asked his permission to print it in a school reader. "My God! when will they listen to me for whole and good?" If this was his "best," he said, "what can the worst be like?") (*Walt Whitman: A Life*, p. 29)

It is on that great long poem that came to be called *Song of Myself*, in its 1855 incarnation of 1,336 lines (before Whitman tinkered with it in later editions of *Leaves of Grass*), that Whitman's reputation chiefly rests—or ought to. (Other works in the 1855 edition are also great: certainly "The Sleepers" and "Faces," and perhaps "I Sing the Body Electric.") The later "Out of the Cradle Endlessly Rocking," "When Lilacs Last in the Dooryard Bloom'd," and "Crossing Brooklyn Ferry" are also great and substantial poems. Some of the erotic poems in the "Calamus" section of the *Leaves* are powerful, as are a few of the Civil War poems in the "Drum Taps" section. Also worth study are the various poems with "Song" in their titles, a grouping that includes "Salut au Monde!" and "Our Old Feuillage."

Why not take Whitman at his word? If students can read 300-page novels, surely they can read a hundred pages of his best work.

Additional Writing Ideas

For academic or research papers, students could explore some of the following ideas:

• 1. *Whitman and the Spiritual*: A good introduction to the mystical tradition may be found in *The Perennial Philosophy* by Aldous Huxley (New York: Harper & Row, 1970; first published 1945). *Cosmic Consciousness*, by Whitman's disciple, Dr. R. M. Bucke (New York: Dutton, 1991), was praised by the poet, who claimed that "it thoroughly delineates me" (Kaplan, pp. 37–38). The psychologist William James's *The Varieties of Religious Experience* (New York: Penguin Books and other publishers) was originally published in 1902 and contains a good deal of material on Whitman. The connection between the metaphysics of Hinduism and Whitman can be probed in "Whitman and Indian Thought" by V. K. Chari (excerpted in Bradley and Blodgett) and in Chari's book *Whitman in the Light of Vedantic Mysticism—An Interpretation* (Lincoln: University of Nebraska Press, 1964). For a contrast to Whitman's view of the One in a poem like *Song of Myself*, see "The Eleventh Teaching: The Vision of Krishna's Totality" in *The Bhagavad-Gita: Krishna's Counsel in Time of War*, translated by Barbara Stoler Miller (New York: Bantam Books, 1986), which keeps the verse form of the original. The recent translation of the *Bhagavad Gita* by Stephen Mitchell may also be consulted (New York: Harmony Books/Random House, 2000). Transcendentalism, the sociophilosophical movement of the nineteenth century that had a powerful impact on Whitman, may be scrutinized in *The Transcendentalists: An Anthology*, edited by Perry Miller (Cambridge, Mass.: Harvard University Press, 1950). See also *Transcendentalism in New England: A History* by Octavius Brooks Frothingham (Gloucester, Mass.: Peter Smith, 1965; originally published 1876) and, for short articles, *The Transcendentalist Revolt Against Materialism*, edited with an introduction by George F. Whicher (Boston: D. C. Heath & Co., 1949). The biographies of Whitman and Gay Wilson Allen's biography of Emerson also look into the relationship between Whitman and Transcendentalist thought.

• 2. *Poems on the Assassination of Abraham Lincoln*: Not surprisingly, many poets besides Whitman wrote tributes when Lincoln was murdered. Some of them were collected in *Poems of American History* edited by Burton Egbert Stevenson (Boston: Houghton Mifflin, 1922), pp. 537–544. To find this fascinating book, long out of print, you will have to hunt it down in libraries or on the Internet, but the search is worth it. Students can compare other elegies to Whitman's "O Captain! My Captain!" and "When Lilacs Last in the Dooryard Bloom'd." The assignment could be extended to compare the reaction of poets to John F. Kennedy's assassination in *Of Poetry and Power* (New York: Basic Books, 1964).

• 3. *Emerson and Whitman*: For many years the poet and great essayist Ralph Waldo Emerson beat the drum for a new kind of American poetry. Whitman was quite familiar with Emerson's essays and lectures and with the chief ideas of the Transcendentalist movement "fathered" by Emerson. (When Whitman sent him a copy of *Leaves of Grass* in 1855, Emerson wrote back to say that Whitman's book was "the most extraordinary piece of wit & wisdom that America has yet contributed" [Kaplan, pp. 202–203].) Students could read Emerson's essays "The Transcendentalist" and "The Poet" (see Emerson's *Selected Essays*, edited by Larzer Ziff [New York: Penguin Books, 1982]) to search for his ideas about the new American poet, and judge how applicable they are to Whitman. *Waldo Emerson: A Biography* by Gay Wilson Allen (New York: Viking Press, 1981), should also be consulted. In addition, Allen has published a standard Whitman biography, and knows the intellectual terrain of this period. For further consultation, see *Emerson Among the Eccentrics: A Group Portrait* by Carlos Baker (New York: Viking Press, 1996). The book's introduction and epilogue, by James R. Mellow, places Emerson among his peers. A recent and highly regarded biography is *Emerson: The Mind on Fire* by Robert D. Richardson, Jr. (Berkeley: University of California Press, 1995).

• 4. *Contemporaries and Followers of Whitman*: Older poetry anthologies and histories of American poetry (such as *A Short History of American Poetry* by Donald Barlow Stauffer [New York: Dutton, 1974]) contain interesting selections from and commentaries on the poetry of Whitman's contemporaries. Beginning with Emerson, students could compare and contrast the writings of various poets to those of Whitman: William Gilmore Simms (1806–1870); Henry Wadsworth Longfellow (1807–1882); John Greenleaf Whittier (1807–1892); Edgar Allan Poe (1809–1849); Oliver Wendell Holmes (1809–1894); Christopher Pearse Cranch (1813–1872), whose curious poem "Correspondences" may have influenced Whitman's long prosaic line or been influenced by him (see

American Poetry: The Nineteenth Century, pp. 590–592, cited below); Jones Very (1813–1880); Henry David Thoreau (1817–1862); Herman Melville and James Russell Lowell (both 1819–1891), born the same year as Whitman, who outlived them by one year; Frederick Goddard Tuckerman (1821–1873); and Bayard Taylor (1825–1878). A wonderful place to track these poets is the magnificent two-volume edition of *American Poetry: The Nineteenth Century* (New York: The Library of America, 1993).

Whitman disciples whose work could be examined include Edward Carpenter (1844–1929), Carl Sandburg (1878–1967), Robinson Jeffers (1887–1962), Kenneth Fearing (1902–1961), and Allen Ginsberg (1926–1997). Ginsberg was perhaps the chief poet-advocate of Whitman in the post-World War II period, and had much to say about him in his essays and interviews. See his *Deliberate Prose: Selected Essays 1952–1995* edited by Bill Morgan (New York: HarperCollins, 2000) and *Spontaneous Mind: Selected Interviews 1958–1996*, preface by Václav Havel, edited by David Carter (New York: HarperCollins, 2001). Antler, a younger poet who accounts himself a disciple of both Whitman and Ginsberg, writes everything from protest poems (the brilliant long poem *Factory*) to lyrics that are often beautiful, often hilariously funny. His work may be found in *Antler: The Selected Poems* (New York: Soft Skull Press, 2000).

• 5. *Whitman's Poetic Language*: In the foreword to *An American Primer*, Whitman said: "I sometimes think that the *Leaves* is only a language experiment." Using *An American Primer* as a guide, students could put Whitman's language "under the microscope," studying what makes it visceral and what gives it its spiritual quality. What are his favorite words? From what sources does he derive his vocabulary? The same could be done for his rhetorical devices—anaphora, epistrophe, etc.

• 6. *Whitman's Prose Works*: Whitman's prefaces to his various editions of *Leaves of Grass* repay close reading. Students will find them collected in Bradley and Blodgett. *An American Primer* is a delightful excursion into the American language, and could be updated by students to include current slang and catch-phrases. Students could also write their own chapters based on *Specimen Days*. Other prose works, including short fiction and a novel, have been published in the monumental *Collected Writings of Walt Whitman*, currently being issued by New York University Press.

• 7. *"Walking Around" Poetry*: Whitman is one of a number of poets who have written poems "on foot" (or who create the illusion of doing so). For other masters of this genre, see work by Guillaume Apollinaire (in translations from the French), Charles Reznikoff, and Frank O'Hara.

The "walking around" poem is predominantly a city genre, so it is no surprise that all of these poets (and there are others) lived in New York or Paris. (A very good discussion of this kind of poem may be found in *Walks in the World: Representation and Experience in Modern American Poetry* by Roger Gilbert [Princeton, N.J.: Princeton University Press, 1991].)

How the Poets See Whitman: A Little Survey

Many poets have responded to *Leaves of Grass* with tributes of their own. Students can do reports on some of the poets who have been influenced by him or who have answered him in their own work. The poets that I have chosen below represent a small sampling of these responses. The source book for such investigations is *Walt Whitman: The Measure of His Song*, edited by Jim Perlman, Ed Folsom, and Dan Campion (Duluth, Minnesota: Holy Cow! Press, 1998), a vast collection of tributes and poems dedicated to Whitman by writers and poets from all over the world, ranging from 1855 to the 1990s.

Whitman found his first receptive readers among the poets of England (William Michael Rossetti, Swinburne, Tennyson, and Hopkins), but the first poets of reputation to be influenced by him were French. Jules Laforgue translated parts of *Leaves of Grass* into French and experimented with Whitman's long free-verse line. Early in the twentieth century, Valery Larbaud wrote travelogue-type poems about the "open road" so dear to Whitman. In Portugal, Fernando Pessoa invented a wonderfully crazy "Salutation to Walt Whitman" that sounds like T. S. Eliot's timid J. Alfred Prufrock going wild after reading *Song of Myself*. In the 1920s and 1930s, writers like Sherwood Anderson (who wrote poetry as well as fiction) and Carl Sandburg were deeply influenced by Whitman. Hart Crane dedicated a section of his long poem "The Bridge" to Whitman, ending it: "My hand / in yours, / Walt Whitman—/ so—." D. H. Lawrence, best known for his novels, used Whitman's long line in some of his greatest poems, including "Snake" and "Bavarian Gentians." Federico García Lorca, visiting the United States in 1929–1930, wrote an "Ode to Walt Whitman" that appeared in his book *Poet in New York*. Langston Hughes wrote, "I, too, sing America. // I am the darker brother," in one of his most famous poems, and many of his other poems reveal that he had carefully read his Whitman. The Chilean poet Pablo Neruda showed Whitman's influence especially in his long poem *Residence on Earth*. Neruda had this to say in an address given in New York City in 1972:

I was barely fifteen when I discovered Walt Whitman, my primary creditor. I stand here among you today still owing this marvelous debt that has helped me live.

To renegotiate this debt is to begin by making it public, by proclaiming myself the humble servant of the poet who measured the earth with long, slow strides, pausing everywhere to love and to examine, to learn, to teach, and to admire. That man, that lyric moralist, chose a difficult road; he was a torrential and didactic bard. These two qualities seem antithetical, more appropriate for a caudillo than for a writer. But what really matters is that the professor's chair, teaching, the apprenticeship to life held no fear for Walt Whitman, and he accepted the responsibility of teaching with candor and eloquence. Clearly, he feared neither morality nor immorality, nor did he attempt to define the boundaries between pure and impure poetry. He is the first absolute poet, and it was his intention not only to sing but to impart his vast vision of the relationships of men and of nations. In this sense, his obvious nationalism is part of an organic universality. He considers himself indebted to happiness and sorrow, to advanced cultures and primitive societies.

Greatness has many faces, but I, a poet who writes in Spanish, learned more from Walt Whitman than from Cervantes. In Whitman's poetry the ignorant are never humbled, and the human condition is never derided.

We are still living in a Whitmanesque epoch; in spite of painful birth pangs, we are witnessing the emergence of new men and new societies. The bard complained of the all-powerful European influence that continued to dominate the literature of his time. In fact, it was he, Walt Whitman, in the persona of a specific geography, who for the first time in history brought honor to an American name. The colonialism of the most brilliant nations created centuries of silence; in three centuries of Spanish domination we had no more than two or three outstanding writers in all America. (*Passions and Impressions*, pp. 376–377)

William Carlos Williams asserted that Keats and Whitman were the first two poets to make their mark on him. His judgment of Whitman was divided. On the one hand, Whitman broke new ground by his use of the American vernacular, a development that Williams thoroughly approved of and followed in his own poetic practice. On the other hand, Williams felt that Whitman didn't know what to do with the free verse he had invented:

Whitman to me was an instrument, one thing: he started us on the course of our researches into the nature of the line by breaking finally with English prosody. After him there has been for us no line. There will be none until we invent it. Almost everything I do is of no more interest to me than the technical addition it makes toward the discovery of a workable metric in the new mode. (*The Selected Letters of William Carlos Williams*, pp. 286–287)

Eleven years later, in 1961, Williams told an interviewer that "Whitman's line is too long for the modern poet. At the present time I have been trying to approach a shorter line which I haven't quite been able to nail." This line would be "more terse, and absolutely not the stretching out of the line that Whitman did" (*Interviews with William Carlos Williams*, p. 39). Interestingly enough, Williams told his interviewer: "I don't hear any Biblical form in [Whitman's] poems" (ibid., p. 42).

Poet Allen Ginsberg has proven to be Whitman's most outspoken contemporary champion, though Ginsberg's long line was also shaped by the unrhymed poems of William Blake. In an interview, Ginsberg remembered his days as a college student at Columbia (in the 1940s) and the attitude toward Whitman that prevailed:

> He was taught but he was much insulted. I remember, around the time of the writing of *On the Road* [by Jack Kerouac], a young favored instructor at Columbia College told me that Whitman was not a serious writer because he had no discipline and William Carlos Williams was an awkward provincial, no craft, and Shelley was a sort of silly fool! So there was no genuine professional poetics taught at Columbia, there was a complete obliteration and amnesia of the entire great mind of gnostic western philosophy or Hindu Buddhist eastern philosophy, no acceptance or conception of a possibility of a cosmic consciousness as a day to day experience or motivation or even once in a lifetime experience. It was all considered as some sort of cranky pathology. So Whitman was put down as a "negativist crude yea-sayer who probably had a frustrated homosexual libido and so was generalizing his pathology into oceanic consciousness of a morbid nature which had nothing to do with the real task of real men in a real world surrounded by dangerous communist enemies" [laughs] or something like that. (*Composed on the Tongue*, pp. 69–70)

Ginsberg adapted the rhythm of his poem "Howl" (1956) in part from the anaphora-laden *Song of Myself.* The long line was also employed in "Kaddish" (1961), the deeply moving elegy for his mother, and in his tribute to Whitman, "In a Supermarket in California":

> What thoughts I have of you tonight, Walt Whitman, for I walked down the sidestreets under the trees with a headache self-conscious looking at the full moon.
>
> In my hungry fatigue, and shopping for images, I went into the neon fruit supermarket, dreaming of your enumerations!
>
> What peaches and what penumbras! Whole families shopping at night! Aisles full of husbands! Wives in the avocados, babies in the tomatoes!—and you, García Lorca, what were you doing down by the watermelons?

(*Howl and Other Poems*, p. 23)

Louis Simpson carried on an argument with Whitman's prophetic poems—in particular, "Song of the Redwoods" and "Song of the Open Road"—in his book called *At the End of the Open Road* (1963). His "Walt Whitman at Bear Mountain" challenges the optimistic view of America and the faith in progress that came to be major Whitman themes. Its first stanzas read:

> Neither on horseback nor seated,
> But like himself, squarely on two feet,
> The poet of death and lilacs
> Loafs by the footpath. Even the bronze looks alive
> Where it is folded like cloth. And he seems friendly.
>
> "Where is the Mississippi panorama
> And the girl who played the piano?
> Where are you, Walt?
> The Open Road goes to the used car lot.
>
> "Where is the nation you promised?
> These houses built of wood sustain
> Colossal snows,
> And the light above the street is sick to death.
>
> "As for the people—see how they neglect you!
> Only a poet pauses to read the inscription."

Simpson has some superb observations as well as penetrating criticisms to make of Whitman:

> Whitman's "philosophy" . . . consists of two or three ideas. One, it is possible to merge in your feelings with others, and it is possible for others to merge in their feelings with you. Two, if this occurs over a distance, or over a span of time, it seems to annihilate space and time. This is a kind of immortality. Three, in order to convey your feelings to others you must, by a process of empathic observation, using all your senses, take things into yourself and express them again. The senses are "dumb ministers" of feeling . . . through them we know one another. The poet is the manager of this process—he puts what we feel and see into words. (*Selected Prose*, p. 322)

Some other poets who have adopted Whitman's long line for their own use include Robinson Jeffers, Kenneth Fearing, the Italian writer Cesare Pavese, and Kenneth Koch, whose poem "Faces" (which focuses on the same theme as the Whitman poem of 1855 that was eventually given this title) shows the hallmark Whitmanic anaphora :

The face of the gypsy watching the bird gun firing into the colony of
    seals; but it was filled with blanks;
The face of the old knoll watching his hills grow up before him;
The face of the New England fruit juice proprietor watching his whole
    supplies being overturned by a herd of wild bulls;
The face of a lemur watching the other primates become more
    developed;
The face of gold, as the entire world goes on the silver standard, but
    gold remains extremely valuable and is the basis for international
    exchange;
The face of the sky, as the air becomes increasingly filled with smoke
    and planes;
The face of the young girl painted as Saint Urbana by Perugino,
    whose large silver eyes are focused on the green pomegranate held
    by a baby (it is Jesus) in the same painting;
The face of the sea after there has been a storm, and the face of the
    valley
When the clouds have blown away and it is going to be a pleasant day
    and the pencils come out for their picnic;
The face of the clouds . . .

(*The Pleasures of Peace*, p. 86)

Charles Reznikoff was perhaps the greatest poet of New York City
after Whitman. His street scenes and mini-narratives also employ the
long line and focus on the experiences of ordinary people:

She sat by the window opening into the airshaft,
and looked across the parapet
at the new moon.

She would have taken the hairpins out of her carefully coiled hair,
and thrown herself on the bed in tears;
but he was coming and her mouth had to be pinned into a smile.
If he would have her, she would marry whatever he was.

A knock. She lit the gas and opened her door.
Her aunt and the man—skin loose under his eyes, the face slashed with
    wrinkles.
"Come in," she said as gently as she could and smiled.

(*Complete Poems*, p. 32)

In "Musical Shuttle," Harvey Shapiro remembers his youthful reading of Whitman's "Out of the Cradle Endlessly Rocking." Both poems are about the origins of the impulse to write poetry, which Whitman says came to him "Out of the mocking-bird's throat, the musical shuttle," as he watched the mating of two birds near the Long Island surf. Shapiro also finds himself on the Long Island shore:

> [. . .]
> I walked the shore
> Where cold rocks mourned in water
> Like the planets lost in air.
> Ocean was a low sound.
> The gate-keeper suddenly gone,
> Whatever the heart cried
> Voice tied to dark sound.
> The shuttle went way back then,
> Hooking me up to the first song
> That ever chimed in my head.
> Under a sky gone slick with stars,
> The aria tumbling forth:
> Bird and star . . .

(*National Cold Storage Company*, p. 52)

Whitman's followers are by now, of course, legion. His long line has passed into the public domain, where any poet can pick it up and bend it to his or her needs. That so many writers have done it constitutes yet another tribute to Whitman's genius. What we ought to remember is that Whitman forged his poetics in his own way. This, more than any tradition, seems to be the path for the American writer. If we use Walt Whitman as a guide, it ought to be to help us toward our own originality.

Bibliography

I. References Quoted in This Article

A. Books and Articles

Ginsberg, Allen. *Composed on the Tongue.* Edited by Donald Allen. Bolinas, Calif.: Grey Fox Press, 1979. Interviews and essays by Ginsberg.
Koch, Kenneth, and Kate Farrell. *Sleeping on the Wing: An Anthology of Modern Poetry with Essays on Reading and Writing.* New York: Random House, 1981; Vintage Books, 1982.

Neihardt, John G. *Black Elk Speaks: Being the Life Story of a Holy Man of the Oglala Sioux.* Lincoln: University of Nebraska Press, 1961; originally published in 1932. A new edition of this book was published in paperback in 2001, with added notes, a useful map, and new introductory material.

Neruda, Pablo. *Passions and Impressions.* Edited by Matilde Neruda and Miguel Otero Silva, translated by Margaret Sayers Peden. New York: Farrar, Straus & Giroux, 1983.

Simpson, Louis. *Selected Prose.* New York: Paragon House, 1989.

Whitman, Walt. The Malcolm Cowley edition of the 1855 *Leaves of Grass.* (See "Texts," below, for full bibliographical entry.)

———. *An American Primer: With Facsimiles of the Original Manuscript.* Edited by Horace Traubel. San Francisco: City Lights Books, 1970; reprinted Duluth, Minn.: Holy Cow! Press, 1987; originally published in 1904.

Williams, William Carlos. *The Selected Letters of William Carlos Williams.* Edited with an introduction by John C. Thirlwall. New York: McDowell, Obolensky, 1957.

———. *Interviews with William Carlos Williams: "Speaking Straight Ahead."* Edited by Linda Walsheimer Wagner. New York: New Directions, 1976.

B. Books of Poetry

Crane, Hart. *The Complete Poems and Selected Letters and Prose.* Edited with an introduction and notes by Brom Weber. Garden City, N.Y.: Doubleday & Co., 1966.

Ginsberg, Allen. *Howl and Other Poems.* Introduction by William Carlos Williams. San Francisco: City Lights Books, 1956.

Jeffers, Robinson. *The Selected Poetry.* New York: Random House, 1938.

Koch, Kenneth. *The Pleasures of Peace and Other Poems.* New York: Grove Press, 1969.

Larbaud, Valery. *The Poems of A. O. Barnabooth.* Translated by Ron Padgett and Bill Zavatsky. Tokyo: Mushinsha Ltd., 1977.

Lorca, Federico García. *Poet in New York.* Translated by Greg Simon and Steven F. White. Edited with an introduction and notes by Christopher Maurer. New York: Farrar, Straus & Giroux, 1988.

Neruda, Pablo. *Residence on Earth.* Translated by Donald D. Walsh. New York: New Directions, 1973.

Pavese, Cesare. *Hard Labor.* Translated and with an introduction by William Arrowsmith. Baltimore and London: The Johns Hopkins University Press, 1979.

Pessoa, Fernando. *Selected Poems.* Translated by Edwin Honig with an introduction by Octavio Paz. Chicago: The Swallow Press, 1971.

Reznikoff, Charles. *The Complete Poems 1918–1975.* Santa Rosa, Calif.: Black Sparrow, 1989.

Shapiro, Harvey. *National Cold Storage Company: New and Selected Poems.* Middletown, Conn.: Wesleyan University Press, 1988.

Simpson, Louis. *At the End of the Open Road.* Middletown, Conn.: Wesleyan University Press, 1963.

Williams, William Carlos. *The Collected Poems, Volume I: 1909–1939.* Edited by A. Walton Litz and Christopher MacGowan. New York: New Directions, 1986.

———. *The Collected Poems, Volume II: 1939–1962.* Edited by Christopher MacGowan. New York: New Directions, 1988.

II. Texts

Whitman, Walt. *An American Primer.* San Francisco: City Lights Books, 1970; republished Duluth, Minn.: Holy Cow! Press, 1987; originally published in 1904. First edited and issued by Whitman's disciple, Horace Traubel, in 1904, this never-completed meditation on language is one of Whitman's most delightful texts. It may be used as a starting point for further discussions of Whitman's use of language, and the nature of American English in general.

———. *Leaves of Grass: The First (1855) Edition.* Edited, with an introduction, by Malcolm Cowley. New York: Penguin Books, 1986; originally published in 1959. Cowley's excellent introduction makes as much sense out of the "structure" of Whitman's amorphous *Song of Myself* as any critic has. The virtue of this edition is that it gives us, with line numbers, the texts of important Whitman poems in their first—and purest—state. Unfortunately there are no explanatory notes to the poems, and Viking Penguin should get on the ball and commission someone to write them. There are too many odd vocabulary words and idiosyncratic usages for a high school student (even a college student) to cut through. (For those who might want a more durable version of this book, a hardcover edition is published by Barnes and Noble.)

————. *The Complete Poems.* Edited by Francis Murphy. New York: Penguin Books, 1975. A fine edition, if a bit bulky to handle. Murphy includes the 1855 text of *Song of Myself,* and there are good notes to the poems. Also included are the 1855, 1856, 1872, and 1876 prefaces to the book.

————. *Leaves of Grass: Authoritative Texts; Prefaces; Whitman on His Art; Criticism.* Edited by Sculley Bradley and Harold W. Blodgett. New York: Norton, 1973; originally published in 1965. An excellent resource volume, but for library consultation rather than high school classroom use. Includes all of Whitman's poetry that one would want to read— uncollected poems, unpublished poems, manuscript fragments. Whitman's pronouncements "On His Art" are here, as well as thirty critical essays and reviews. (One of them—an unsigned, laudatory review—is by Walt himself.) Especially interesting is "Whitman and Indian Thought" by V. K. Chari, who notes that although "the absence of any established evidence that Whitman studied the Hindu books has remained a serious hurdle in Whitman research, . . . [in] the years during which *Leaves* was in the making there was a considerable vogue in America for Hindu religious ideas. . . ." (pp. 926–927)

————. *Poetry and Prose.* New York: The Library of America, 1982. Edited by Justin Kaplan, who wrote the notes and a chronology, this volume includes the 1855 and 1892 ("Deathbed") edition of *Song of Myself,* as well as *Specimen Days, Democratic Vistas,* and virtually all of Whitman's important texts.

III. Critical Biographies and Collections of Essays

Allen, Gay Wilson. *The Solitary Singer: A Critical Biography of Walt Whitman.* New York: Grove Press, 1955. Still the most thorough look at Whitman's life and career.

Allen, Gay Wilson and Ed Folsom, editors. *Walt Whitman & the World.* Iowa City: University of Iowa Press, 1995. Appreciations of Whitman from England to Sweden. A fascinating collection for the breadth of interest that it exhibits in Whitman's work.

Folsom, Ed, editor. *Walt Whitman: The Centennial Essays.* Iowa City: University of Iowa Press, 1994. A wide-ranging collection of essays assembled by a dedicated Whitman scholar.

Greenspan, Ezra. *The Cambridge Companion to Walt Whitman.* Cambridge and New York: Cambridge University Press, 1995. Contains a number of solid essays about Whitman's life and writings. My personal favorite is Greenspan's "Some Remarks on the Poetics of 'Participle-Loving Whitman,'" which discusses one of Whitman's favorite stylistic devices.

Kaplan, Justin. *Walt Whitman: A Life*. New York: Simon & Schuster, 1980. A highly readable "popular" biography, Kaplan's judgment about the nature of Whitman's spirituality is worth quoting: "Whitman was not a 'mystic.' Conversion, discipline, renunciation of the self, the body, and the world are alien to *Leaves of Grass*. . . . He had shared the experience of countless people, irreligious by common standards, who had flashes of illumination or ecstasy. . . . The rhythm of these experiences is sexual and urgent . . . and he invoked it and prolonged it through poetry . . ." (p. 190). Be that as it may, Kaplan's very description points to the centrality of the "illumination or ecstasy" that Whitman experienced. Students might especially profit from a reading of chapters 8–9 (pp. 146–183), which describe the various sciences and pseudo-sciences of the age (such as phrenology) that had a profound effect on Whitman.

Loving, Jerome. *Walt Whitman: The Song of Himself*. Berkeley, Los Angeles, London: University of California Press, 1999. The most recent Whitman biography and a first-rate piece of work. Among Loving's contentions is that we have no absolute proof that Whitman was gay.

Martin, Robert K. *The Continuing Presence of Walt Whitman: The Life After the Life*. Iowa City: University of Iowa Press, 1992. "Martin's collection is particularly strong on the investigation of Whitman's homosexuality, his homotextuality, and his influence on gay writers and will clearly become the most aggressive gathering of essays ever published on this increasingly prominent aspect of Whitman and his work," reads the book jacket copy in part.

Reynolds, David S. *Walt Whitman's America: A Cultural Biography*. New York: Knopf, 1995. An important recent survey of Whitman and his times that has much information of importance about the poet for student and teacher alike.

Reynolds, David S., ed. *A Historical Guide to Walt Whitman*. New York and Oxford: Oxford University Press, 2000. Six essays on Whitman, including Reynolds' brief biography, a valuable "Illustrated Chronology" of Whitman's life, and a brief "Bibliographical Essay" by Reynolds.

Schmidgall, Gary. *Walt Whitman: A Gay Life*. New York: Dutton, 1997. The book jacket tells us: "*Walt Whitman: A Gay Life* is the first biography to illuminate the vital connection between Whitman's life as a homosexual and his legacy as a landmark literary artist."

Thomas, M. Wynn. *The Lunar Light of Whitman's Poetry*. Cambridge, Mass., and London: Harvard University Press, 1987. Another recent and highly regarded study of Whitman and his work.

Warren, James Perrin. *Walt Whitman's Language Experiment*. University Park and London: Pennsylvania State University Press, 1990. That's what Whitman once claimed, that his *Leaves of Grass* was a "language experiment." Warren investigates the idea thoroughly.

Zweig, Paul. *Walt Whitman: The Making of the Poet*. New York: Basic Books, 1984. Zweig carefully builds up the history of Whitman's development as a poet in this scrupulously researched and thoughtful book. He too dismisses any real "illumination": "Whitman's version of the peace that passeth all understanding is of the body and from the body. It expands like a gathering sexual storm and 'droops' like the subsidence of feeling after the sexual climax. [We] will never know whether Whitman experienced such a moment and became a poet because of it" (p. 254). Zweig's position is interesting because he himself has recounted his own search for enlightenment as a devotee of Swami Muktananda in his fascinating autobiographical book *Three Journeys*.

IV. Essays

These essays can be read and reported on by high school students, or used in term papers. It is important to note that chief among Whitman's defenders have been poets like D. H. Lawrence, Donald Hall, Kenneth Rexroth, Randall Jarrell, Cesare Pavese, Karl Shapiro, Guy Davenport, and William Carlos Williams.

Davenport, Guy. "Whitman." In *The Geography of the Imagination: Forty Essays*. San Francisco: North Point Press, 1981. A beautifully written and insightful essay: "[Whitman] closed the widening distance between poet and audience. He talks to us face to face, so that our choice is between listening and turning away. And in turning away there is the uneasy feeling that we are turning our backs on the very stars and on ourselves" (p. 70). "Whitman's fond gaze was for grace that is unaware of itself; his constant pointing to beauty in common robust people was a discovery. Custom said that beauty was elsewhere" (p. 71).

Gross, Harvey. *Sound and Form in Modern Poetry: A Study of Prosody from Thomas Hardy to Robert Lowell*. Ann Arbor: University of Michigan Press, 1964. Contains a provocative study of Whitman's prosody, which Gross calls "formal and ceremonious. . . . His proper mode is not speech but invocation; not conversation, but chant and ceremony" (p. 84). He tells us that "Whitman's basic contribution was the substitution of syntax for meter as the controlling prosodic element in his poetry" (p. 85). The effect of the lines is a musical one, depending on devices such as syntactical parallelism, anaphora, and ellipsis. The danger is that "Whitman's nonmetrical prosody is as capable of doggerel as Poe's metronome" (p. 88).

Hall, Donald. "Whitman: The Invisible World." In *To Keep Moving: Essays 1959–1969*. Geneva, N.Y.: Hobart & William Smith Colleges Press, in association with *Seneca Review*, 1980. "Many of Whitman's admirers . . . speak of his catalogues, his multiplication of things. Yet, the seen world hardly exists for him, because he spiritualizes everything." An excellent essay, originally written to introduce a selection of Whitman's verse to readers in Great Britain.

———. "The Long Foreground of Walt Whitman." In *The Weather for Poetry: Essays, Reviews, and Notes on Poetry, 1977–81*. Ann Arbor: University of Michigan Press, 1982. An excellent review of Justin Kaplan's Whitman biography.

Jarrell, Randall. "Some Lines from Whitman." In *Poetry and the Age*. New York: Random House Vintage Books, 1955; originally published 1953. A crucial essay in the rehabilitation of Whitman's reputation, focusing on this "poet of the greatest and oddest delicacy and originality and sensitivity, so far as words are concerned."

Lawrence, D. H. "Whitman." In *Studies in Classic American Literature*. New York: Penguin, 1964; originally published in 1923. A wonderfully cranky piece of creative griping, in which Lawrence takes Whitman to task for the loss of self exhibited in the American poet's passion for "merging." Lawrence links Whitman to faceless mass society, i.e., conformity. In brief, the wish to attain to Allness threatens Lawrence's ego. His thrashings-about are a delight to witness, especially in the light of his acknowledgment of Whitman as a "very great poet." This essay also appears in Bradley and Blodgett.

Marx, Leo, editor. *The Americanness of Walt Whitman*. Boston: D. C. Heath & Co., Problems in American Civilization series, 1960). The text of the 1891–92 edition of *Song of Myself*, accompanied by essays from de Tocqueville, Edward Dowden, John Jay Chapman, George Santayana, Van Wyck Brooks, R. W. B. Lewis, and Richard Chase. Also here are Lawrence's and Jarrell's essays.

Miller, Edwin Haviland. *Walt Whitman's "Song of Myself": A Mosaic of Interpretations*. Iowa City: University of Iowa Press, 1989. A fascinating and very useful volume that moves through Whitman's long poem line by line, citing critical articles that offer interpretations and giving their sources. Included is the 1855 text of *Song of Myself* and an extensive bibliography.

Miller, James E., Karl Shapiro, and Bernice Slote. *Start with the Sun: Studies in the Whitman Tradition*. Lincoln: University of Nebraska Press, 1960. Notable for Shapiro's essay on "Cosmic Consciousness" and Miller's "The Poetics of the Cosmic Poem," this collection extends the Whitman tradition to the work of D. H. Lawrence, Hart Crane, Dylan Thomas, and Henry Miller. Shapiro's "The First White Aboriginal" also appears in this volume.

Padgett, Ron, editor, with Bill Zavatsky. "Free Verse" in *Poetic Forms*. New York: Teachers & Writers Collaborative, 1988. This cassette interview is a discussion of free verse, with reference to the history of the form and Whitman's practice.

Pavese, Cesare. "Interpretation of Walt Whitman, Poet." In *American Literature: Essays and Opinions*, translated with an introduction by Edwin Fussell. Berkeley, Los Angeles, and London: University of California Press, 1970. An engaging essay by this important Italian fiction writer and poet, whose own long-lined poems show the influence of Whitman's free verse. Also in Bradley and Blodgett.

Pearce, Roy Harvey, editor. *Whitman: A Collection of Critical Essays*. Englewood Cliffs, N.J.: Prentice-Hall, 1962. An excellent collection of essays that contains the Lawrence essay as well as essays or book chapters by Pearce, William Carlos Williams, Ezra Pound, James Miller, Jr., F. O. Matthiessen, Charles Feidelson, Jr., R. W. B. Lewis, Richard Chase, and others.

Perlman, Jim, Ed Folsom, and Dan Campion, editors. *Walt Whitman: The Measure of His Song* (Minneapolis: Holy Cow! Press, 1998). This wonderful and massive (531 pages) collection of poems, letters, and essays ranges from 1855 to the 1990s and gathers tributes from many poets of various cultures.

Rexroth, Kenneth. "Walt Whitman: Leaves of Grass." In *Classics Revisited*. New York: Avon Books Discus Edition, 1969. A fine essay in which Rexroth points out that, among the many great nineteenth-century writers who became "self-alienated outcasts," Whitman "successfully refused alienation" (p. 249).

———. *American Poetry in the Twentieth Century*. New York: The Seabury Press/Continuum Books, 1971. Whitman is "the only American poet who from his day to ours has been a major world writer and who has influenced writers in every language—from Rabindranath Tagore, Francis Jammes, Emile Verhaeren, or Blaise Cendrars to the contemporary

Matabele poet, Raymond Kunene" (p. 18). The entire book is worth reading, both for Rexroth's fluent style and his brilliant observations.

Shapiro, Karl. "The First White Aboriginal." In *In Defense of Ignorance*. New York: Random House/Vintage Books, 1965; originally published in 1960. Another important essay that contributed to the rehabilitation of Whitman's reputation. Shapiro begins with a comparison of Whitman and D. H. Lawrence, then settles down to delineate Whitman's philosophy: "He is the one mystical writer of any consequence America has produced, the most original religious thinker we have; the poet of the greatest achievement; the first profound innovator; the most accomplished artist as well—but nobody says this nowadays. For in the twentieth century Walt Whitman is almost completely shunned by his fellows. He has no audience, neither a general audience nor a literary clique. Official criticism ignores him completely; modern neo-classicism, as it calls itself, acknowledges him with embarrassment" (p. 188).

Zavatsky, Bill. "Free Verse." In *The Teachers & Writers Handbook of Poetic Forms*, edited by Ron Padgett. New York: Teachers & Writers Collaborative, 1987. A short essay on free verse, with an example chosen from *Song of Myself* and suggestions for further reading and writing.

Emily Dickinson

Terry Blackhawk

Mixing It Up with Dickinson

Two High School Poetry Workshops

ATTEMPTING TO UNDERSTAND Emily Dickinson sometimes puts me in mind of the last lines of her Poem 1400—"That those who know her know her less/ The nearer her they get—." The mystery and delight, ambiguity and power of Dickinson's genius make her, in my opinion, almost a force of Nature, something to be reckoned with yet always beyond our grasp. She stands as a model of fiercely determined artistic choice, of incomparable linguistic artistry, and of an independent woman's insistence, as Adrienne Rich put it, ". . . to have it out at last/ on [her] own premises." In 1998, thanks to an NBC Classics in the Classroom Writing Residency, I was able to bring the power of her words to a class of eleventh graders at Detroit's Henry Ford High School, where I had been working as poet-in-residence. I was curious to know how Detroit teens would respond to her, and I wanted to see how her writing could trigger theirs. Later that spring, I used Dickinson as the focus of a series of poetry workshops at Western Michigan University with high school students attending the Michigan Youth Arts Festival.

"Dear World": Dickinson in Detroit

Because so many unfortunate biographical myths, oversimplifications and distortions abound about Emily Dickinson, Roberta Herter (the classroom teacher at Henry Ford High School) and I decided to start our study of Dickinson by presenting students with her letters, thus giving them a chance to know something of her voice, style, and biography. One of the most erroneous stereotypes of the poet is that of a mad isolate who renounced the world around her. While it is true that, for the latter part of her life, Dickinson avoided visitors and "never left her Father's grounds," she was nevertheless deeply engaged with many friends and relatives, chiefly through letters.

The portion of her correspondence discovered to date includes nearly 1,200 letters addressed to more than ninety correspondents and has been compiled in a three-volume collection, *The Letters of Emily Dickinson* edited by Thomas Johnson. Given the sheer volume of her correspondence, Roberta and I felt fortunate to discover a thoughtful, classroom-friendly selection of letters from a commercially-produced resource—*Reading Emily's Mail* by Linda Boxleitner—which arranges some of the better-known letters into useful groupings and provides exercises on describing the author's voice and identifying poetic language. The students worked in groups of three or four, examining packets of letters addressed either to Dickinson's cousins, to her girlhood friends, to the publisher Thomas Wentworth Higginson, to the mysterious "Master," to Judge Otis Lord (suggested by some as the recipient of the passionate "Master" letters), or to Helen Hunt Jackson, a fellow writer and friend. The students responded almost immediately to the passion and emotion in Dickinson's writing, were perplexed and intrigued by some of her phrasings, and were curious about the Master letters, which I showed them in facsimile.

After a couple of days with the letters and some discussion of Dickinson's life, family, and home, I felt that the students were ready to begin looking at some poems. Among the first poems I gave them, along with "This is my letter to the world" and "She staked her feathers—gained an Arc," was "Some keep the Sabbath":

324

Some keep the Sabbath going to Church—
I keep it, staying at Home—
With a Bobolink for a Chorister—
And an Orchard, for a Dome—

Some keep the Sabbath in Surplice—
I just wear my Wings—
And instead of tolling the Bell, for Church,
Our little Sexton—sings.

God preaches, a noted Clergyman—
And the sermon is never long,
So instead of getting to Heaven, at last—
I'm going, all along.

I put two columns on the board with the titles EMILY and CHURCH, and asked the students to identify contrasts between Dickinson's way of worship and that of the church: that of her Bobolink to the church's choir, the sky instead of the dome, and so on. The students were quick to identify the differences and to appreciate her lack of orthodoxy, her worship of nature, and her independence. For these teens, many of whom come from highly religious families, the idea of personal, self-determined worship was surprisingly appealing. Next I talked about the patriarchal relations in Dickinson's family and explained how she had never entered into the church her family attended, despite the fact that by her father's doing it had been built right across the street from their home. I also told the story of how she'd been a "no-hoper"—i.e., she had refused to declare herself as "saved" for Christ during revival season at Mt. Holyoke when she was a student there. One student, Tanisha, raised her fist in the air on that one, a right-on sister gesture that amazed and delighted me.

Throughout our conversation, I tried to stress Dickinson's independence of thought and lifestyle. I agree with the views of many contemporary critics who see Dickinson's rejection of nineteenth-century society as a willed and ultimately triumphant assertion of her own individualism. She was determined not to be trapped by the "dimity convictions" or restricted definitions of what was possible for a woman of her time. By retreating inside her tightly drawn boundaries and "selecting her own Society," she retained control over her emotional life and created space for her genius. But another quality I love to stress about Dickinson is her sense of humor. How can we fail to admire the wit of a poet who tells us "I like a look of Agony/Because I know it's true"; who, when her mother tells her to turn over a new leaf, writes, "I call that the Foliage Admonition"; or who deflates ministerial pomposity with "He spoke upon Breadth/Till it argued him narrow"?

Continuing our discussion of "Some keep the Sabbath," I wrote *circumference* on the board, drew a big circle with *known* on the inside and *unknown* on the outside and talked about the limits of knowing that ever perplexed and attracted Dickinson. I mentioned her idea that "The Brain is wider than the Sky" and discussed "My Business is Circumference"—a declaration she made early in her life (Letter 268). Dickinson's preoccupation with her concept of circumference coincides with her desire to transcend received knowledge; for instance, in Letter 950 she commented, "The Bible dealt with the Centre, not with the Circumference—." Engagement with circumference creates "vaster attitudes" that erase boundaries between dual concepts such as the known/the unknown, inside/outside, life/death, and so on. The imagery in many of Dickinson's poems carries the reader into vast, ungrounded territory, resulting in a letting-go of conventional concepts.

Finally, I mentioned that reaching beyond the limits of circumference rewarded Dickinson with moments of sacred revelation, and I connected her isolation from the world with these intense spiritual and intellectual preoccupations. Her commitment to this project of "knowing" what cannot be known—the "uncertain certainty" as she so aptly puts it in Poem 1411—must have undergirded many of her life choices. In fact, a concordance to Dickinson reveals that "know" is the most frequent verb Dickinson employs in her poetry. I wrapped up the session by emphasizing Dickinson's desire to probe the unknowable and answer unanswerable questions. I asked the students to generate a list of questions, then pick one to answer in a short poem, as a sort of "mini-exercise," trying to connect it with Dickinson and her desire to probe "the uncertain certainty." Before class ended, each student had shared a question.

Why ask why?
Where did time come from?
What did I do to deserve so much agony and pain?
Will my life end in suicide?
Will death take my mother the same way he took my father?
Why am I so tired?
Why is everybody so down?
Why am I so confused?
Why did I come to school today?
Why do I want to climb out of this window?
Why do I feel so crazy?
Why do they say the earth moves but we can't feel it?
How does the sun light up so many places at one time?
Why does Ashley have on all black?

The next day we read more poems, and I gave them choices for writing using Dickinson's first lines as springboards. They began, and the hour filled quickly. Many chose to do their own versions of "This is my Letter to the World"—pieces which, not surprisingly for a group of Detroit teens, took on racism, crime, and urban violence. Dale used the entree to take issue with a world in which he felt freedom was a sham. His world, or white racist society, is "always watching / scared to see us united." Krystal addressed a world filled with crime and violence before "retreating into her little ranch (house)." "Do you miss me?" she queried, "Because I do not miss you." Rachael expressed a similar bitterness:

Dear World

You never told me about unfairness.
I had to experience that myself.
You never assured me of my safety
but threw me in the arms of danger.

You never wrote to me.
From Day One you showed me
I wasn't accepted.
Every obstacle I passed, you
disowned me more.

You were my only hope
but when I needed you the most
you turned your back on me.

This is my first and last letter to
the world, just to express my gratitude
and tell you thank you, thank you
for nothing.

    —Rachael Head

After a number of students had shared their drafts, I told them that on my next visit they could choose to deal with poems about God, birds, or pain, since I'd collected packets of poems on each of these topics. They decided that God was too controversial, birds were boring, but pain was something they could all identify with. I began our next session by asking them to identify what kinds of things cause pain and to give reasons for what they had to say. The list was lengthy, ranging from physical injury, having a friend move away, losing a loved one, and not being able to help someone in need, to racism and parental abuse. They opened up and were willing to tell their stories, for which I was appreciative. I view this kind of storytelling and sharing of personal experiences as an important part of writing. As each student shares a story, others listen and formulate or reflect on their own experiences. Dale described his anguish at seeing a woman on a bus going into an epileptic seizure and not being able to help her. Martina had recently been in an emergency room with an asthma attack and described the smell of fear and the panicky feeling of not being able to breathe.

The Dickinson poems I selected on this topic ranged from the acerbic to the tender to the Gothic or surreal.

479

She dealt her pretty words like Blades—
How glittering they shone—
And every One unbared a Nerve
Or wantoned with a Bone—

She never deemed—she hurt—
That—is not Steel's Affair—

A vulgar grimace in the Flesh—
How ill the Creatures bear—

To Ache is human—not polite—
The Film upon the eye
Mortality's old Custom—
Just locking up—to Die.

1078

The Bustle in a House
The Morning after Death
Is solemnest of industries
Enacted upon Earth—

The Sweeping up the Heart
And putting Love away
We shall not want to use again
Until Eternity.

599

There is a pain—so utter—
It swallows substance up—
Then covers the Abyss with Trance—
So Memory can step
Around—across—upon it—
As one within a Swoon—
Goes safely—where an open eye—
Would drop Him—Bone by Bone.

Once we had read the poems, I told the students how "The Bustle in a House" meant so much to a friend who had recently lost her husband, and how her daughter had set the poem to music and sung it at the funeral service. The students were taken with lines such as "The Sweeping up the Heart" and intrigued by "There is a pain—so utter," especially by its concluding image of walking over the abyss in a swoon. I asked them to think of an experience or a topic related to pain and then to make a list of images, in three columns (sight / sound / other senses), that related to their topic. After they had spent some time on this, I asked the students to start a poem and encouraged them to freely borrow lines or phrases of Dickinson's language, if they found them useful. As they had previously with "This is my letter to the World," some chose to use one of Dickinson's lines as a first line. The pieces seemed to have personal significance for the students. Brandii wrote about her grandfather who had recently died. Shannon adapted Dickinson's rhythms to indict an abusive parent. Will focused on the time his father left the family for good. I had a feeling that something had opened up and felt optimistic about the lesson to come.

When I arrived for the next session, the students were closed, quiet, almost refusing to talk. It seemed necessary to widen the discussion beyond matters of pain, so I asked them to look at Dickinson's two Eden poems, with some discussion about the sexuality in those poems. On several occasions, the students had expressed curiosity as to whether "she had a man." I did not want to lecture on the mysteries and controversies surrounding Dickinson's love life; clearly she was a passionate person. Whether she had lovers or who they may have been are to this day matters of speculation. I did mention, however, that there are a number of candidates for her affections championed by various scholars on a list ranging from Otis Lord to Charles Wadsworth to Samuel Bowles to her sister-in-law Sue. More to the point, I simply wanted them to experience a different side of Dickinson's writing.

211

Come slowly—Eden!
Lips unused to Thee—
Bashful—sip thy Jessamines—
As the fainting Bee—

Reaching late his flower,
Round her chamber hums—
Counts his nectars—
Enters—and is lost in Balms.

249

Wild Nights—Wild Nights!
Were I with thee
Wild Nights should be
Our luxury!

Futile—the Winds—
To a Heart in port—
Done with the Compass—
Done with the Chart!

Rowing in Eden—
Ah, the Sea!
Might I but moor—Tonight—
In Thee!

We ended this session in individual conferences, as students revised and polished their Dickinson-inspired poems. Some were close to being finished. Bridgett had been taken with "The Bustle in a House" and used its second line ("the morning after death"—changing *morning* to *mourning*) as her first line, and its last phrase "until Eternity" as her last line. Bridgett's poem felt empty of imagery to me, but when I raised that issue, she argued that if Dickinson could use abstract terms, why couldn't she? I was aware that Bridgett, whose forthrightness in writing about sexual abuse had shown us all how poetry could help deal with personal horror, might not take to too much prodding on this issue, so I stopped pushing. Besides that, I had loved her assertive question! Her revision efforts centered around balancing stanzas and choosing some precise words. Her poem ended:

> awakened nerves mourn
> memories of pain
> left behind, a shattered Heart
> [. . .]
> and you, a breathless child
> lost within reality
> a hidden love
>
> that shall not surface again
> until Eternity.

Shannon also began and ended with Dickinson's language. In addition to the poem's first line, the second line of Shannon's third stanza altered "She dealt her pretty words like blades" to "what pretty words she deals." There were some rough spots in the rhythm, so I encouraged Shannon to regularize the form, using her final stanza as her guide. We discussed how she could make other stanzas fit her rhyme scheme and how she could eliminate unnecessary syllables. I felt that her poem made strong use of the senses to express the emotions of its speaker and was pleased at how willing she was to confront a painful relationship.

> There is a pain so utter
> you can feel it in your bones—
> the angry words, red faces—
> children startled from their rooms.
>
> The yells and tears and sweat
> as she pushes you into the wall—
> your saliva mingles in the air
> with the leftover pizza smell.

While you're down, she curses you
and what pretty words she deals.
You hear fine china breaking
with every slash you feel.

Oh, it hurts you scream in your mind,
not daring to let her hear,
'cause she'll bare white teeth and say
"To ache is human, my dear."

—*Shannon Sullivan*

Our final session focused on exploring Dickinson's poetry in conjunction with visual art. While I was working at Henry Ford, I received as a gift *Language as Object: Emily Dickinson and Contemporary Art*, an art book published in conjunction with an exhibit at the Mead Art Museum at Amherst College. This marvelous collection of photography, sculpture, painting, collage, and poetry inspired by Dickinson contains images and scenes that provide other paths to understanding her, and expresses the power and mystery of her work in many haunting ways. For our final session, I brought in color xeroxes of some of my favorite reproductions in the book. I asked the students to choose one and then to meditate on it. Next, they were to freewrite or free-list words and phrases that came to mind and see if or how new language inspired by the artwork might connect with their drafts. Ashley chose Carla Rae Johnson's *Lectern for Emily Dickinson*, working in one of the earlier "unanswerable" questions to good effect.

Climbing the stairway
to nowhere
step by step
to the beat of silence
holding on
to the rail for balance.
Where did time come from?
Time seems to fall
from the sky
only to come
to a closed door.
The knock falls silent
interrupts the creak
of the staircase.
Isolated.

Insulated.
Dilapidated.
Confused.
Quiet.

—*Ashley Little*

Will, whose poem was about his father's abandonment of the family, selected Joseph Cornell's *Toward the Blue Peninsula: for Emily Dickinson.* I had first seen Will on the previous Halloween when he had come to school dressed as Jason from "Friday the Thirteenth" and refused to take off his hockey mask. The only white kid in the class, he had seemed angry and defensive. By the spring, however, his good nature was evident as he teased and joked with his classmates. I was pleased that he felt comfortable enough to write about what was surely one of his great losses in life. His first draft had covered more than a page, but once he encountered the sparseness of the Cornell image, he whittled his poem down to only the bare and necessary essentials.

There is a pain
like I was locked in a cell
that only had two windows
not even a door.
The pain comes from my Father
who tells me I don't want you no more,
tells me to go ask a barely known man
will he take me.
Pain like my life in a cell
the walls coming in and crunching me
into a powdery dust.

—*Will Morris*

"Walking toward you without knowing": Michigan Youth Arts Festival, Kalamazoo

My goal for the short (two-day) but intensive workshop sessions held at Western Michigan University was to "mix it up" as much as possible. The high school-age students who attend this workshop are already committed, self-identified poets whose work has earned them an invitation to the Festival. I used many of the strategies (artwork, questions, borrowed lines) I employed with the students at Henry Ford High School, as well as a set of mini-assignments adapted from "Twenty Little Poetry Projects" by Jim Simmerman, which I had just enjoyed using myself in a Detroit Writer's Voice poetry workshop. I also introduced poems by contemporary poets Adrienne Rich and Lewis Turco.

At our first session (Friday morning), I began by telling the kids that teachers usually approach them with questions. This time I wanted them to pose the questions. I instructed them to write a list of questions, any questions at all. After a few minutes I asked each participant to select a question, which I then put on the board—questions that ranged from the sublime to the ridiculous, the personal to the mundane. Poetry, I told them, gets us into places where we are faced with unanswerable questions, and thus challenges us. Then I asked the students to write a poem that gives a mundane question an extraordinary answer, or to pick a complex, unanswerable question and answer it in a poem that is fairly simple. After a time, I had them all choose partners and read their poems to each other. (I find that this is a good way for the kids to loosen up and to begin talking in productive ways about their work.)

I then introduced Dickinson, characterizing her as someone whose mission was to probe the unanswerable. These students already had some familiarity with her. Many had bits and pieces of poems in their heads—first stanzas of "Because I could not stop for Death" or "There's a certain slant of light." We went around the room and shared what of Dickinson we knew by heart. I recited "Split the Lark," which I'd prepared on a handout. They were interested in the reference to "sceptic Thomas," which I explained—as is often the case with Dickinson—has many possible interpretations. (It may allude to "doubting Thomas" in the New Testament; to Sir Thomas Browne, who tried to find the soul by dissecting human bodies; or to Dickinson's friend and mentor Thomas Higginson; or to all three.)

The discussion ranged widely. The students expressed some of the usual stereotypes about Dickinson—as mad, fearful, a "ghost." I countered their assumptions by describing her social standing in her hometown of Amherst, her stubbornness toward religion and patriarchy, and her humor. To create some common ground, I provided what background I could, trying to give a picture of her complexity and intensity. I discussed the Gothic grotesqueries in some of her poems, *circumference* as her "Business," and *immortality* as her "Flood subject." I brought up the transcendental ideal of surpassing limits and characterized Dickinson as eccentric, brilliant, passionate, and intellectual. Some critics, I told them, tend to see Dickinson through their own political or psychological lenses (Grabowsky's agoraphobic Dickinson, Cody's Freudian Dickinson, Paglia's Emily as dominatrix). I discussed the publishing that she did during her lifetime, the discovery of her poems, the fascicles (chapbooks), and how her letters have survived and can be read as poems. We ended by reading Lewis Turco's poem "Winter Bouquet," which is composed from language gathered from Dickinson's letters.

We began our afternoon session by looking at a number of poems from the handout, reading and commenting. The students and I took turns reading, and quite a few poems were heard aloud this way: *Wild Nights! . . . Much Madness is divinest Sense . . . The Bustle in a House . . . After great pain . . . The Lightning is a yellow Fork . . . Come slowly—Eden! . . . These are the nights that Beetles love.* I put a selection of her first lines on the board and asked the students to choose one as a springboard into their own poems. They wrote for a while, and some seemed to enjoy playing with her language and ideas. Eleuheu used rap rhythms to jazz up the idea of circumference, and Tom took off into a "Wild Nights" that was all his own. Kaitlin's personal "slant of light" owes a number of debts to Dickinson. Her final stanza adapts imagery and rhythm from "Safe in their Alabaster Chambers."

Emily's in My Bed

"There's a certain slant of light"
across the milky skin
of cheeks and nose and eyelids
stopping only to begin.

"Dust is the only secret"
this vivid light reveals
in small specs of passion
churned up by porcelain wheels.

   —*Kaitlin Russell*

Others complained that Dickinson's rhythms were inhibiting. Her voice seemed to lock onto theirs in some cases. Gina wailed, "This sounds like Dr. Seuss!" and Geoff complained that he "*hates* Emily Dickinson." "Go ahead," I said, "quarrel with her." I didn't want to force Dickinson down their throats.

Saturday morning. Because we were all in a new space, away from home and immersed in the Festival, I began the next day's session by asking the students to jot down several things they had noticed on their way from dorm to workshop that morning. Then I talked about how modern poets have been influenced by Dickinson. We read Adrienne Rich's "I Am in Danger—Sir—" and discussed how Rich uses the second person "you" to address and pay homage to Dickinson while also posing the question

"Who are you?" Another unanswerable question, Lindsey astutely pointed out.

Using the same collection of visual art inspired by Dickinson that I had used at Henry Ford, I spread out color xeroxes, asking the students each to come up and choose one. Then I asked them either to revisit their drafts from the previous day, or to begin a new piece. As well as suggesting that they try writing letters to Dickinson, I gave them some other ideas, which I listed on the board:

Use as much language as you can suggested by the artwork you selected.
Include an observation from your morning walk to class.
Include an example of synaesthesia.
Include a statement that makes no sense at all.
Include a line in which all the words are in alphabetical order: e.g., Artists breathe color.
Use a phrase from a song or an old-fashioned (or parental) saying.
Include a metaphor using a plant, music, or tool.

Geoff's choice of artwork—a paper cutout of a human profile incorporated into the body of a fish (*Head in Fish* by Mary Frank)—showed a new appreciation of Dickinson and her transcendental desires.

"Why Must Everything Burn Free?"

This golden halibut—
heart beating energy
glowing life
burning, radiating, rising
like the Phoenix from the inside—

you are free.
I was once like you
my fires extinguished.
Now, I sit and watch
your leaps of faith.

One day I would
like to be like you
again. To jump from
here, from the world,
to some place new.

I would like the strength
and courage
to free myself from
the evening's sea.

—*Geoff Denstaedt*

Poem Hands by Leslie Dill

Midnight

There's a certain slant of light
that slides across my walls
when someone pulls
into the driveway.
There's a certain music
that is night, as it whispers
past my window and
collects on my pillow.
Night time music, like
what the planets murmur
to shooting stars.

The streetlight warm,
direct shadows across
the pavement. A certain imitation
of sunlight.

The doorknobs begin being
philosophical, so I begin to sleep.
The bed pockets me,

the blankets soothe me.
Night pulls on my eyelids
and moves branches with soft amber hands
tattooed with poetry.

There's this certain sleep of mine,
knees tucked under my chin, drooling
the anticipation of a soft cotton morning
onto my mattress as I dream
about multiplying life
by the power of two.

—Paul Kostrzewa

Paul explained that "Multiplying life by the power of two" was from a song by the Indigo Girls. "Cotton morning" was his example of synaesthesia, and "soft amber hands tattooed with poetry" came from Leslie Dill's painting *Poem Hands*. "A certain imitation of sunlight" and the echoing "certain sleep of mine" adapted Dickinson's "a certain slant of light." The doorknob line was Paul's nonsense statement, and the "night time music" is his metaphor.

Megan's picture showed Emily with a wine glass. Her poem addressed Dickinson, using the mysterious mirror figure to blur her own identity with that of the poet.

Emily, this night the wine
in your glass is untouched, held
away from you like a sickness.
I wonder if your legs have ever hurt
as mine did this morning
when I came down the stairs
walking toward you without knowing.
And now you stand in front of the mirror
but you don't look in. You will not see
the wistful stare in your eyes,
or the way your mouth smiles but stays
taut as the string of a violin.

Emily, does the light sometimes
scream at you?
In the mornings, coming out
to touch your flowers,
the sun will wilt you in your
heavy dress. Outside, there
is nothing to be done about this.

I know, for I have tried.
But in your room, where nothing
passes through, you are safe
from sun and even air
and the people downstairs
who have given you this wine
you cannot drink.

I tell you to let your hair down
from its coil at your neck,
let the glass fall from your hand.
The red wine will seep
into the floor, will intoxicate
the woodwork. Tomorrow,
when you wake,
the stain will be dry
and easily forgotten.

—*Megan van Leeuwen*

I wish to express my thanks to Roberta Herter, sponsoring teacher at Henry Ford High School, who brought me into her classroom as poet-in-residence under a Michigan Council for Arts and Cultural Affairs grant. I also wish to acknowledge the National Endowment for the Humanities, which provided me with a Teacher-Scholar Award in 1992–3, allowing me to spend a sabbatical year studying Dickinson's life and work, and Professor Jane Eberwein of Oakland University, who served as a valued mentor and guide to my research on that project. Thanks also to Teachers & Writers Collaborative for making the NBC Classics in the Classroom grant available. Finally, my enduring gratitude to Louise Harrison, creative writing coordinator for the Michigan Youth Arts Festival, for her friendship, support, and love of kids and poetry.

Bibliography

American Poetry: The Nineteenth Century. Volume Two: Melville to Stickney, American Indian Poetry, Folk Songs and Spirituals. New York: The Library of America, 1993.

Boxleitner, Linda. *Reading Emily's Mail.* Portland, Me.: J. Weston Walch, 1994.

Dickinson, Emily. *The Complete Poems of Emily Dickinson.* Edited by Thomas H. Johnson. Boston: Little, Brown, 1960.

Dickinson, Emily. *The Letters of Emily Dickinson.* Edited by Thomas H. Johnson and Theodora Ward. 3 vols. Cambridge, Mass.: Harvard University Press, 1981.

Eberwein, Jane, ed. *An Emily Dickinson Encyclopedia.* Westport, Conn.: Greenwood Press, 1998.

Rich, Adrienne. "'I am in Danger—Sir—'." In *Necessities of Life.* New York: Norton, 1966.

Simmerman, Jim. "Twenty Little Poetry Projects." In *The Practice of Poetry.* Edited by Robin Behn and Chase Twichell. New York: Harper Collins, 1992.

Turco, Lewis. "Winter Bouquet." In *Ecstatic Occasions, Expedient Forms.* Edited by David Lehman. Ann Arbor: University of Michigan Press, 1987.

Appendix: The Michigan Youth Arts Festival Workshop Handout

Poems by Emily Dickinson

1128

These are the Nights that Beetles love—
From Eminence remote
Drives ponderous perpendicular
His figure intimate
The terror of the Children
The merriment of men
Depositing his Thunder
He hoists abroad again—
A Bomb upon the Ceiling
Is an improving thing—
It keeps the nerves progressive
Conjecture flourishing—
Too dear the Summer evening
Without discreet alarm—
Supplied by Entomology
With its remaining charm

1173

The Lightning is a yellow Fork
From Tables in the sky
By inadvertent fingers dropt
The awful Cutlery

Of mansions never quite disclosed
And never quite concealed
The Apparatus of the Dark
To ignorance revealed.

211

Come slowly—Eden!
Lips unused to Thee—
Bashful—sip they Jessamines—
As the fainting Bee—
Reaching late his flower,
Round her chamber hums—
Counts his nectars—
Enters—and is lost in Balms.

249

Wild Nights—Wild Nights!
Were I with thee
Wild Nights should be
Our luxury!

Futile—the Winds—
To a Heart in port—
Done with the Compass—
Done with the Chart!

Rowing in Eden—
Ah, the Sea!
Might I but moor—Tonight—
In Thee!

341

After great pain, a formal feeling comes—
The Nerves sit ceremonious, like Tombs—
The stiff Heart questions was it He, that bore,
And Yesterday, or Centuries before?

The Feet, mechanical, go round—
Of Ground, or Air, or Ought—
A Wooden way
Regardless grown,
A Quartz contentment, like a stone—

This is the Hour of Lead—
Remembered, if outlived,
As Freezing persons, recollect the snow—
First—Chill—then Stupor—then the letting go—

1078

The Bustle in a House
The Morning after Death
Is solemnest of industries
Enacted upon Earth—

The Sweeping up the Heart
And putting Love away
We shall not want to use again
Until Eternity.

435

Much Madness is divinest Sense—
To a discerning Eye—
Much Sense—the starkest Madness—
'Tis the Majority
In this, as All, prevail—
Assent—and you are sane—
Demur—you're straightway dangerous—
And handled with a Chain—

861

Split the Lark—and you'll find the Music—
Bulb after Bulb, in Silver rolled—
Scantily dealt to the Summer Morning
Saved for your Ear when Lutes be old.

Loose the Flood—you shall find it patent—
Gush after Gush, reserved for you—
Scarlet Experiment! Sceptic Thomas!
Now, do you doubt that your Bird was true?

Mark Twain

Henry James

Gary Lenhart

Mark Twain, Henry James, and Travel Writing

THE FRONTIER MYTH has so pervaded American thought that it has largely obscured the context in which nineteenth-century American literature was written. But as we look more closely at the canonical texts of that time, we are reminded that James Fenimore Cooper wrote many of his books in Naples and Paris, that Washington Irving wrote "The Legend of Sleepy Hollow" in England during a seventeen-year European sojourn, and that Henry Wadsworth Longfellow began translating Dante during the second of four extended trips to Italy. In essays such as "The American Scholar" and "The Poet," Ralph Waldo Emerson presented an ardent brief on behalf of staying home and creating a New World literature, but even he cherished the trip to England during which he met Coleridge and began his long friendship with Thomas Carlyle. Mallarmé's translations of Poe, Wilde's enthusiasm for Whitman, Nietzsche's reading of Emerson, and Tolstoy's debts to Thoreau are evidence that American voices were certainly heard in Europe. With the exceptions of Walt Whitman* and Emily Dickinson, almost every major nineteenth-century American writer traveled to the European continent. Many wrote about their experiences, providing a fresh eye on the Old World for readers who had never been there.

Travel writing continues to be popular, occupying extensive shelf space in bookstores and popping up frequently atop best seller lists. Foreign settings disrupt our habits of perception. You are made aware of things that in familiar settings fade into the background, and life has a new soundtrack. As we try to find our bearings in foreign locales, the results are fresh and surprising. Being temporarily displaced makes it easier to pierce the veils of our assumptions and see anew our own environments.

---

* Whitman loved to travel, but his major trips were to New Orleans, Canada, and the frontier states that have since become the American Midwest. He was also greatly influenced by the German philosophy and Italian opera fashionable in mid-nineteenth-century Manhattan.

To prepare college students for a writing assignment that is a variation of one favored by novelist William Burroughs—who instructed students to take long walks, look closely at everything, and then describe what they encountered—I first try to dislocate them with accounts of travel in distant lands. There are many to choose from; among my favorites are travel narratives by Herman Melville, Margaret Fuller, Willa Cather, and James Baldwin. Whenever possible, I enjoy reading with students descriptions of the same exotic places by two or more writers with different sensibilities. Few complement each other with greater gusto than these two descriptions of Florence, by Henry James and Mark Twain.

The following were published eight years apart (1869 and 1877)—two tourists in the same city, taking walks along the same river at about the same hour of the evening. For one, it was his first and only visit to Florence; the other returned at regular intervals throughout the remainder of his life.

I had never known Florence more herself, or in other words more attaching, than I found her for a week in that brilliant October. She sat in the sunshine beside her yellow river like the little treasure-city she has always seemed, without commerce, without other industry than the manufacture of mosaic paperweights and alabaster Cupids, without actuality or energy or earnestness or any of those rugged virtues which in most cases are deemed indispensable for civic cohesion; with nothing but the little unaugmented stock of her medieval memories, her tender-coloured mountains, her churches and palaces, pictures and statues. There were very few strangers; one's detested fellow-pilgrim was infrequent; the native population itself seemed scanty; the sound of wheels in the streets was but occasional; by eight o'clock at night, apparently, every one had gone to bed, and the musing wanderer, still wandering and still musing, had the place to himself—had the thick shadow-masses of the great palaces, and the shafts of moonlight striking the polygonal paving-stones, and the empty bridges, and the silvered yellow of the Arno, and the stillness broken only by a homeward step, a step accompanied by a snatch of song from a warm Italian voice. My room at the inn looked out on the river and was flooded all day with sunshine. There was an absurd orange-coloured paper on the walls; the Arno, of a hue not altogether different, flowed beneath; and on the other side of it rose a line of sallow houses, of extreme antiquity, crumbling and mouldering, bulging and protruding over the stream. . . . All this brightness and yellowness was a perpetual delight; it was part of that indefinable charming colour which Florence always seems to wear as you look up and down at it from the river, and from the bridges and quays. . . .

It is true indeed that I might after a certain time grow weary of a regular afternoon stroll among the Florentine lanes; of sitting on low parapets, in intervals of flower-topped wall, and looking across at Fiesole or down the rich-hued valley of the Arno; of pausing at the open gates of villas and wondering at the height of cypresses and the depth of loggias; of walking home in the fading light and noting on a dozen westward-looking surfaces the glow of the opposite sunset. But for a week or so this was all delightful. (*Collected Travel Writings: The Continent*, pp. 400–403)

Florence pleased us for a while. I think we appreciated the great figure of David in the grand square, and the sculptured group they call the Rape of the Sabines. We wandered through the endless collections of paintings and statues of the Pitti and Ufizzi galleries, of course. I make this statement in self-defense; there let it stop. I could not rest under the imputation that I visited Florence and did not traverse its weary miles of picture galleries. We tried indolently to recollect something about the Guelphs and Ghibellines and the other historical cutthroats whose quarrels and assassinations make up so large a share of Florentine history, but the subject was not attractive. . . .

We went to the church of Santa Croce, from time to time, in Florence, to weep over the tombs of Michelangelo, Raphael, and Machiavelli . . . and between times we used to go and stand on the bridges and admire the Arno. It is popular to admire the Arno. It is a great historical creek with four feet in the channel and some scows floating around. It would be a very plausible river if they would pump some water into it. They all call it a river, and they honestly think it is a river, do these dark and bloody Florentines. They even help out the delusion by building bridges over it. I do not see why they are too good to wade. . . .

I got lost in Florence at nine o'clock one night, and stayed lost in that labyrinth of narrow streets and long rows of vast buildings that all look alike until toward three o'clock in the morning. It was a pleasant night and at first there were a good many people abroad, and there were cheerful lights about. Later I grew accustomed to prowling about mysterious drifts and tunnels and astonishing myself with coming around corners expecting to find the hotel staring me in the face, and not finding it doing anything of the kind. Later still, I felt tired. I soon felt remarkably tired. But there was no one abroad now—not even a policeman. I walked till I was out of all patience and very hot and thirsty. At last, somewhere after one o'clock, I came unexpectedly to one of the city gates. I knew then that I was very far from the hotel. The soldiers thought I wanted to leave the city, and they sprang up and barred the way with their muskets. I said:

"Hotel d'Europe!"

It was all the Italian I knew, and I was not certain whether that was Italian or French. The soldiers looked stupidly at each other and at me, and shook their heads and took me into custody. (*The Innocents Abroad* and *Roughing It*, pp. 192–5)

What have we learned about the city, the river, and the tourists, I ask my students. How is it that the writers respond so differently to the same vistas and paths? What is the tone of each passage? What assumptions underlie the authors' responses to Florence's manners, buildings, art, industry, public security, even quiet evenings? What do the two descriptions tell of their authors?

The first passage, of course, is by James; the second by Twain. The descriptions contrast productively the refined aesthete and the debunking democrat. While Twain didn't rest in Florence long, as his party was soon on its way South and to the Holy Land, James returned to Florence many times—although he preferred to write about Rome, the cosmopolitan character and scale of which were more to his taste. There are other passages in Twain's *The Innocents Abroad* and James's *Travel Writings* that might be compared fruitfully, particularly those about St. Peter's, the Colosseum, the Campagna, and St. John Lateran in Rome. Whatever the site, Twain entertains with cranky Yankee blasts at the barbarities of European social hierarchy, religion, and technological underdevelopment—all themes that would inspire *A Connecticut Yankee in King Arthur's Court* and *Joan of Arc*. James, on the other hand, is ever deferential to the established culture of the Old World, finding the "source of an incalculable part of our present conception of Beauty" (p. 481) in practices and institutions he can't fully approve of. This admiration and appreciation for the Old World can be seen in his *Portrait of a Lady* and *The Golden Bowl*, as well as many of his other novels.

For the past ten years I have split my teaching about evenly between an Ivy League college, where almost every student spends at least one term abroad, and a community college, where far fewer students have been overseas, and those often as part of their military service. For the purpose of this assignment, having been to Italy may make some difference to students, but probably less than the "snobby," deferential tone of James's prose, Twain's condescending rudeness toward his hosts, or the "'racial' prejudice" (p. 134) of both. (If those present a problem, gently urge students to articulate why.)

I ask students at both colleges to write travelogues from their memories of some journey to a foreign place, or to visit someplace local where they have never been. The latter journey may be down the block, to a local diner or ethnic restaurant, an expensive clothing store or the town dump, to a courtroom, or health club. Some students imitate the Twain and James passages by simply taking a walk, trying to encounter every-thing they see with the fresh eyes of a tourist. To emphasize the impor-tance of estrangement to this assignment, I remind them that Twain wrote his passage on the basis of one week in Florence, and though James spent much more time in Italy, it was always as a tourist, a "mere man of pleasure" (p. 101). Working from memory may obscure details and clut-ter vistas with nostalgic significance, so frequently the second option pro-duces stronger writing. If students choose to write about the local diner, however, ask them to imagine themselves a visitor from another country. With both approaches, the successful pieces explore not only what it means to see something afresh, but also what biases govern how we expe-rience the "foreign." I am frequently surprised by the shock to even rel-atively sophisticated students that people in other cultures choose to do things in foreign ways.

By offering students the contrasting views of Florence (and, implic-itly, Italy and, to some extent, Europe) provided by Twain and James, I encourage them to see that there is no "correct" way to respond to new or foreign places—whether they are writing as Americans abroad or as "for-eigners" in the United States. Perhaps the woman who spent an entire term in Italy yearning to return home and vowing never to live abroad again would have written just as honestly without Twain's example. Per-haps the young man who returned from Barcelona vowing that after grad-uation he would return to live and work in Europe would have hymned Europe's refinements without the inspiration of James. Most students fall between these extremes, sometimes exalting like Twain the qualities of home, sometimes echoing James's awe in the face of imposing beauty. Ideally, all recognize that personality affects perception, that impressions and expression can't be divided—that what we see and how we describe it says as much about who we are as where we have been.

Bibliography

James, Henry. *Collected Travel Writings: The Continent*. New York: The Library of America, 1993.

Twain, Mark. *The Innocents Abroad. Roughing It*. New York: The Library of America, 1984.

Mark Twain

Yvonne Murphy

"Stretchers," Hairballs, and Whoopin' in the Fog

Teaching Elements of Fiction with Mark Twain's *Adventures of Huckleberry Finn*

ALTHOUGH I AM A POET, sometimes I teach fiction writing, helping students to complete a long story. We usually spend a class period or two (depending on the level of detail and interest of the students) on each element of a story: setting, plot, action, characterization, dialogue, etc. Then we work for a few more days to tie the pieces together into a cohesive whole and to revise.

It can become a rather arduous process. The students, at times, complain that it appears as if they've undertaken an endless project. Ultimately, though, the students feel proud of their stories and gain a real sense of the dedication and hard work that goes into a finished piece. A longer individual project like this also gives them a strong sense of accomplishment, and the faith that they can rely on themselves to see their work through to the end. It is an excellent way, too, for me, a poet, to grow as a teacher and extend my own creative abilities.

Of course, if the students' concentration slips or if a majority of them complain about the length of the project, we take a break and try to do something fresh with our material. For example, in the middle of a long fiction writing project, I might have the students spend a day writing haiku based on their settings. Maybe we'll draw pictures of an important scene, to try to get a new perspective on it. Or we'll write letters from one character to another to uncover motivations and personalities. We might not even write for a day or two, spending class time in teams of two or three, serving as mutual "consultants." As consultants, we take turns reading each other's work and suggesting helpful ideas. Some days, though, we might take a complete break from our project and write another poem or a song. I have a smorgasbord approach to teaching writing: I don't like to go into a classroom and teach only one idea or skill. I much prefer the organic approach of giving access to many potential skills and then sitting back to see what grows. Sometimes I see immediate results; other times an idea will reappear as a brilliant mutation in subsequent works.

This year, in a residency sponsored by Teachers & Writers Collaborative and NBC, I used Mark Twain's *Adventures of Huckleberry Finn* as a model to teach fiction writing to high school juniors and seniors. I've loved *Huckleberry Finn* since my own high school days and have used it before for smaller lessons at a number of grade levels. When I was a teenager, *Huckleberry Finn* enchanted me with its tale of a young outsider, Huck, making his own way downriver in a seemingly vast, dangerous world. Huck's adventure, to me, was made even sweeter by the constant, albeit conflicted, companionship of his one devoted friend, Jim. I spent many of my own teen days feeling alone and looking for adventure in the form of escape and friendship. Of course, I thought I was all alone in my strangeness. I wasn't all that unusual. From my recent experience teaching eleventh and twelfth graders at Furr High School in Houston, Texas, I am able to understand how normal and vital these feelings actually are.

The NBC residency was an excellent opportunity for me to try something I had long thought of: to use one book, *Huckleberry Finn*, continuously for my longer fiction lessons. In the past, I had always used sections from different books. I was interested to see how an intensive reading of one book would add to the overall experience. It also happened that the classroom teacher I worked with also wanted to teach *Huckleberry Finn*. It was a lucky coincidence that showed the students two different approaches to the same text, each perspective adding to a deeper comprehension of the other and a deeper retention of both.

What follows are a few lessons from my ten-week residency with the students. The Dialect, Superstition, and Parents lessons I describe below could be used as one-time assignments. A perfectly fine story could be written by combining just two of the elements mentioned below. Other writers would certainly highlight elements of fiction I haven't mentioned. There are myriad ways to combine the parts of this project. The trick here is remaining in tune with the class rhythm and knowing when to adjust your plans.

1. Dialects

The first pages of the book are best for this exercise, although dialect from any part of the narrative would suit the purpose here. One edition of *The Adventures of Huckleberry Finn* I found (the Signet Classic) includes Twain's explanation of his use of dialects. To start the lesson, I read this out loud to my students and ask them if they know what a dialect is. We then stumble through a definition of *dialect* and its difference from the word *vernacular*. To complicate matters, I throw the words *slang* and *jargon* into the mix and we try to give examples of jargon vs. examples of dialect. This part of the lesson is really fun, because I am originally from—as Texans say—"Up North." For this lesson, I try to exaggerate the sounds and particularities of a more general Northern dialect. Then, I offer some dialect from my hometown, Rochester, N.Y. The students give examples of their own dialects, everything from street talk to private family language. We laugh as one student does what he perceives to be a Californian "surfer dude" dialect. Many of my students are familiar with Cajun and Creole dialects, having relatives from nearby Louisiana.

Next, I read from the opening chapter of *Huckleberry Finn*. The class discusses Huck's speech and notes some of the particularities that seem to construct a dialect—phrases, pronunciations, spellings, individual words. For example, in the first paragraph, Huck uses the word *stretchers* to suggest that the book previous to his, *The Adventures of Tom Sawyer*, isn't completely true. The class mulls that word over, comparing it to other words they use or have heard used to mean a white lie. We spend a few more minutes thinking about what makes dialects, and then the conversation turns to the assumptions we make about certain dialects—intelligence, class, race, culture, gender. This turn is emblematic, in my experience, of high school students' thinking: they have an immanent desire to understand the greater social world outside.

The following are some of the dialect pieces written after our class discussion:

My Great-Grandmother

Ma Sha I tell ya, Louisiana is haunted. I tell ya dem plantashuns full wit dem ghosts. Souls of spooks runnin round. I tell ya dey made me play wit dat gul at ha home, and Sha it was a face, of a pritty woman, starin at us. I say look at dat womun, den ha face disapeered. Scared me haf to death. But no Sha, yall got to go see dat big house on da byu. Da snakes, Ohh Sha da snakes came in big groups. One chased me an aunty Lily clean cross da feeld. Lily ran all-da-way ta Tut and Cyset house and dey laffed and laffed at dat fool, oh ye, I was talkin bout dat house, the chilren couldn't sleep in dat house. No, da spirit was takin da cover off da children but da mayd sat, *sho as I'm here you gone let dem alone*. Well, Sha, I'm finsta take my nap ni, good nite Sha.

—*Tiffani Burton*

JUAN: Wuz up, dawg!

JOSE: Chale homes.

JUAN: Say, dawg, let's go cruisin' around in my G-ride.

JOSE: You talkin' about that hooptie?

JUAN: That ain't no hooptie foo. All it need is a paint job, some rims, and a system.

JOSE: How much you got it for?

JUAN: For five bills from that player down the street.

JOSE: Chale!

JUAN For real foo.

—*Juan Alvarado*

Well a sometimes I be on da cut chilling wit my homies and dis fine honey walk up. I be like *yo what's ya name?* So, I'm making her down and thangs and she seems down for whatever. Later on I call the brawd up to see what she bout cause if it's like dat it's all good. We chill and get freaky and thangs so my stomach starts to talk: *it's time to get some vittles up in here.* You heard me! So later on I told da chie I'll holla at her later and I was out the dow....

—*Paul Tatum*

2. Superstitions

This part of our project was charming and delightful. I came into the classroom one morning and started by discussing the word *superstition*. Then I asked the students to spend seven minutes writing down a list of all of the superstitions that either they or their family held. Volunteers then read their lists out loud. Many of us laughed with recognition when we heard "Don't step on a crack, you'll break your momma's back!" and "Say 'bread and butter' when something like a pole comes between you and a friend when you're out walking." We giggled as some very peculiar and idiosyncratic superstitions were read. "I never heard of that!" someone would inevitably shout with glee. "That's *bent!*" Translation: weird.

Next, I read from Chapter Four of *Huckleberry Finn*, in which Huck talks about Miss Watson's superstitions and tells the reader about Jim's auspicious "hairball." The class loved hearing this after our previous discussion. I asked them to spend fifteen to twenty minutes making up their own unheard-of superstitions. I mentioned that these ideas, besides being pleasurable, might come in handy later, when we would be coming up with character sketches or trying to create a plot twist in our stories. When the students finished writing, I asked again for volunteers to read.

Without hesitation, everyone read from their lists. Peals of laughter and amazement ensued.

Here were a few of our invented superstitions:

If you break the frame of your watch, you can expect to age faster.
—*Henry Cantu*

If you say five "n" words in one sentence, your nose will bleed.
—*Derrick Allen*

If you give to the poor, you'll have a good life.
—*Christina Hermosillo*

If a dog looks at you for a long time and doesn't bark, you're going to get a dog bite.
—*Karla Vazquez*

If you wear red on Wednesday, a new love is coming.
—*Erik Alvarado*

Don't sneeze in a church or you will have to change your religion.
—*Firas Hussein*

If you break a glass figurine, you'll have ten days of worrying about your hair being cut off.
—*Jeanette Cantu*

If you use a butter knife to eat a steak, you'll throw up everything you ate that day.
—*Juan Alvarado*

3. Parents

Undoubtedly, one of the more disturbing and real aspects of this novel is Huck's estranged and abusive relationship with his rough, vagrant father. Chapter Five details a rather sudden and violent return of Huck's father, when he berates Huck for going to school and beats him for learning to read. Huck's father accuses him of becoming "swelled-up" with himself and threatens that he'll "learn people to bring up a boy to put on airs over his own father and let on to be better'n he is." Then he forces him to sit down and read for him. When he is satisfied that Huck can read, he knocks the book out of his hands and says: "Now looky here; you stop that putting on frills. I won't have it. I'll lay for you, my smarty; and if I catch you about that school I'll tan you good." Later on, Huck's dad gets drunk and hallucinates that snakes are attacking him. He then has a fit, going as far as to threaten killing Huck. The chapter ends with Huck's sitting vigil with a loaded gun pointed at his sleeping father.

This scene has a lot of impact on any young person with a troubled relationship. In any high school, in any town or city, there are teens who understand this scene on an intimate level. After I read this chapter, I don't spend the usual time discussing and analyzing it. The issues seem too raw and all too real. Instead, I read the chapter and clarify any technical questions the students have. Then I tell them they can write about a real or fictional disagreement between a child and a parent, or about any other troubled or complicated relationship. I do point out the use of dialogue in this scene and stress that they might try incorporating dialogue in their own writing.

Here are two responses:

My T-Jones

My mother: You need to make up your mind on who you want to be with. You're not going to be going out with all those different boys. You are only supposed to have one boyfriend. *Me to my mother*: Momma, I'm not ready to settle down. I haven't found the right person yet. I'm not trying to be like Niecie. *My mother says*: Well, I can't keep up with all these boys, what happened to the boy you brought to the house from Cleveland, TX? What's his name again? *Me*: Who, Marcus? He act like he too busy to call me so I moved on and found someone else. *Momma*: And where is your jacket? You're not leaving this house without a jacket. *Me*: Momma I know, it's right here. You know I never leave the house without it. *Momma*: And some boy called you last night, I forgot his name, there's so many of them. *Me*: Ha ha ha! *Momma*: You know what time to be in the house and if the boy have a pager, give me the pager number and let me know what kind of car he drive. *Me*: O.K., Momma, I'm gone. Bye bye.

—*Charndre Jones*

Midnight

"Jasmine, can't you hear me?" her mother yells while Jasmine stares into the kitchen table, almost seeing through it, she finally realizes someone is speaking to her. "Girl are you deaf or something or are you just plain stupid? You're daydreaming again, it won't get you anywhere girl, I already told you many times. Jasmine, I need you to go to the store for me." "But mom!" "Don't but mom me little girl, just do as you have been told to do so! I swear you're not good for anything Jasmine, all you want to do is complain, Mom this and Mom that, look at you now, you're just sitting there looking awkward. Tell me Jasmine what are you thinking about when you stare off into space?" Her mother won't understand how free Jasmine feels to daydream, she's safe in her own world, trouble-free, no disappointments to face. "Get the hell out of my house." "What?" "You heard me, get the hell out and don't come back until you learn how to take an order." "An order, listen to your drunk ass talk about order. You complain that I don't do anything, well hell at least when I do something I'm sober and not falling all over myself with every step I take. But if this is the way you want it well then so be it. I don't know why I ever left my dad's house." "I'll tell you why, because he didn't want your ass there, this is why little girl." "SHUT UP! I can't stand being here anymore! I have to get out of this hellhole." "Be my guest, this is one less mouth I have to feed." "Oh, you never even feed the ones that you have now. Anyway you want me gone fine, let me just get my things so I can go." "Things, what things? Oh no honey, you didn't buy one piece of clothing, everything that was bought, was bought with my money. Understand, my money. You have worked not one day in your miserable life." "Well then you can take those clothes and shove them up your ass!" As Jasmine walks out the door sobbing like a two-year-old, she turns and looks at her mother for one last time.

—*Jeannette Rubalcava*

4. Setting

In order to help students get started on their long stories, I decided this time to start with settings. I began by asking the class to give their own reasons why a setting is crucial to a story. "Because you've got to know where the story takes place," one person remarked. "It gives the flavor of the story." Another added, "The setting could be a crucial part of the action later on." I stressed that one of the best ways to create a setting is to include strikingly specific details. We spent a minute deciding what would make a detail "strikingly specific." I asked them if a blue sky is that striking. They said no, too ordinary. I asked if it is specific? They replied that it could be specific, depending on the weather; however, we agreed that there are ways to make even "blue" more specific. Clear blue, like the color of contact lenses? An ominous, darker blue, like the sky just about to fill up with storming?

I then read from chapter 9 of *Huckleberry Finn*, where Huck describes his cave dwelling and, subsequently, the outbreak of a heavy thunderstorm. The students were particularly impressed with the ways in which Twain's description mingles the five senses. They also commented on

Twain's ability to describe the storm with a certain poetic beauty while maintaining the dialect and integrity of his main character. We discussed the importance of seeing the setting through our characters' eyes. In the following passage, Twain describes the storm through Huck:

> Directly it began to rain, and it rained like all fury, too, and I never see the wind blow so. It was one of these regular summer storms. It would get so dark that it looked all blue-black outside, and lovely; and the rain would thrash along by so thick that the trees off a little ways looked dim and spider-webby; and here would come a blast of wind that would bend the trees down and turn up the pale underside of the leaves; and then a perfect ripper of a gust would follow along and set the branches to tossing their arms as if they was just wild; and next, when it was just about the bluest and the blackest— *fst!* it was as bright as glory, and you'd have a little glimpse of tree-tops a-plunging about away off yonder in the storm, hundreds of yards further than you could see before; dark as sin again in a second, and now you'd hear the thunder let go with an awful crash, and then go rumbling, grumbling, tumbling down the sky towards the under side of the world, like rolling empty barrels downstairs—where it's long stairs and they bounce a good deal, you know. (pp. 671–2)

After reading the passage, I asked the students to comment on elements that stood out to them. They shouted out a variety of responses, but we dwelled on the trees being *spiderwebby* and the thunder sounding like "empty barrels." I asked them to consider why these examples worked so well. We discussed how word choices and the senses can affect the physical and emotional impact of an image. We toyed around with different ways to describe a tree: "skeletal," "laughing," "thick-rooted," "smooth." In turn, I encouraged them to concentrate on word choice and description in their own stories.

Below are three brief examples of settings by members of the class:

Corona

Corona is a ranch about nine hours from Houston. I know the place because my cousin lives there, it is a gorgeous place. My cousin stays at a two-story house which is not very far from the river. A block and a half and the river is in your sight. When its current is running, the water is crystal clear. Anything dropped in there could be found. Across the river is the woods which we hunt in. At night it's all real dark, the only light seen is the one from a taco stand which is across from the highway. The way of living there is by growing crops or having animals. My cousin does both. At dawn, my cousin, his father, and I go work at the place where he has oranges and avocados, which is called a *huerta*. The way of irrigation is getting water from the river. The only thing I wouldn't like to happen in Corona is a freeze because all the crops would go to waste. This is what happened with El Niño the last time it struck. My cousins lost their crops and money. Now he is selling cattle in other nearby ranches. There is a *tinaco* that holds water for the little town and mad owls nest in it. Owls don't like to be mocked or aggravated. They will attack you if you whistle like them, or that is what is told. When I go to the plaza to play soccer with all my friends the days go by fast. Then I ask to be walked home 'cause darkness comes and there is no light at all. On the way to my cousin's house I treat to cokes and chips. After I get home I have to shout out so some of my cousins will open the gate and hold the dogs back while I run inside the house.

—*Joe Serna*

Haunted House

Glance at this place and you would think it was abandoned. The path made by its constant visitors is hidden by the yard's abundance of greenery like a rain forest. The house's entrances and exits are boarded up and sealed, or at least it appears that way. Little dogs and other animals dare not to step into the yard because they know its secrets or maybe because they've been hurt by one of the abandoned syringes. Little kids think of the house as haunted. But these kids must know about the house's secrets because inside the house live the dead. Zombies roam around with eyes that are bloody red all wanting one thing and doing anything for it. The bugs crawl all over the house, with more brains than the inhabitants inside. The air has an old stench of burning because they have no heat. Your vision inside the house is a blur because the action inside the house is immense. You can hear the screaming and shouting of the zombies trying to get what they crave for. Then, out of nowhere a flood of blinding blue, white, and red lights uncover the hidden secrets of the house and in a flash the blue troops raid the zombies and have exorcised the house from its secrets.

—*Derrick Allen*

The Maze

This place is altogether different. Each corner isn't the same. When you first enter into the maze it seems easy but looks can be deceiving. You have four ways you can go but three out of the four are wrong. These three have something waiting to kill you. You can't climb out, you have to go in with the right choices to make. The walls are gray and are steadily moving. If you try to climb them you slip and fall into quicksand. The things that you meet on the wrong way all lead to death. One is disease, two is drugs, and three, crime. The only right way leads to prosperity and hope. If you can't take the maze of life and try to climb out, you fall into an early grave. It starts out simple but it gets harder and harder as you go and grow in knowledge. You have to make the right choices instead of the wrong ones. The sound comes when someone trips up and is overcome with wrongdoing. This sound is a screaming for help but no one answers the call. You only smell fresh scents of perfume and summer.

—*Paul Tatum*

5. Characterization

Next we turn to characterization. Once we have written a setting for the story, it seems natural to put a person or creature in that place. For characterization, we look closely at what we know about Huck and Jim. I list their names on the board and ask the class to provide information that we know about each character. Since we are already deep into the novel, I don't feel it necessary to read a selection here (if I were to start this project with characterization, I would choose to read any number of descriptions of Huck or Jim from the beginning of the book, when they first are introduced). When we finish our lists, I ask the students to tell me what kind of information is on the board under each character's name. "Their appearance," someone suggests. "Where they're from," I hear another voice say, soon followed by: "name," "age," "race," "physical condition," "hair color," "education," "language," "superstitions," "family situation," "wealth," "marital status," "job" and so on. From this response, I start a new list on the board under the heading of *Characteristics*. We discuss how the word *character* is implicit in that word.

Next, I ask the class if there are any qualities or characteristics of people that we have left off our list. This takes a moment's thought because many of the students are caught up in defining their characters by physical details. "How about their goals in life?" I ask. "What about their fears? Regrets? Loves? Their thoughts? Their capacity to care?" A whole new line of thinking begins: students start suggesting less superficial qualities, such as the way their characters see the world, their characters' inner struggles, ways in which a character is proud of himself or herself. I then suggest that the students use these lists to write a sketch or brief description of their main characters. I take a moment to ask them what a sketch is and how it relates to a larger drawing or painting, and then apply their responses as metaphors for how their character sketches will fit into the creation of their longer stories. I advise them that they might try writing their sketches in the character's voice, from the character's point of view, in order to get a closer sense of them.

Here are some examples of our main characters:

Saint

Saint, yeah, that's what people that know me call me. My real name is Santiago and I'm going to let you in on a little about my life. You know, people may see me and they'll probably think I'm a tough, mean person. And, you want to know something? I am. You're probably wondering: *if this is a tough man as he says he is, then why would he want to talk to me for?* Many times when you're alone and don't have someone to talk to, it's hard. I started living on the streets from the time I was ten years old. You're probably thinking that I'm homeless, but I'm not. For your information, I have my own house. It may not be a fancy house but I would say that I'm a lucky person to have a roof over my head. Many times when I go out in the streets, and by the way I live in L.A., Los Angeles on the South Side in a real bad neighborhood.... As I was saying, many times when I go out on the streets it's pitiful to see many of my race, Mexicans, and others living in the street, homeless. Everybody can make a change if they want to, but they choose not to. You know it's all in the mind and attitude of the person. I would have never thought that I would have been around so much pain and suffering.

—*Vicente Magana*

Alzheimer's (My Great Aunt)

I tried to express myself, but couldn't find the
Words. I'd have beautiful feelings and
Moments one minute and the next I didn't
Even remember that I had felt happy or excited.
I felt very confused, almost all the time.
I didn't know how or what to feel.
You cared for me so many years and as you
Were growing up, you saw how my
Mind and memory deteriorated. I wanted to
Give you so much advice and tell you stories
About my life and share my life experiences
With you, and yet, I couldn't even carry on a
Conversation. It's amazing how this disease
Just creeps in slowly, like a thief in the night
And eventually consumes and affects your
Entire life. You can't remember your family
And don't recognize your surroundings.

Then, all of a sudden I'd get brief moments
Of memory and recognition and everything was
Peaceful, but before I knew it I'd have a memory
BLACKOUT and the conclusion would set in
All over again. It was terrible.
I felt like a prisoner in my own body.

   —*Nelly Cavazos*

Far from Home

My eyes are at sea level, my body not that much bigger than a fifty-cent coin. My brownish outside helps me blend in with the white sand, but clashes with the muddy dirt. Out here I am open prey, there I had not a care in the world. On the muddy sand seagulls constantly swoop down, and try to grab me for a quick snack. But that is the life of a sand crab far away from home. The beautiful waters of my home brought a hollowed-out log to me. I went exploring on the log and accidentally fell in. My tiny little legs would climb the steep walls, but I would fall due to the massive water decay on the log.

    On this voyage I have met fellow sand crabs native to the area. They have taught me how to find food in this strange land. Although I am treated well, I need to find my home. The waters of these parts are too cold for my body to handle. The constant change of weather is too much to bear.

   —*Terence Williams*

6. Adding Drama

Next, I make sure that the students understand the differences between plot, drama, and theme. These distinctions are often difficult for the novice writer. The plot, I tell the class, is just a series of events, it's what happened. I give them an example of a plot: my morning so far—I got up, ate cereal, fed the cats, got dressed, left the apartment, got in my car, and drove to school. This is a plot. It moves the story from point A to point B. I tell this example in as bland a tone as possible, to underscore its humdrum quality. However, I add that the *theme* of a story is the meaning or meanings found within the events, while the drama is not what happens in a story, but *how* it happens.

    To illustrate this idea, I tell them I am about to read from the beginning of Chapter Fifteen of *Huckleberry Finn*. Jim is on the raft, a fog rolls in, and Huck, in a canoe near the raft, gets separated from Jim, but eventually is reunited with him. This plot sounds good, but not overly thrilling. We then discuss the different ways in which Huck might react to this sequence of events. We also take turns describing how the plot might be carried out, what details a writer might or might not choose to dwell on. I tell the students that we are now talking about the drama of the scene. After this, I read the passage and ask the class to close their eyes and imagine the scene as I'm reading it. The scene is full of intense drama. Twain describes the fog in such a manner that the reader is both scared and mystified alongside Huck. At one point, Huck, who has been whooping a call out into the night in hopes that he'll find Jim, insists, "I couldn't tell nothing about voices in a fog, for nothing don't look natural nor sound natural in a fog." I read this section in a dramatic and suspenseful manner. The scene lends itself perfectly to this kind of reading and it keeps students on the edge of their seats. Sometimes I stop reading before the end of the scene, causing students to beg me to finish. I don't do this to be cruel, but rather to illustrate to the young writers how suspense or drama will keep their readers moving from paragraph to paragraph, turning page after page.

After I finish reading, I ask the students to try to create a scene for their story that incorporates more drama. I suggest that they look back over what they've written so far and decide how they could intensify the action or suspense of the plot. Is there something dramatic that could happen with the setting, between the characters, in the dialogue? I remind them that their goal is to try to keep the reader wanting more, to keep them literally "on the edge of their seats."

Below are some excerpts from longer stories written in the class. I hope they keep you wanting more!

Watcher in the Woods

My favorite place is the woods. The woods at night are creepy and scary. Stepping into the woods at night was like stepping into a closet and closing the door behind me because the trees cover the moonlight. The trees felt like they were right behind me. Leaves and branches hit against me feeling like I'm catching a beating. When the branches were swinging from one side to the other you can hear a little whistling sound because of the wind blowing. Owls in trees look scary because you can only see their eyes, which look like headlights.

I could tell I wasn't alone because I could hear steps. It sounded like someone or something was stepping on popcorn. As I walked slowly it walked slowly, too, making it sound like we were stepping on firecrackers. When I turned around to see what it was, it was just a measly raccoon who at first I thought was a skunk. I decided to still continue through the woods. Although I was scared, it just felt like an adventure to me and I wanted to continue.

Pacing along the trail I felt myself trembling like it was cold, thinking anything I heard from now on would be a raccoon but I was soon wrong. When I ran into a big bear I didn't think the bear saw me at first but when I tried to run it heard me and stood up growling. I knew then that I had to stop from whatever I was doing and try not to make a sound. Each sound the bear made, I stepped away thinking that it wouldn't hear me. One time it did and it ran up on me, literally throwing me into a tree. After that, I didn't know what hit me but I knew if I was to play dead the bear would let me be. . . .

—*Cheryl Woodley*

Neighborhood Life

It's dark, gloomy. For some reason it's always raining. People are on the corner hanging out. Many of the houses are torn down, some are boarded up. Haze is everywhere, also. Not a sunny day seems to pass. Homeless men try to warm themselves up by using old barrels to start fires to keep warm. Gunshots are always heard at night, also with screams that follow. Police sirens are heard, too.

There is a young boy who wishes he could get out. He saw his older brother die in front of him. Ever since that he has been scared for life. Ten years had passed and the boy, Arron and his friends are chilling on the corner, smoking weed. Juan asks Javier what's going down this weekend. Arron answered that the party's at Brenda's house. All of a sudden, a blue car pulls out in front of them, a group of guys pull out, giving Arron and his homeboys a mean look. Just about when they are getting ready to fight, a couple of cop cars pull up and the young men in the blue car leave. Arron and his friends all go to the store. When they walk up to the store, Arron sees Brenda, "Hey, what up girl!" "Nothing much Arron, still coming to my party?" "Yeah, I'll be there." They stared at each other for a while then said goodbye. Javier: "Hey, man how come you didn't mac* to her?" "It ain't like that." Juan: "Why not?" "Even though I've known her since eighth grade, it's just been hard for me to talk to her in that way." Javier: "Man, you're just scared of what she'd tell you." Arron: "Besides, she got a man." Juan: "F**k that, that's never stopped you before." Javier: "Yeah, what is it, our player has just met love and it's with that girl?" Arron: "Man, let's drop this and get the 40 oz. and roll. . . ."

—*Erik Alvarado*

---

* Slang for "put the moves on."

Bibliography

Twain, Mark. *The Adventures of Tom Sawyer. Life on the Mississippi. Adventures of Huckleberry Finn. Pudd'nhead Wilson.* New York: The Library of America, 1982.

Gertrude Stein

Daniel Kane

Book Was There

Teaching Gertrude Stein's *Tender Buttons* to Young and Old

> *Elephant beaten with candy and little pops and chews all bolts and reckless reckless rats, this is this.*[1]
>
> *Book was there, it was there. Book was there.*[2]

TENDER BUTTONS may be Gertrude Stein's most notorious and challenging work. It's also hilarious, repetitive, whimsical, and fascinating. Recently, I taught *Tender Buttons* to two very different groups of students in Brooklyn—to college students at Kingsborough Community College, and to a group of third graders in Williamsburg. I encountered two distinctly different reactions. The college students reacted with hostility to Stein, while the third graders greeted her text with the same unabashed enthusiasm they might express when faced with a stray and harmless puppy that suddenly appears in their bedroom.

Several different things need to happen, I think, for older students—students who are no longer "innocent" and apt to be hardened and cynical—to appreciate *Tender Buttons*. Even if they don't like Stein at first, her work elicits heated discussions about what constitutes art, and what modern art is. Afterwards, many get past their initial resistance, and some even come to really like Stein's uniqueness.

First, one thing that can help when introducing Stein to older students is to discuss early twentieth-century art—Cubist painting in particular. *Tender Buttons* was published in 1914, the same year as the legendary Armory Show, which introduced American audiences to Cubism and Dada for the first time via the work of Pablo Picasso, Marcel Duchamp, Paul Cézanne, and others. If you are going to teach Stein, I suggest that you put up pictures of these artists' works in your classroom—I must admit I didn't do this with my own classes, and I now wish I had! Students will have all those unusual and surprising images on the wall to look at as they hear the eccentric and wonderful language of Stein's own work. In a 1913 article on Stein, Mabel Dodge linked Stein's aesthetics as a writer with those of Picasso as a painter, suggesting that Stein's language could be understood as a series of rhythmical and cadenced sounds existing outside the realm of linguistic reference. In other words, *Tender Buttons* is a kind of poem-picture-song that doesn't have to make traditional "sense" to be enjoyed.

With this in mind, read "Rooms" (either alone or with students), the last piece in the *Tender Buttons* series, a long, uninterrupted prose poem that begins with the phrase, "Act so that there is no use in a centre." Meditate on this phrase for awhile. You might conclude (as I have) that *Tender Buttons* is a musical form containing theme and variations—the theme being the continuous challenge to and rejuvenation of meaning-in-language. Notice how "Rooms" has all sorts of phrases suggesting or repeating the word *spreading*: "And then the spreading"; "If the centre has the place then there is distribution"; "Now when there is separation there is the division." In a way, Stein seems to be telling us that the moment we try and make sense out of something, whatever sense we've made immediately starts to open itself up to alternative interpretations—sense spreads around and away from us, and we're left watching meaning disperse like a flock of geese headed north. Stein's advice to "Act so that there is no use in a centre" invites us to collaborate in a kind of joyful anarchy of meaning (there is no center, no *central* meaning, and no need for it) that re-imagines words as material that can at once break apart and revitalize a feeble, boring language.

In addition, you have to get your older students to see that the experience of reading Stein is *fun*. You need to let them know that language doesn't *have* to be tied down to familiar forms of communication such as "Pass the salt" or "Do you want to dance?" Ask your students to imagine that words can act like musical notes—you might want to provide examples of musical-sounding words, like *bomb* or *shazzam* or *tutti-frutti*. When you read sections from *Tender Buttons* out loud to your students, really try and accentuate the rhythms and the wackiness of Stein's language—read the poems quickly, giggle as you read, move your body around.

Even so, I would caution you that you'll probably have to work hard to get older students past their initial resistance to Stein. My community college students in Brooklyn ranged in age from 19 to 71, and many of them had immigrated to the U.S. from all over the world—from South and Central America, Eastern Europe, and Africa. One might think that this diversity would result in an equally diverse set of responses to Stein. After all, my group was generally remarkably sophisticated—Ilya had presented his own translations of several poems by Vladimir Mayakovsky, for example, and Ayesha had described the concept behind Gerard Manley Hopkins's sprung rhythm eloquently and passionately. As my usual practice in presenting poems to this group included reading work aloud, I proceeded to read the following:

A Dog

A little monkey goes like a donkey that means to say that means to say that more sighs last goes. Leave with it. A little monkey goes like a donkey.

A White Hunter

A white hunter is nearly crazy.[3]

When I looked up from the page, even some of the students who were usually "on my side" looked stunned and horrified. Indeed, Yelena—a Russian student who was forceful in her defense of the "difficult" poets most of her classmates were often quick to dismiss—was the first to respond, and it was with a phrase I'd never expected to hear from her: "That's ridiculous. I could do that myself." Deb, the class septuagenarian and troublemaker, quickly seconded Yelena's critique, telling me that I was using my authority as professor to "dress" a poem that didn't deserve to be read as "poetry" in the first place. (She minded us of the old "Emperor has no clothes" story.)

A bit deflated, I didn't have the time or nerve to mount a defense of Stein's *Tender Buttons* right then, but I left determined to promote Stein as a source of intelligence and poetic pleasure.

The following day, I walked into class armed with reproductions of Jackson Pollock's *Autumn Rhythm* and Réné Magritte's *Ceçi n'est pas une pipe* (the famous painting of a pipe with the words "This is not a pipe" written directly underneath the image). I chose these images not so much because I thought they were pertinent to Stein (who, after all, knew and championed the work of other painters including Picasso and Matisse), but because I knew some of my students were already familiar with the two paintings. Before bringing up Stein to them, I showed them the Pollock. Most students were well-acquainted with Pollock thanks to an art history class at the college, and so were ready to discuss the image in terms of its "energy" and "wild beauty." We discussed how Pollock had created *Autumn Rhythm* by dripping paint on the canvas. A few students did snicker at Pollock and our ensuing conversation, but for the most part had no problem accepting Pollock as an "artist," and his painting as "art."

I informed the students that Pollock had faced resistance from the general public when his work first appeared. Magazine headlines proclaimed him "Jack the Dripper," I told them, and the public perception was that his technique was somehow not "artistic" or "skillful" enough to warrant the label of "real art." The most common criticism Pollock faced was that "anyone could do" what he did—the implication being that his paintings should therefore not be taken seriously. I noticed that a couple of students glanced at Yelena after I said this, maybe recalling that she had condemned Stein the day before with similar sentiments.

I showed my students the Magritte image. This work generated a delightful conversation that was as playful as the painting itself. Jimmy protested, "Why is he telling us that isn't a pipe. It's a pipe!" as other students laughed and shook their heads in appreciation of Magritte's surrealistic joke. I took this opportunity to talk about how Magritte might be emphasizing the slipperiness and arbitrariness of meaning. We had a spirited and sophisticated conversation, verging on a graduate-level colloquy on poststructuralism. Students did a lot of connecting work, referencing a wide range of media including Simpsons episodes and hip-hop lyrics, which communicated the same kind of dislocative message as the Magritte image.

I then told the students that *Tender Buttons* was written around the same time Marcel Duchamp exhibited a urinal in an art show, that Stein was challenging preconceived notions of what poetry was supposed to be just as Duchamp was attacking notions of what artworks should consist of. This parallel helped most of the students to "get" *Tender Buttons* this time around. That is, they understood that their negative responses to Stein might stem from the "shock of the new."

We read through the first few pages of *Tender Buttons* out loud, pausing every now and then to comment on the rhythmic power of the language. A number of students connected Stein's text to Magritte's pipe painting, pointing out how titles of individual poems had no apparent bearing on the content of the poems themselves. While not all the students ended up loving Stein and *Tender Buttons*, I do believe I got them all to at least respect her as an innovative writer who deserved to be taken seriously—which as far as I'm concerned was a job pretty well done.

My third grade students offered me an entirely fresh set of responses and an initial enthusiasm that stood in marked contrast to the older students' initial reactions. I know a lot of the positive work the third graders did was due to the natural open-mindedness typical of young kids. They haven't yet learned to be cynical and dismissive towards unfamiliar things. Say "aider stop the muncher, muncher munchers"[4] or "stick stick sticking,

sticking with a chicken"[5] to any nine year old and see what happens. Young kids don't need a narrative in order to experience pleasure from a text, while most college students have sadly enough come to judge any reading experience against the standard of a story with a defined beginning, middle, and end. Also, I have a feeling that the kinds of reading they do in class (think back to Dr. Seuss and the fun he had with nonsense and linguistic playfulness!) as well the bizarre and absurd TV shows they watch at home (like Pokémon) help young students accept and even welcome writing that doesn't make conventional sense. Older students who no longer read or watch essentially non-narrative, non-linear books and TV programs are in a sense *out of practice* when it comes to engaging with work that challenges the norm.

The following is a lesson plan for *Tender Buttons* that I drafted after my experience with these third graders. Though this was the best class I ever had at that particular school, there were certain things I might have done differently—hence this is a combination of what I did and what I should have done. I believe you can easily adapt this lesson plan for your own students—and have fun!

A Ten-Step Stein Exercise

1. Before you distribute any handouts, start off by writing Gertrude Stein's name on the board. Then have your students shout out her name at the count of three:

    1...
    2....
    3.....

GERTRUDE STEIN!!!

This way, you'll generate some excitement by indirectly suggesting to your students that Stein's work is something to laugh and shout about.

2. Show your students a picture of Stein—there's a famous portrait of her by Picasso that you could probably find in any library. It's also available on the Internet at the Metropolitan Museum of Art's website. If you don't have the time to look for the picture, you might try drawing an image of Gertrude Stein in chalk on your blackboard (make her big, broad-shouldered, heavy, and round).

3. I've found that kids really like to know a little bit about the author they're being asked to read. Give your students some simple biographi-

cal details about Stein. You might want to start by saying how Stein is a "literary giant"—she did after all influence hundreds of writers, wrote hundreds of poems, plays, essays, and hard-to-categorize works such as *The Autobiography of Alice B. Toklas* (a best-selling autobiography of Stein's own life, as told through the voice of Toklas). Let your students know that Stein was an American by birth, but she lived most of her adult life in France. (You can take this opportunity to show your students where France is on the map). Tell your students that Gertrude Stein was good friends with famous artists and writers including Pablo Picasso, Henri Matisse, and Ernest Hemingway. You can also point out that she lived through two World Wars in Europe, and even served cakes and tea to French and American troops when they weren't too busy fighting the Germans. If you and your students are up to it, you can discuss how Stein lived with a woman by the name of Alice B. Toklas for a great deal of her life.

4. Okay, so now that you've built up Gertrude Stein in your students' imaginations, now what? Before reading excerpts from *Tender Buttons*, ask your students for the words they might use to describe an apple. Write these down on the board (green, red, sour, crunchy, etc.) Tell them that they described "apple" really well, but that you'd like to introduce them to a writer who described "apple" in a completely different—and even crazy—way.

5. Distribute handouts of "Apple," "A Red Hat," and "A Dog" (from *Tender Buttons*). Read the prose-poem "Apple" out loud:

> Apple plum, carpet steak, seed clam, colored wine, calm seen, cold cream, best shake, potatoe, potatoe and no no gold work with pet, a green seen is called bake and change sweet is bready, a little piece a little piece please.
>
> A little piece please. Cane again to the presupposed and ready eucalyptus tree, count out sherry and ripe plates and little corners of a kind of ham. This is use.[6]

6. Ask your students if this is how they might define an apple. (They will most probably answer "No"). You can tell your students that Stein was weird and wonderful and liked to have fun with language, and liked to make people nervous, giggly, and confused with her writing.

7. Ask individual students to read the "A Red Hat" and "A Dog" excerpts out loud—have one student read one line, the next read the next, and so on. Follow their halting reading with your own confident one.

8. Ask your students to count how many times Stein repeats words in these prose poems—for example, count how many times Stein uses the word *little* in "Apple," *grey* in "A Red Hat," and *monkey* in "A Dog." The

point of this is to have your students *hear*, without your telling them, how repetition adds musicality to a piece.

9. Write a collaborative sentence with your students on the board. First, pick an object. (My class chose to describe a bicycle, but any object will do). Then ask your students to describe it in as strange a way as possible. Each student gets to contribute one word to the sentence—feel free to stop after eight or nine words. If you like, scramble up the words of the sentence yourself on the blackboard to make the sentence all the more odd. This way, your students will see the musical and humorous possibilities of turning sense into nonsense. For "a bicycle" we came up with "The rock was rolling big wet bicycle race."

10. For this exercise, have students start by writing a sentence that describes an object. They should try to make the sentence at least six to eight words long—for example, you might write, "A green apple delicious and sour very crunchy." Then have them write a bunch of *new sentences* by simply mixing up, repeating, or even adding new words to their first sentence in all sorts of different ways—try to make it sound like a wild sort of song. For example, you might transform "A green apple delicious and sour very crunchy" into something like:

Sour sour crunchy and green apple delicious very and a crunchy.

If, despite having worked on the collaborative sentence, your students have trouble understanding this exercise, tell them to scramble up words in their sentences the way one would scramble up eggs. Spend the rest of class period helping your students out, kid to kid, table to table.

I found that it was good to tell my students in no uncertain terms that they should write crazy, weird sentences. Indeed, when I told that to one student who was having trouble getting her exercise off the ground, she "got it" immediately and actually said, "Not making sense is fun because it makes it feel like we're not working." Also, for some mysterious reason, this particular class used line breaks more than any other class I've ever had, despite the fact that *Tender Buttons* is written in paragraphs. Maybe it's because Stein's writing is so musical in nature that students somehow manage to naturally employ line breaks as a way of accentuating rhythm. Here are some student poems that came out of this class:

A Book

The book was big and wet rolling on the rock race.

Big and wet rock race the book rolling down the trees.

Rolling tree race big rocks and wet paper down the shake.

Shake rolling paper down rocks book tree and big wet rats.

Big rats rolling book and tree wet rocks down the book and race shakes.

   —*Angela Lin*

A Pencil

It makes bubbles and butter and water.
Water butter make my pencils.

Water

Water you eat water I keep in my room
Water I play if it is a ball water I see in a pepper.
Play pepper water to eat keep the water
in my room hello are you there.

A Ball

Ball I eat I do not play with a ball
I talk will the ball and I have to say
hello are you there.
I play there not with I ball I eat
the ball talk here but there say
hello to the ball ball rock.

   —*Marilyn Cercado*

An Apple

The apple was wet the worm was
wet every thing was wet
The apple rolled down
the worm rolled down
together

> the worm down
> rolled and the
> apple down rolled
> and they down rolled
> together

   —*Lillian Alvarado*

Alligator

The alligator was wet and
riding a big wet bicycle.
The big alligator was riding
a big bicycle.
The big bicycle and the alligator
was riding a big wet black bicycle.

> —*Ronald Wooden*

A Car

A dog is lost and a fat man is lost too.

> —*Robert Torres*

An Ear

An ear can be round
But it can't make a sound.
An ear can be deaf.

> —*April Nieves*

A Car

The car was black blue wheels.
The cars wheels were blue the car was black.
Wheels the cars were the blue car black
Cars the were the blue black car wheels.
Black cars blue were the wheels car.
Blue black cars were wheels the car.
Were wheels the blue black car cars.
Cars the wheels blue cars black car.

> —*Juan Pedraza*

Bibliography

Rothenberg, Jerome and Pierre Joris, editors. *Poems for the Millennium, Volume One: From Fin-de-Siècle to Negritude.* Berkeley: University of California Press, 1995.

Stein, Gertrude. *Writings 1903–1932.* New York: The Library of America, 1998.

Notes

1. Stein, Gertrude. *Gertrude Stein: Writings 1903–1932* (New York: The Library of America, 1998), p. 324.
2. Ibid., p. 325.
3. Ibid., p. 325.
4. Ibid., p. 326.
5. Ibid., p. 341.
6. Ibid., p. 337.

Wallace Stevens

Sam Swope

The Blackbird Is Flying, The Children Must Be Writing

Teaching Wallace Stevens

I

Among twenty snowy mountains,
The only moving thing
Was the eye of the blackbird.

First we went over some hard words—*pantomime, indecipherable, Haddam, lucid, euphonies,* and *equipage.* Then, as I handed out copies of "Thirteen Ways of Looking at a Blackbird," I told my fifth graders, "This is a famous poem written by an American businessman named Wallace Stevens. I'm telling you that so you know you can be a writer and still have another career." I said, "Before we discuss it, I want you to read it silently."

Thirty-six children put their elbows on their desks and leaned over the poem. I had been this class' writer-in-residence for three years and knew them well. They were a smart group, immigrants to Queens, New York, from more than twenty countries, speaking eleven languages. Many were poor, their sights set on doctoring as the clearest way up the American ladder, and although they enjoyed reading and writing, most had the idea that math and science were the only subjects that really mattered.

Their classroom was crowded, not much space for anything but students, tables, and chairs. But it was a bright, tall room, at the top of a fat old schoolhouse made of brick and limestone. The room's windows started eight feet up the wall, so that even when standing you had to look up to look out, and all you ever saw was sky. It was like being in a deep box with the lid ajar.

Twenty snowy mountains. It was late January, but seventy degrees and sunny. We were hot. "El Niño!" cried my students. "Global warming!" What could they know of mountains and of blackbirds? The school had no recess, and when the kids were not in class, most were stuck in tiny apartments, forbidden to play in the city streets. (A handful had visited their native countries, where they ran freely outdoors, but that was only for a few weeks every few years. Mostly, their childhoods were spent in man-made environments, and "nature" was something they knew from books and TV.)

The room was silent as the children read.

II

I was of three minds,
Like a tree
In which there are three blackbirds.

The moving "eye" of the blackbird becomes the "I" that is the poet, the blackbirds an unsettling metaphor for the poet's thoughts. Throughout this poem, Stevens juxtaposes the actual blackbird with the blackbird of his mind. At least I think that's what he's doing, but it's hard to know for sure. It's a fair question: Is "Thirteen Ways of Looking at a Blackbird" too difficult for fifth graders?

Kenneth Koch, a poet whose useful, entertaining books on writing poetry with children have earned him my gratitude and trust, describes in his book *Rose, Where Did You Get That Red?* the way in which adult poems can inspire children to write their own poetry. Koch uses poems by Blake, Donne, Whitman, Lorca, Ashbery, and others, each providing an example of what he calls a "poetry idea." He makes a special pitch for "Thirteen Ways of Looking at a Blackbird," finding in it both a "gamelike quality" that is appealing to children and an obvious poetry idea: Write about an ordinary object in as many different ways as you can. This assignment was well suited for my yearlong unit on The Tree, and I hoped it would help my students approach our subject from new and interesting directions.

I waited for the children to finish reading the poem. One by one they looked up, faces blank. "Uh-oh," I thought. The less confident cast sidelong glances round the room, checking to see if others were as lost as they. I told them, "This is a difficult poem. Don't worry if you didn't understand it. But before we discuss it, I'd like to hear your first reactions."

Not a hand went up. Everywhere I looked, eyes avoided mine.

I called on Simon, a bright-eyed kid with sticking-out ears. Simon was the baby of a Dominican family, so lovable and so well-loved he never was afraid to say he didn't know. "This is like a college poem, Mr. Swope," he said. "Why'd you give us a college poem for?"

"Yeah!" said Angelo. "I didn't understand a word of it!"

"Yeah!" said Alex. "I thought I was falling asleep!"

Smelling blood, everyone perked up, eager to join an uprising—yeah! yeah! yeah!

"It's not a poem!"

"It's like a set of instructions!"

"Directions to see a blackbird!"

"It's a how-to thing!"

"It's got numbers!"

"Yeah, it's like so weird!"

I was of three minds: I am a rotten teacher; this is a rotten class; Stevens is a rotten poet.

III

The blackbird whirled in the autumn winds.
It was a small part of the pantomime.

Stevens's economy of language is impressive. In just two lines he moves us from a single bird to the whole sky. If this were a scene in a movie, the soundtrack would be silent as the camera tracked the bird, then gradually pulled back to reveal an autumn panorama in which the ever-smaller blackbird soared.

"Now I'll read the poem out loud," I said. "Just make yourselves comfortable and listen." I turned out the lights; the room went gray and dusky. Several students put their heads down. It's a marvelous thing, reading to children. My voice, Stevens's poem, blackbirds in the room. No one fidgeted, no one whispered, and when I finished, the poem hung in the air.

"Reactions?"

Students lifted their heads, rubbed their eyes. I called on Miguel, a polite boy whose mother had been a schoolteacher back in Ecuador. He smiled apologetically, sorry to disappoint.

"Come on, Miguel," I said. "What did you think of the poem when you heard it read out loud?"

"When you read it, it made more sense."

"Yes," I said. "In what way did it make more sense?"

He smiled and squirmed, nothing to say.

Sageeta, a thoughtful Indian girl with beaded cornrows, put it this way: "When you read something, you can't explain the feeling—it's the feeling you have, whatever you do."

"What do you mean, 'whatever you do'?"

"When you read this, it's a feeling. It gives you a feeling."

"What feeling?"

"I can't explain it."

Is this enough? To read a poem out loud, cast the spell, give your students a feeling, and move on? Not talk about what can't be talked about? Perhaps, but even if we say that sometimes the reading of a poem is enough, is "Thirteen Ways of Looking at a Blackbird" that sort of poem? I doubt it. If I had let it go, Stevens's words would have whirled in the room and vanished.

It's a tough poem to hold on to. It has no characters, no plot, no humor, no rhyme, no clearcut beat, no uplifting sentiments, and its pleasures are subtle, quiet, abstract, intellectual. Koch is right. "Thirteen Ways of Looking at a Blackbird" is a puzzle, a Cubist collage—precisely the kind of poem you get to know better by talking about it. But how to do that with a room of ten-year-olds?

Following Koch's advice, I focused on the poem's more accessible sections, then asked the children to write about a tree in as many ways as they could. Most came up with four or five separate thoughts, of which these are typical:

> It looks like eyes on the trunk.
> A stick with a beehive on the end.
> I wish it was Spring so my tree could grow leaves.
> A tree is a place that keeps people trapped inside.
> You are the wall I hate that covers the sun when I'm cold.

I was both heartened and disappointed. They had gotten the poetry idea, as Koch promised, yet they hadn't written poems. To help them do so, I decided we'd discuss the poem line by line, but in small groups, and then, using Stevens's poem as a model, write "Thirteen Ways of Looking at a Tree."

Later, after I explained this assignment, Sageeta looked at me and said, "Let me get this straight: You want us to use all thirteen techniques, but with different words, and about a tree?"

"Yes, that's the idea, but if a section seems too hard," I said, "skip it. Make up something all your own."

"No, no, it's not too hard," she said. "No problem."

> The world around the tree
> Was hectic and moving
> Yet it stood still
> With a brave heart.
>
> —*Sageeta*

IV

A man and a woman
Are one.
A man and a woman and a blackbird
Are one.

Here the style of the poem changes. In plain, declarative sentences, Stevens announces a spiritual idea of unity. We are all one. There's nothing more to say.

I met with students in groups of five or six. What a difference intimacy makes! One group was all boys, and by the time we got to this part of the poem, each of them was fighting to be heard. Simon, the boy who scolded me for giving them a college poem, was so eager to talk he couldn't sit still.

"Simon, please don't stand on your chair."

"But I want to say what section IV means!"

"Okay, what's section IV mean?"

"It means a man and a woman get married and become one because they love each other so they're not two separate people."

Cesar disagreed. "No, it means like the man and woman do like a matrimony and then they look at blackbirds and see the blackbirds do the same."

"But a man and a woman and a blackbird are not going to get married!" said Lorenzo.

"No, not like get married exactly," explained Cesar, "but birds, people, they do basically the same—"

"No!" said Simon. "He said that a woman and a man and a blackbird are one. He's not comparing them."

"Then what is Stevens doing with the blackbird here?" I asked Simon.

He went quiet for a moment, then he said, "It might be that that bird's their pet."

Everyone liked this idea. "Maybe they are bird lovers," suggested Lorenzo. "The man and the woman, they get married, so then they treat the blackbird like a child."

Cesar smiled, happy at that thought. "Part of the family," he sighed.

You are one.
So am I.
But trees are part of us
Also.

    —*Noelia*

V

I do not know which to prefer,
The beauty of inflections
Or the beauty of innuendoes,
The blackbird whistling
Or just after.

I begged him, "Salvador, write! Write something! Try!"

He hadn't written a thing for months, rarely had his homework, and in class he couldn't sit still. Salvador was immensely confident, capable of unusual, interesting thought, yet he was also lazy and disorganized, angry and socially awkward. He often drew while other children wrote, but he wasn't very good at it, and what he drew upset me.

"May I see?"

Salvador had scrunched his drawing in a corner of the page. It was typically sloppy and mostly indecipherable. There were scratchy men with limbs that didn't bend, and there were guns and bombs. At least he had a bird, an eagle decently drawn, but even it was bleeding from the heart. There were blotches of explosion and lots of smudgy death, not the joyful ruin happy children draw, no flashing zigzag lines and gaudy colors.

"Oh, Salvador," I said. "Why are your pictures always so violent?"

He smiled, happy to be noticed, and continued drawing. We had had this conversation many times before.

"It worries me, Salvador. It makes me feel like you're not happy."

"Oh, I'm happy, Mr. Swope. I just like drawing violence, that's all."

I knew him well enough to say, "This picture makes me think you're going to grow up and be a mass murderer, Salvador, and I think you can do a little better than that."

Salvador giggled as he kept on drawing.

"Do me a favor. Stop drawing and try to write. Write at least one way of looking at a tree, okay? You can do this."

"Okay," he said, and cheerfully pulled out his writing folder.

It grows big
but he
is small
although
big things
are happening inside.

    —*Salvador*

There are no euphonies here, and even though his poem isn't perfectly clear, it has some interesting innuendo going on, a lot of promise. I gave it a *Good!!!*

But it's hard to know what I responded to—the poem itself, or the boy behind it; my student as he was, or as I wanted him to be.

VI

Icicles filled the long window
With barbaric glass.
The shadow of the blackbird
Crossed it, to and fro.
The mood
Traced in the shadow
An indecipherable cause.

This section was a class favorite, with its prison made of ice, its menacing shadow, and its goosebumps sort of evil. Yet when I asked Soo-jung how she'd do something similar, but with a tree, she shook her head and told me that was hard.

Her classmates disagreed.

"I know!"

"Through the icy window—"

"The tree—"

"Or its shadow—"

"It looks like a monster or something—"

"Suddenly the wind blows and you see this branch—"

"And it looks like a hand—"

"Yeah, and you get scared—"

"And you see a UFO!"

As other children huddled round and spun this silly horror, Soo-jung sat in silence. She was often quiet, not always by choice. Sometimes she'd join in a discussion, then startle us by going mute, eyes looking out at me as from a cell. She couldn't speak, not even when she wanted to. No one could explain these strange and sudden silences, least of all Soo-jung. It was as if she were under a curse, and in a way, she was.

Soo-jung had emigrated from Korea with her parents at age four. Three years later her mother up and left. Soo-jung's father didn't tell his daughter why or where her mother had gone, and Soo-jung never heard from her again. This is the stuff that fairy tales are made of: abandoned daughters locked in towers, wounded birds and goblins dancing in a circle, "No one loves you! No one loves you!"

When you suffer as a child and have the blackbird's shadow in your heart, do you lose the fun of fear, the happiness of horror? Throughout the years I had her as a student, Soo-jung never once wrote of a happy ever-after. No prince ever rode into her stories.

We want to know our students, and knowing, try to help. I searched her writing, certain that I understood, but is her life, as I have told it, her deciphered cause? Am I so wise? Can I say I know this child so well I see into the window of her soul? What arrogance is that?

Soo-jung's only comment on this section of the poem was, "I don't like looking out an icy window 'cause I feel like it's destroying my eyesight."

"Because you can't focus?"

"Exactly."

The tree is an angel
That god sent down
To watch over the earth.
But in the winter
The snow covers its eyes
So it can't see.

　　—*Soo-jung*

VII

O thin men of Haddam,
Why do you imagine golden birds?
Do you not see how the blackbird
Walks around the feet
Of the women about you?

It's hard to look at the world and really see it.

To get the kids outside and under, on, and around trees, we traveled to Central Park once a month and spent the day there, observing, writing, and playing. One day we were outside, and the kids were drawing trees. I was watching Angelo, a skinny Cuban kid with shiny blackbird hair.

"Angelo, why are you coloring the tree trunks brown?"

"'Cause that's what color they are."

"Take a look around you. What color is the bark?"

He squinted at some nearby trees and said, "It's brown."

"No, it's not. It's gray."

"No, it's not. It's brown."

"Look!" I told him. "Use your eyes!"

Angelo looked again, and when he saw that I was right, he said, "I don't care what color real trees are. In comics, trees are brown."

Angelo's parents were divorced. To support her son and daughters, his mother worked six days a week as a receptionist. She was a kind, decent woman with a sad smile, and she always looked tired. She came to school several times, worried about Angelo. He didn't read books, was bored by school, didn't do his homework, hadn't tested well. All he cared about was comics and cartoons. What should she do?

"Buy him paper and paints and markers," I said. "Send him to art class."

"I don't want to encourage him."

"His comics are really good. Maybe he'll be an artist."

"That's what I'm scared of," she said. "An artist's life is very hard."

"It's scary, yes. But if he is an artist, there's nothing you can do. You won't change that. It'll be better for Angelo, and better for you, if you encourage him."

This made her sad.

"Don't worry, he'll be fine. I think he's got a gift. Besides, there's money in cartoons."

It was easy to see him as an artist type. Angelo was a loner. He was quiet and sensitive, quick to cry, but he had a rattlesnake temper when roused. He loved to dance. Although happy if I let him make a comic and not write, if I didn't, Angelo would make a comic anyway, drawing one in words. It didn't matter what sort of writing I got him to do—essay or story or poem—it was always a comic strip struggling to get out.

When Angelo handed in his "Thirteen Ways of Looking at a Tree," I asked him, "While you were writing this, did you glance at a real tree even once?"

"No."

I threw up my hands and said, "Angelo!"

"Heh, heh, heh," he answered, mimicking Beavis.

But Angelo was right, just following the master. I don't imagine Wallace Stevens sat on some old rock while writing of the blackbirds at his feet.

O crazy mimes of Staten Island
Stop giving free performances
to the tree, can't you see the
Tree is one of you, you mimes,
The Tree is a very still mime!

　　—Angelo

VIII

I know noble accents
And lucid, inescapable rhythms;
But I know, too,
That the blackbird is involved
In what I know.

In the beginning was the thump, screech, and grunt. Then came words, or was the whistle first? Long before our noble accents, back when speech was being made, what models did our early wordsmiths use? Where did the sounds of language come from—the whoosh of wind, a gurgling stream, the songbird warble? Somewhere lost in time did Nature help to shape our tongue, and so inform our thought? Is that what Stevens meant: "the blackbird is involved in what I know"?

I asked Fatma, a gloomy Pakistani child and the school's top speller, what she had made of "Thirteen Ways." She hadn't liked it: "The thing is, it doesn't say very much, but then you don't understand it."

Good point. Even when his words are simple, reading Stevens is like trying to understand a language you don't know very well. You have to do a lot of guessing.

But Noelia, a carefree Caribbean child, showed her gap-toothed smile and said, "That's why I like this poem."

"Explain."

"Because I didn't understand it!"

"But why do you like that?"

"Because I learn new things," she said. "And it's kind of weird."

"Weird is good?"

"Oh, yeah! Weird is def-i-nite-ly good."

Noelia loved the funniness of words, their boing-a-doing and tickle: "In-you-EN-doe!" "YOU-fun-knees!" But with Stevens I suspect she loved the word *equipage* best of all, and when I said, "That word is kind of fun to say. Let's say it all together," Noelia pogoed up and down and shouted out of sync, "Equipage! Equipage! Equipage!"

Later, I told this story to a friend of mine, a fan of Wallace Stevens and a poet. When I was done, she asked, "That's how you pronounce it? Are you sure that it's eh-kip'-ij?"

"No, I'm not sure," I said. "How would you pronounce it?"

"It's French. I think it's eh'-kee-pahj."

"My God, how stupid, yes, of course you're right." Whatever was I thinking?

But then I looked *equipage* up, and found we both were wrong. A French word, yes, but come to us by way of England, its Gallic murmur filtered through a Henry Higgins nose. It's ek'-wuh-pij.

> The hands of
> the tree
> reach for the
> sunlight
> —*Lorenzo*

IX

> When the blackbird flew out of sight,
> It marked the edge
> Of one of many circles.

If Stevens were my student, I'd have written in the margin: "Interesting image, Wallace, but I'm not quite sure what you're referring to here. What circles do you mean exactly?"

I think about my students. I can see them in my mind—or sort of can—the whole class in a circle, holding hands.

> When the
> tree shakes
> its arms
> I still see the
> mark
> left behind.
> —*Polly*

X

> At the sight of blackbirds
> Flying in a green light,
> Even the bawds of euphony
> Would cry out sharply.

I told each group, "I have no idea what this section means. Don't bother imitating it. Just make up something of your own. Now, let's move on."

I didn't understand the section, true enough, but that's not why I hurried to get past it. I wanted to move on because of the word *bawd*. I had looked it up, expecting it to mean "a libertine," but *bawd* instead means "prostitute."

It wasn't that I didn't think the kids could handle that. They watched TV, they flipped the bird, they spat out words both coarse and sexual. Some of them knew a lot more than they should. My worry was their parents, who didn't know how much their children knew (or half-knew, even worse) about the whores who nightly worked the nearby strip with all the garish lights. My worry was the school board and the armies of the right.

> I looked out my window
> And there the tree stood,
> Gazing into my eyes
> Like it knew something.
> —*Sageeta*

XI

> He rode over Connecticut
> In a glass coach.
> Once, a fear pierced him,
> In that he mistook
> The shadow of his equipage
> For blackbirds.

This one's fun. The glass coach crossing Connecticut is a nice touch, almost surreal, with the rider—I see someone noble—vulnerable, exposed, as though inside a bubble. Then the sudden fear, a gasp!

"How would you do that, but with a tree?" I asked one of the groups, and had them write.

Whip-smart Polly needed time to think, but not too much. That girl could get her words down quick.

> As I ride the bus
> along the road
> I see the tree
> moving but not
> me, am I crazy?
> —*Polly*

Yes! She'd even got the startle right, the shock we feel when things aren't what we think.

Polly came from Hong Kong, skinny as a stick, and everything with her was fast, fast, fast. On Field Day when the whistle blew, off she'd fly and leave the rest behind. In class, no sooner did I give a task than snap! she had it done—and neatly, too. And when it came to math, her hand shot up, the numbers figured out inside her calculator head. There's more: eager to grow up, she was the first to place a hand upon her hip, to roll her eyes and say to me, "Oh, please!" And long before the other girls, Polly played the teen and wore short shorts, her shirttails knotted up above her little belly button.

On parent-teacher night, she brought her mom and dad to school. They knew only Chinese, so Polly told them what I said. We spoke, her parents smiled and nodded, looked confused, and left. A topsy-turvy world, the daughter telling grown-ups how things are. There were a lot of things that Polly didn't know, of course, but what's a ruthlessly efficient girl to do? To be not lost, she grabbed whatever models she could find, and they were all around her: Spice Girls! *Baywatch! Titanic!*

To counteract, I offer Art. Yet what can any poem do—a match's flicker in Times Square! And though the battle's always hard, it's harder still with poems as strange as Stevens's with its winter thoughts, all mind, no easy heart. But maybe that's why Polly worked with it so well. Clever thing, she tackled it like math.

> Two birds on a
> tree. Two minds
> in one. As two
> minds in one
> thought.
> —*Polly*

Brava! Not only had she understood the birds as metaphors for thought, but she extended that and made them metaphors for love. I told her, "Polly, this is really good. Profound, in fact, and beautifully expressed."

She said, "I got this idea from a commercial."

"What idea?"

"The two always stick together," she said and slyly smiled.

I didn't understand, but Polly swatted at the air and gave a huff and told me, "Never mind!"

Noelia turned to me and said, "It's from a toothpaste commercial, and part of it is tartar control and part is whitening, and together they are one."

XII

> The river is moving.
> The blackbird must be flying.

Jessica always thought too much, which made her stories so complex and so confused that the only way she could think to end them was to write: "To Be Continued!" And when she made her first attempts to mimic Stevens, her words were typically perplexing:

> The land was
> of five minds
> like my tree.

I said to her, "Don't think. Just write whatever comes into your head!" When our work that day was done, among the other bits she handed in was this:

> My tree is so big
> that no one
> really notices.

Some days later, I read this poem to the class and Jessica cried out, "But that's not mine!"

"It has your name. It's in your handwriting."

"I'd remember if I wrote it."

I handed her her paper, which she studied, disbelieving.

"You wrote it, that's for sure, and good for you," I said. "That is a good poem."

Jessica looked surprised. "It is?"

"Yes."

"Oh!" she said, and beamed with pride.

Then she got to thinking, and later said to me, as if confessing, "That poem I wrote that you liked? I don't know what it means."

XIII

> It was evening all afternoon.
> It was snowing
> And it was going to snow.
> The blackbird sat
> In the cedar-limbs.

There's a lot of quiet in this poem.

Earlier, when Salvador discussed the blackbird whirling in the silent autumn winds, he said, "I think what Wallace was trying to say is like the blackbird would make no noise when he was going through the wind and so he was like part of the stillness of what was around him."

"But if he was part of the stillness," said Maya, "he shouldn't be moving, right?"

"Stillness can also mean quiet," I said. "It doesn't only mean motionless."

"Oh," said Maya, dreamy-eyed, her straight black hair so long that it was like a cape.

I asked Tomás, "What is Stevens doing in the last section?"

Speaking softly, Tomás said, "It's the end of his poem, so it's gonna be like it's gonna be darkness, and it's snowing a little, but it was gonna snow more, so he has to go home."

"Why does the poet end with this simple image?"

"Because he probably doesn't want to write no more and so he wants to end it in a way that people can understand."

"Mmm-hmmmm. How do we know that it's ending?"

"He's saying it's evening and he has to go to sleep or something."

Sleep, perhaps, or maybe there is here a deeper stillness, the blackbird on the snowy limb a metaphor for death. Many children heard the poem's darker echoes, but Maya, who loved horror, reveled in them. "Isn't thirteen a dreaded number?" she had asked me with a hopeful smile. "Isn't black an evil color?"

"Yes," I said. "That's in the poem, too."

Maya was a model student with a peaceful, pleasant manner. When we studied Stevens, I did not sense that anything was wrong, and did not know that her favorite uncle had just died, or that her best friend in the class had recently betrayed her. It wasn't until sometime later that her mother called to tell me Maya was often overwhelmed with tears and cried out to her parents, "I want to die! I want to die!"

As still as night
as night is
still
The wind blows
the bird chirps
the dog barks
but still
the tree is still.
The bark falls off
but there is no sign
of pain, or suffering.
How can this be?
No pain,

no nothing that a
human has.
So giving
and strong,
nothing really
in its way.

   —*Maya*

We worked with Stevens for two weeks. And then, at the end of a February day, several children read their poems to the class, and we said goodbye to blackbirds. Everyone was tired, yet everyone seemed happy. It was time to go home.

"All right," I said. "That was good. Thank you. That was very interesting."

When I asked Simon if he liked the poem now, his face lit up. "Oh, yeah, a lot!" he said, and others quickly cried out they did, too—oh, yeah! yeah! yeah!

Bibliography

Stevens, Wallace. *Collected Poetry and Prose.* New York: The Library of America, 1997.

William Carlos Williams

Charles North

"January Morning," or What Will You Not Be Experiencing?

Teaching William Carlos Williams's Poem

EARLY IN HIS POETIC CAREER, William Carlos Williams wrote a delightful little ode to, of all things, his own nose ("Smell!")[1] in which he calls his nose and himself "tactless asses," unable to stem their "indiscriminate, always unashamed" attraction to all things including the "rank" and "unlovely." "What," he exclaims, "will you not be smelling?" The poem ends: "Must you taste everything? Must you know everything? / Must you have a part in everything?"

The answer to these playful questions, not merely for his nose but for Williams the poet, is Yes! (including the exclamation point). It is as though he can't help noticing and being excited by his surroundings, especially those parts that others often overlook: the unappealing, the apparently trivial or commonplace, the unlovely. And like his great predecessor Walt Whitman, he has the rare ability to make the unpromising details of life striking and even beautiful. These qualities make Williams's poetry a wonderful model for student writers.

Williams's pleasure in his surroundings is nowhere more evident than in "January Morning," a "Suite" of notations having to do with what it is like to be alive on a winter morning in New Jersey in the vicinity of the Hudson River.

January Morning
Suite:

I

I have discovered that most of
the beauties of travel are due to
the strange hours we keep to see them:

the domes of the Church of
the Paulist Fathers in Weehawken
against a smoky dawn—the heart stirred—
are beautiful as Saint Peters
approached after years of anticipation.

          II

Though the operation was postponed
I saw the tall probationers
in their tan uniforms
                              hurrying to breakfast!

          III

—and from basement entries
neatly coiffed, middle aged gentlemen
with orderly moustaches and
well-brushed coats

          IV

—and the sun, dipping into the avenues
streaking the tops of
the irregular red houselets,
                                        and
the gay shadows dropping and dropping.

          V

—and a young horse with a green bed-quilt
on his withers shaking his head:
bared teeth and nozzle high in the air!

          VI

—and a semicircle of dirt-colored men
about a fire bursting from an old
ash can,

          VII

               —and the worn,
blue car rails (like the sky!)
gleaming among the cobbles!

VIII

—and the rickety ferry-boat "Arden"!
What an object to be called "Arden"
among the great piers,—on the
ever new river!
                    "Put me a Touchstone
at the wheel, white gulls, and we'll
follow the ghost of the *Half Moon*
to the North West Passage—and through!
(at Albany!) for all that!"

IX

Exquisite brown waves—long
circlets of silver moving over you!
enough with crumbling ice crusts among you!
The sky has come down to you,
lighter than tiny bubbles, face to
face with you!
                    His spirit is
a white gull with delicate pink feet
and a snowy breast for you to
hold to your lips delicately!

X

The young doctor is dancing with happiness
in the sparkling wind, alone
at the prow of the ferry! He notices
the curdy barnacles and broken ice crusts
left at the slip's base by the low tide
and thinks of summer and green
shell-crusted ledges among
                    the emerald eel-grass!

XI

Who knows the Palisades as I do
knows the river breaks east from them
above the city—but they continue south
—under the sky—to bear a crest of
little peering houses that brighten
with dawn behind the moody
water-loving giants of Manhattan.

XII

Long yellow rushes bending
above the white snow patches;
purple and gold ribbon
of the distant wood:
            what an angle
you make with each other as
you lie there in contemplation.

XIII

Work hard all your young days
and they'll find you too, some morning
staring up under
your chiffonier at its warped
bass-wood bottom and your soul—
out!
—among the little sparrows
behind the shutter.

XIV

—and the flapping flags are at
half mast for the dead admiral.

XV

All this—
            was for you, old woman.
I wanted to write a poem
that you would understand.
For what good is it to me
if you can't understand it?
            But you got to try hard—
But—
    Well, you know how
the young girls run giggling
on Park Avenue after dark
when they ought to be home in bed?
Well,
that's the way it is with me somehow.[2]

The poem's fifteen sections come in no apparent order and are "unparallel," i.e., varied in content, tone, length, shape, rhetorical strategy, etc.

What is immediately striking is how vividly and exuberantly Williams records what he notices. Williams's animated (and animating) sense of things is infectious and inspiring, as is his clear joy in being alive.

What might be called the democracy of his approach—a great variety of things treated with equal respect, emphasis, and enthusiasm—is displayed in the way Williams writes as much as in what he writes about. He is determined to avoid Poetry with a capital P. The language he uses is colloquial and conversational and includes frequent exclamations, interruptions, afterthoughts that give the impression of someone speaking off the cuff, and words that strike some readers as "nonpoetic." Rather than formal devices such as regular stanzas, he prefers casual, even fragmentary notation: *this*, he seems to be saying, is *poetry* as much as anything else is. Even the length and shape of his enjambed lines, a number of which end with "little" words (*of, to, the, as*) add to this air of quick notation.

What Williams does in "January Morning" is, in effect, to follow his nose from one perception, feeling, idea, or association to another. At one point he is struck by "middle aged gentlemen / with orderly moustaches," then by the sun on the roofs of little houses, then by a horse rearing. In section VIII, the name of the ferry he is on provokes a miniature cadenza of associations: from "Arden" to *As You Like It* to Henrik Hudson and the Northwest Passage. One thing follows another not in a logical sense, but rather in the order it appears in the poet's awareness.

*   *   *

"January Morning" is one of my favorite Williams poems, and I have had success using it in college poetry-writing classes. It is essentially a list poem wherein each section is free to take on whatever characteristics the writer chooses. That freedom is inspiring to many students. They can choose almost anything as a springboard—a season, a place, an idea, a feeling, a name, an activity, even a conventional topic—and then follow their noses without predetermining any aspect of the individual sections. Nor need the final product resemble "January Morning." The important thing is to set out to write freely, with the permission Williams's poetry grants us to try new ways and to be honest rather than censor or tailor our feelings to some socially acceptable notion of what is fitting.

One method that often helps is to have students draft twenty sections, and then choose the best fifteen (or ten or five). Or they can simply brainstorm at first, with no thought about sections. This type of poem can also be thought of as Theme and Variations; but it is important to establish that the "theme" can be as firm or as flimsy as the writer likes. That is to say, it's perfectly all right for the nominal subject to be just that, an "excuse" for writing a poem that will find its own way thereafter. I have even suggested to some students, after discussing "January Morning" with them in some detail, that they begin with a title, and then purposely disregard the title in writing the poem. Sometimes Williams's exuberance and concreteness carry over into their poems even so, and the superficial discrepancy between the poem's title and body adds an intriguing dimension.

As a poet myself, I find a great many things about "January Morning" inspiring. Williams's way of writing as though he is right in the middle of what he writes about—rather than scribbling on a prescription pad at midnight after a sixteen-hour day as a physician, as was often the case— gives his poems an extraordinary immediacy. His stops and restarts and qualifications, as in the final section of the poem—which is also a playful but at bottom serious comment on his poetry in general—give the impression that he discovers what to write in the process of writing. His frequent use of a simple "and" to begin a section propels his poem forward. Students who follow their noses in this fashion often find themselves pleasantly surprised by what they come up with. The surprise is part of the excitement in writing poetry, as well as what makes many of the best traditional and contemporary poems exciting for readers. Of course Williams's poetic effects are not as easy to come by as he makes it seem; making it seem so is his gift. It is in fact rare for a writer to be so attentive to surroundings as well as to inner states, and to render both so vividly. What Williams says to the woman in the final section is equally important for student writers: "You got to try hard." But trying hard doesn't necessarily mean laboring over lines or individual words; especially for beginning poets, that approach to poetry can kill off all enthusiasm. Trying hard can mean trying to be as free and inclusive and honest as Williams is. What should be made clear to students is that regardless of the model, the composition of their poems is in every respect up to them, the goal being to produce writing that reflects at least some of the qualities of Williams's poem.

There are many other ways to present "January Morning" as a model, such as by focusing on its "dailiness" and general down-to-earthness. Also noteworthy are the specific settings and place names Williams uses throughout his poetry; not that everything must be identified, but that real names and specific locales contribute to a poem's immediacy, in addition to being, for most modern readers, more evocative than old-fashioned allusions to mythical places like Xanadu or Arcady. In general, reading "January Morning" with the class, with close attention to Williams's poetic choices—despite his self-proclaimed "indiscriminate" attractions, he is in fact highly discriminating as a poet—can help students see that the poem's variety is a vital part of its remaining fresh and compelling from beginning to end.

I have found that the differences between Williams's style—including the look of his poems on the page—and the more orderly arrangements of the majority of poems students encounter in their anthologies often stimulate them to experiment, and in some cases encourage students who were disinclined to write poetry at all. In either case, the important thing is to experience the sheer excitement of writing poems. As a bonus, once students begin to pay close attention to a poem like "January Morning" and try to assimilate some of its qualities into their own writing, they begin to find a wide range of poetry accessible to them as readers and, in turn, find themselves inspired by it as writers.

Bibliography

American Poetry: The Twentieth Century. Volume One: Henry Adams to Dorothy Williams. New York: The Library of America, 2000.

Williams, William Carlos. *The Collected Poems of William Carlos Williams, Volume I.* A. Walton Litz and Christopher McGowan, editors. New York: New Directions, 1986.

Notes

1. William Carlos Williams, *The Collected Poems of William Carlos Williams, Volume I*, A. Walton Litz and Christopher McGowan, editors. (New York: New Directions, 1986), p. 92.

2. In *American Poetry. The Twentieth Century. Volume One: Henry Adams to Dorothy Williams* (New York: The Library of America, 2000), p. 430.

Raymond Chandler

Lewis Warsh

Watching the Detective

The Singular Art of Raymond Chandler

RAYMOND CHANDLER'S WRITINGS are a maze of enticing contradictions and paradoxes. The most obvious one involves Chandler's whole
oeuvre: he was a writer of detective stories or crime fiction—a genre of
writing not usually associated with serious literature—who is frequently
discussed in the same breath as many of the most distinguished literary
figures of the past century. When we think of detective stories we think
of cheap paperbacks with lurid covers that we might read to fall asleep or
lull us into mindlessness on a long plane ride, books that might give pleasure while we're reading them but which (like most TV shows and many
movies) are instantly forgettable. Chandler's novels are replete with murder, adultery and police corruption—all the elements we usually associate
with crime fiction—and feature an ascetic, brooding, alcoholic private
detective, Philip Marlowe, one of the most endearing and strangely
heroic characters in twentieth-century American literature. Yet here we
have Chandler's collected works, published in two volumes by the Library
of America. Chandler's inclusion in The Library of America confirms
what most serious readers of fiction already know: rather than mere
entertainments, these groundbreaking novels deserve a shelf of their own.

What exactly did Chandler do to raise the standard of the crime
novel? How, in Chandler's own words, was he able to take "a cheap,
shoddy, and utterly lost kind of writing, and make of it something that
intellectuals claw each other about?" (*Raymond Chandler Speaking*, p. 74)
Is he *really* worthy of being read in the company of the great American
modernists, Ernest Hemingway or William Faulkner, or even in the company of such gritty realists as John Steinbeck, Theodore Dreiser, or Sherwood Anderson? Where is the "art" in his work? In what way, especially,
might his writing be inspiring to a young writer? Why, instead of dis-
carding his books after we finish them, do we turn to them again—even
though we know the ending, who is innocent and who is guilty? We want
to re-read his books not to find out what happens at the end but for the
pleasure of the writing itself.

Instead of treating crime fiction as a separate genre in class, I try to integrate Chandler's work into a course focused on twentieth-century realist fiction. Chandler's novels inspire discussions about the nature of realism and give the students an opportunity to formulate their own idea of what constitutes a "realistic" piece of writing. Is reality a fixed idea that we all agree upon, or is it more subjective? Does Chandler's description of the world coincide with a version of reality that we all understand and accept?

Chandler's writing—especially his use of dialogue and his descriptive writing—also act as excellent models in creative writing courses. The best examples of crime fiction are models of storytelling. What a good crime writer knows how to do is keep the reader interested. A reading of one of Chandler's novels might focus on the techniques he uses to move the action forward. Another topic of discussion might be the way he uses humor to diffuse the tension. Teaching crime fiction also stimulates class debate about what makes a piece of writing literature, and whether Chandler's books meet those criteria. (For some students, reading Chandler's work in a classroom feels like a subversive act.)

Chandler was not the first writer to raise the standards of crime fiction. Dashiell Hammett, though several years younger than Chandler, had already written several novels, most notably *The Maltese Falcon* and *The Thin Man*, before Chandler wrote his first story. Hammett's major innovation was his use of the private detective, in his case Sam Spade, as a heroic figure. Unfortunately, Hammett stopped writing in the mid-1930s, and it is Chandler, whose best work came later, whom most people consider to be the writer who transformed crime writing into literature.

Chandler's reputation is based on six novels, all of which he wrote after the age of fifty. Of these six, *The Big Sleep, Farewell, My Lovely,* and *The Long Goodbye* are generally considered the best. Chandler's novels are all told from the first-person point of view of Philip Marlowe and all take place in Los Angeles, a city that was (in the 1940s) a work in progress, populated by refugees from the rest of the country who arrived at the new frontier—as Chandler himself did—hoping for a fresh break. Marlowe is emblematic of the contradictory nature of Chandler's work—a hero with attitude, a tough guy with the soul of a romantic, an alcoholic loner with an existential longing for the meaning of life. Existentialist thinkers such as Albert Camus, a contemporary of Chandler's, concluded that the meaning of life was found in the gratuitous act of helping others—of easing the burdens of people in pain—but for Marlowe this code of life isn't so simple, especially in the Inferno of Southern California, where the police are as ethically corrupt as the worst criminal. Marlowe, without family or lover, has little apparent interest in material comforts, other than alcohol and tobacco and maybe two meals a day; nor is he that interested in sex. Marlowe's closest brush with romance, with Eileen Wade in *The Long Goodbye*, is interrupted almost before it begins. Nor does he covet money that he doesn't deserve: many of his wealthy clients offer him huge sums with the unrealistic hope that he'll be able to solve their problems, but he invariably turns them down. The message is that he's a man who can't be bought or influenced; he refuses to put himself in a position where he's in anyone's debt. Each incident in the complicated plots of these books is a mini-drama that exemplifies Marlowe's code or philosophy. The extreme intricacies of the plots are Chandler's way of minimizing their importance, and of cuing the reader to the writing. "Pay attention to my language," he seems to be saying. "The story is only a prop for the way I use words."

One of Chandler's great strengths is his power of observation. His books are layered with passages of descriptive brilliance, especially of people and places. Chandler's apprenticeship as a writer was a long one. Often called "the poet of the detective novel," Chandler wrote only poetry until he was forty-five. That same year (1933), he published his first story, and *The Big Sleep* did not come out until 1939. It's inspiring to think that it's possible to begin a successful career as a novelist at such a late age, and instructive as well. He became expert at observing people both as physical specimens (their features, gestures, and clothing) and as psychological beings. Learning the accurate names of things is part of it, and part of the long apprenticeship, since names of people and things, as well as descriptions of places we know intimately, are what we learn as we proceed through life. "It took me three years," Chandler once wrote, "before I could learn how to get a character to leave a room convincingly." What makes his writing special is that he was able to convey the magic of everyday experiences and of objects and things that are so commonplace we no longer notice them. He never uses a word simply to fill in the holes in a sentence. As in great poetry, every word in a Chandler sentence reverberates beyond itself. Much the way aspiring painters spend time in a museum "copying" the works of old masters, Chandler's descriptions lend themselves to imitation, in the best sense, by aspiring writers.

Chandler's prose is a great model. A valuable classroom exercise is to have students write descriptions of people they know well—in as much detail, and as realistically, as possible. Each description must include at least one simile. A follow-up exercise is to describe people the student doesn't know personally in the same amount of detail. It's always interesting to see how subjective, and telling, an ostensibly "objective" description of a person is.

Here are a few models culled from Chandler's books:

(1) She was twenty or so, small and delicately put together, but she looked durable. She wore pale blue slacks and they looked well on her. She walked as if she were floating. Her hair was a fine tawny wave cut much shorter than the current fashion of pageboy tresses curled at the bottom. Her eyes were slate gray, and had almost no expression when they looked at me. She came over near me and smiled with her mouth and she had little sharp predatory teeth, as white as fresh orange pith, and as shiny as porcelain. They glistened between her thin too taut lips. Her face lacked color and didn't look too healthy. (*The Big Sleep*, p. 590)

(2) The girl and I stood looking at each other. She tried to keep a calm little smile on her face but her face was too tired to be bothered. It kept going blank on her. The smile would wash off like water off sand and her pale skin had a harsh granular texture under the stunned and stupid blankness of her eyes. A whitish tongue licked at the corners of her mouth. A pretty, spoiled and not very bright little girl who had gone very, very wrong, and nobody was doing anything about it. To hell with the rich. They made me sick. (*The Big Sleep*, p. 636)

(3) He was a gray man, all gray, except for his polished black shoes and two scarlet diamonds in his gray satin tie that looked like the diamonds on roulette layouts. His shirt was gray and his double-breasted suit of soft, beautifully cut flannel. Seeing Carmen he took a gray hat off and his hair underneath it was gray and as fine as if it had been sifted through gauze. His thick gray eyebrows had that undeniably sporty look. He had a long chin, a nose with a hook to it, thoughtful gray eyes that had a slanted look because the fold of skin over his upper lid came down over the corner of the lid itself. (*The Big Sleep*, p. 639)

(4) He was looking up at the dusty windows with a sort of ecstatic fixity of expression, like a hunky immigrant catching his first sight of The Statue of Liberty. He was a big man but not more than six feet five inches tall and not wider than a beer truck . . . His arms hung loose at his sides and a forgotten cigar smoked behind his enormous fingers . . . He wore a shaggy borsalino hat, a rough gray sports coat with white golf balls on it for buttons, a brown shirt, a yellow tie, pleated gray flannel slacks and alligator shoes with white explosions on the toes. From his outer breast pocket cascaded a show handkerchief of the same brilliant yellow as the tie. There were a couple of colored feathers tucked into the band of his hat, but he didn't really need them. (*Farewell, My Lovely*, p. 767)

(5) There was a cornflower in the lapel of his white coat and his pale blue eyes looked faded out by comparison. The violet scarf was loose enough to show that he wore no tie and that he had a thick, soft brown neck, like the neck of a strong woman. His features were a little on the heavy side, but handsome, he had an inch more of height than I had, which made him six feet one. His blond hair was arranged, by art or nature, in three precise blond ledges which reminded me of steps. . . . Apart from all this he had the general appearance of a lad who would wear a white flannel suit with a violet scarf around his neck and a cornflower in his lapel. (*Farewell, My Lovely*, p. 800)

In each of these brief descriptive passages we learn a great deal about the observer. Chandler somehow manages to blur the boundary between the person observed and the person observing. He does this by shaping an attitude that encloses the observed person in an aura of language. We both see the person being observed and learn how the observer/narrator feels about the person he's seeing. Marlowe is conscious not only of what the person looks like but of the social class to which he or she aspires. Embedded in the language are attitudes—in this case, sociological and political. "To hell with the rich. They made me sick." The way a person moves, leaving the room, say, tells us something about that person: is he or she shy, aggressive, rude? What do you say when you say "goodbye," and in what context do you use one phrase or another?

Chandler's descriptive language is basically connotative. In the first example, he uses the word *durable* to describe a young woman's body and to offset the phrase "delicately put together." *Durable* isn't a word we usually associate with the animate world. It will more likely describe a machine, such as a car, a tractor, or an article of clothing made from a fabric that's meant to last. Bodies aren't "durable," they're vulnerable. Yet there's also something appropriate about the use of this word; people are, as the twentieth-century French philosophers Felix Guattari and Gilles Deleuze point out in their theoretical work *Anti-Oedipus*, kinds of machines at times (eating machines, drinking machines, sex machines, sleep machines). Time and again, Chandler makes us raise our eyebrows in astonishment at his choice of language, and sends our thoughts spiraling in directions we never considered before. His descriptive writing is a kind of muted surrealism: often out-of-kilter but never totally discordant. Let's look at a few more of the descriptive passages above.

In the second example, Chandler uses a simile to describe the expression on a girl's face when she's drunk or stoned—"the smile would wash off like water off sand." The girl has no control over her expression. Notice the string of adjectives—*harsh, granular, whitish, stupid, stunned, pretty, spoiled, bright*; note the repetitions as well: *blank/blankness, little smile/little girl.*

In the third example, the repetition is even more pronounced: the word *gray* appears in almost every line. What is most fascinating about the fourth example is the precision of detail—"a rough gray sports coat with white golf balls on it for buttons." It's like a photograph with a zoom lens. And in example 5, Chandler gives a taste of his humor, and self-mockery, as if to say: what do all these descriptive details add up to, anyway?

In discussing Chandler's descriptive writing with students, try to focus on use of simile, on accuracy of detail, on adjectives. Encourage students to keep lists of types of clothing—what's in style now, what was in style last year—and different styles of hair. Chandler's portraits of people are instructive in that they are always dealing with the specific—his character is never simply wearing a hat, but a "borsolino" hat. Young students especially are apt to use generalizations in their descriptive work: point out to them the generic nature of such writing, and the exactitude with which Chandler gives us his people. At the same time, sometimes simply using a brand name to describe something isn't enough. A "borsolino" hat gives us the name without describing it, especially when the brand is no longer in fashion.

Have your students write outside—on the subways or buses, or while standing on a street corner—and encourage them to include as much specific detail as possible about everyone and everything they see. Jack Kerouac, who wrote in the 1950s and 1960s, was also a master of descriptive writing, and would call the writing he did out of doors a kind of "sketching"—comparable to the artist who paints or draws *en plein air.* (Another master of detail, from another century, was Walt Whitman—like Chandler, a super realist, for whom the whole world was his subject.) Concentrate on facial descriptions—the shape of eyes, noses, mouths, chins. In example 3: "His thick gray eyebrows had that undeniable sporty look." The word open to question here is *sporty*—on the border between connotation and definition, subjective and objective. The word is filled with implications. Like Gustave Flaubert, the French nineteenth-century novelist, Chandler was obsessed with *le mot juste*—the perfect word, the right word, the exact word. And sometimes his choice of the perfect word has a strange, almost eerie, effect on our experience as readers.

Chandler was also a master of the way people talk. In the mid-1940s he worked in Hollywood as a screen writer and received Academy Award nominations for his scripts for *Double Indemnity* (1944) and *The Blue Dahlia* (1946). These movies are worth seeing, but the best example of Chandler's dialogue is in the film version of *The Big Sleep.* The movie was directed by Howard Hawks, and William Faulkner wrote the screenplay. Humphrey Bogart played the role of Philip Marlowe. Faulkner wisely kept much of Chandler's own dialogue intact. The best scenes are between Bogart and Lauren Bacall, who plays the part of Vivian Sternwood. The other films made from Chandler's novels—*Farewell, My Lovely*, starring Robert Mitchum, and *The Long Goodbye*, with Eliot Gould in the Marlowe role—are not nearly as good, but also worth seeing, perhaps as part of an in-depth study of crime novels and film noir.

The writer whom Chandler most admired and who influenced him most was Ernest Hemingway. The ties between Chandler and Hemingway are especially noticeable in the way they both handle dialogue. Both writers were masters at capturing the nuances of the human voice as well as the correct usage of language in a very specific situation. A good model to use along with Chandler would be Hemingway's short story "Hills Like White Elephants," which consists almost entirely of dialogue. This section from Chapter 24 of *Farewell, My Lovely*, in which Marlowe encounters two corrupt cops, one of whom he names Hemingway, is one of the best examples of his skill at capturing the colloquial voice:

> At the bottom of the shaft we got out and walked along the narrow hallway and out of the black door. It was crisp clear air outside, high enough to be above the drift of foggy spray from the ocean. I breathed deeply.
>
> The big man still had hold of my arm. There was a car standing there, a plain dark sedan, with private plates.
>
> The big man opened the front door and complained: "It ain't really up to your class, pally. But a little air will set you up fine. Would that be all right with you? We wouldn't want to do anything that you wouldn't like us to do, pally."
>
> "Where's the Indian?"
>
> He shook his head a little and pushed me into the car. I got into the right side of the front seat. "Oh, yeah, the Indian," he said. "You got to shoot him with a bow and arrow. That's the law. We got him in the back of the car."
>
> I looked in the back of the car. It was empty.
>
> "Hell, he ain't there," the big one said. "Somebody must of glommed him off. You can't leave nothing in a unlocked car any more."
>
> "Hurry up," the man with the mustache said, and got into the back seat. Hemingway went around and pushed his hard stomach behind the wheel. He started the car. We turned and drifted off down the driveway lined with wild geraniums. A cold wind lifted off the sea. The stars were too far off. They said nothing.
>
> We reached the bottom of the drive and turned out onto the concrete mountain road and drifted without haste along that.

"How come you don't have a car with you, pally?"

"Amthor sent for me."

"Why would that be, pally?"

"It must have been he wanted to see me."

"This guy is good," Hemingway said. "He figures things out." He spit out of the side of the car and made a turn nicely and let the car ride its motor down the hill. "He says you called him up on the phone and tried to put the bite on him. So he figures he better have a look-see what kind of guy he is doing business with—if he is doing business. So he sends his own car."

"On account of he knows he is going to call some cops he knows and I won't need mine to get home with," I said. "Okey, Hemingway."

"Yeah, that again. Okey. Well, he has a dictaphone under his table and his secretary takes it all down and when we come she reads it back to Mister Blanc here."

I turned and looked at Mister Blaze. He was smoking a cigar, peacefully, as though he had his slippers on. He didn't look at me."

"Like hell she did," I said. "More likely a stock bunch of notes they had all fixed up for a case like that."

"Maybe you would like to tell us why you wanted to see this guy," Hemingway suggested politely.

"You mean while I still have part of my face?"

"Aw, we ain't those kind of boys at all," he said, with a large gesture.

"You know Amthor pretty well, don't you, Hemingway?"

"Mr. Blaze kind of knows him. Me, I just do what the orders is."

"Who the hell is Mister Blaze?"

"That's the gentleman in the back seat."

"And besides being in the back seat who the hell is he?"

"Why, Jesus, everybody knows Mr. Blaze."

"All right," I said, suddenly feeling very weary.

There was a little more silence, more curves, more winding ribbons of concrete, more darkness, and more pain.

The big man said: "Now that we are all between pals and no ladies present we really don't give so much time to why you went back up there, but this Hemingway stuff is what really has me down."

"A gag," I said. "An old, old gag."

"Who is this Hemingway person at all?"

"A guy that keeps saying the same thing over and over until you begin to believe it must be good."

"That must take a hell of a long time," the big man said. "For a private dick you certainly have a wandering kind of mind. Are you still wearing your own teeth?"

"Yeah, with a few plugs in them."

"Well, you certainly have been lucky, pally."

Notice how Chandler injects a menacing situation with an undercurrent of humor. Even though the "big man" has the upper hand and Marlowe is the vulnerable one in this situation (the chapter ends with him being dumped from the car), Marlowe has the temerity to needle him by calling him "Hemingway." The cop is more curious than angry—"Who is this Hemingway person?" he wants to know. You get the feeling, from Hemingway's diction, that he's insecure about his intelligence, and that Marlowe is trying to exploit his weakness, not out of cruelty but to throw him off guard. The relationship between private detectives and the police is wary at best, and Marlowe has a problem dealing with people who feel self-important because of their authority. The tone of the banter between Marlowe and the cop—and Marlowe's needling—is what gives the dialogue a life of its own.

Notice, as well, the use of slang and sarcasm. This conversation was written over fifty years ago. One possible exercise might involve students rewriting the conversation using more current colloquialisms. The dialogue in Chandler's novels sounds mild and civilized in comparison to the way such a conversation between similar characters would sound today. Yet despite the relatively mild-mannered language, Chandler's books aren't dated; not in the big sense, since they transcend with ease all notions of high and low art, and in this way are immediately accessible on every level. It would be great to devote a whole advanced high school or college class to Chandler and crime fiction, orbiting back into the past to the work of Chandler's main predecessor, Dashiell Hammett; to his main influence, Ernest Hemingway; to peers such as James M. Cain, Jim Thompson, and Ross MacDonald; and to present-day writers such as James Ellroy, Elmore Leonard, and Charlotte Carter. A close appreciation of the similarities and differences between Hammett's Sam Spade, Chandler's Philip Marlowe, and MacDonald's Lew Archer would be instructive and illuminating. Then, of course, there is the whole field of film and film noir. Quentin Tarrentino's recent movie *Pulp Fiction* owes much of its fast-paced wit to Chandler's tone of mock seriousness. Yet another filmmaker, Takeshi "Beat" Kitano, in his films *Fireworks* and *Sonatine*, has invented a character who might well be Philip Marlowe's half-brother. Taciturn, gentle, and violent almost in the same breath, detached yet purposeful, a modern-day Achilles who defies mythology and courts anonymity, Kitano's character—living on a different continent and in a different era—further validates the enduring nature, and the apparent universality, of Chandler's vision.

Bibliography

Chandler, Raymond. *Late Novels and Other Writings*. New York: The Library of America, 1995.

———— *Stories and Early Novels*. New York: The Library of America, 1995.

Gardinier, Dorothy and Katherine Sorley Walker, editors. *Raymond Chandler Speaking*. Berkeley: University of California Press, 1997.

Hiney, Tom *Raymond Chandler: A Biography*. New York: Grove Press, 1997.

Eugene O'Neill

Jeff S. Dailey

"Life Doesn't Give Us Happy Endings"

Writing with Eugene O'Neill

EUGENE O'NEILL wrote more than twenty short plays between 1913 and 1919. Once he achieved his first commercial success—*Beyond the Horizon* in 1920—he focused on writing longer, more substantial works, such as *Desire Under the Elms, Mourning Becomes Electra*, and *A Long Day's Journey into Night*. The quality of O'Neill's short plays varies—some betray their author's youth, others show great dramatic insight. They are useful for students to read and perform today, as they provide good models for beginning playwrights to follow and exciting situations for student actors; additionally, they are all short enough to be read and performed in one class period.

The following curriculum outlines a variety of activities I use to teach about O'Neill and his plays. For each unit there is at least one writing project. I have included samples taken from the work of my students, all seniors at Grover Cleveland High School—a large, comprehensive 9–12 school in Queens, N.Y., which has a large immigrant population. Typically, we study the plays in class, then the students write first drafts of their assignments as homework. After we have covered all the plays, each student chooses one of the writing assignments to revise for publication or performance.

Before we begin reading the plays, I give students some background on O'Neill and his family. Since all of O'Neill's work is intensely autobiographical, students should know about his parents and brother, about his early introduction to the theater, and about his bouts of depression and alcoholism. As many of the early plays end in suicide, readers should also be aware that both O'Neill and his mother attempted suicide, and that both of his sons were eventually successful at it. Although gloom pervades many of O'Neill's plays, I have found that students do not react emotionally to the many suicides in them. They see them rather as plot devices, as in *Romeo and Juliet*. After all, compared to the mass violence in contemporary film and television, even the bloodiest O'Neill plays seem tame.

Teachers can easily obtain biographical information on O'Neill from print and on-line sources. These range from Internet sites that provide single-page biographies to multi-volume studies (see the bibliography). An excellent and concise source of information can be found in the comprehensive chronology located in the back of each of the volumes of the Library of America edition of O'Neill's plays.

Unit 1: Dramatic Monologues from *Hughie* and *Before Breakfast*

The goal of this first project—which does not require any reading—is for the students to write monologues. I begin by playing a videotape of one of O'Neill's last plays—*Hughie*.

> *Hughie*—synopsis
>
> Erie Smith, a gambler, returns in the early hours of the morning to the New York hotel where he lives. He has been away on an extended drinking binge, brought on by the death of his close friend Hughie, the former night clerk in the hotel. Upon arriving, Erie meets Charles Hughes, the new night clerk, and regales him with stories about his experiences with gamblers and women, and about Hughie.

Although there are two characters in the play, it is a virtual monologue for one character, Erie Smith. Before showing the video, I have students make three columns in their notebooks and label them for Erie, Hughie, and Charlie. While the students watch the tape, they have to write down what information they learn about each "character" (for Hughie is a character, even if he is dead) in the appropriate column.

When the video is finished, the students have to review their notes, decide what is important, and then write a short biographical sketch (or, in the case of Hughie, an obituary) about one of the three men. By doing this, they learn that playwrights do not divulge all the necessary information in chronological order; often it is leaked out in bits and pieces that are left for the audience to assemble.

Here are two student examples:

Erie

Erie was born in Erie, Pennsylvania. His real name is Smith. After grammar school he had to work. Erie ended up being a horse player in Pennsylvania.

Erie has a gambling problem. He has been going to the hotel that Hughie worked in for 15 years. He gave Erie confidence. Hughie then ended up dying. Erie went to Hughie's funeral and he paid $100 for flowers in the shape of a horseshoe. Erie ends up missing Hughie. Then Erie goes to the hotel again and meets Charlie, who reminds him of Hughie. He then ends up being friends with Charlie.

—*Daiana Geca*

Hughie

Hughie was a clerk at a hotel. He was married and had two kids. He died at the age of 43. He liked to be with his friend Erie (Mr. Smith). Hughie liked to gamble, because of the thrill, but never did because he was faithful to his wife's orders and also because his wife would take his money. Hughie was a good husband and a trustful person.

—*Alexis Almonte*

Next we read *Before Breakfast*, O'Neill's only single-character play—Mrs. Rowland is the only speaking character. (Although her husband's arm does extend onstage at one point, he never says anything.) This monologue can be read aloud in class, or can be performed by a student actress. Upon finishing it, the class can discuss the events that preceded the suicide and decide whether or not it was inevitable.

Before Breakfast—synopsis

Mrs. Rowland enters the kitchen in her rundown apartment and finds her husband's clothes scattered about. While picking them up, she finds a love note from his mistress in his jacket pocket. From the kitchen, she berates her hungover husband in the adjoining room, telling him she knows of his infidelity and that he has to get dressed and get a job; she is tired of supporting them. She hands him a basin of water and tells him to shave. While she continues to rebuke him, she hears a crash. Running into the room she finds that her husband has slit this throat.

Students then write their own dramatic monologues. I give them pictures to look at, each of which (cut from the *New York Times Magazine*) shows a single person who is either completing or has just completed an action—working, exercising, crying, etc. The students choose one of the pictures and imagine what has just occurred. They then write monologues, similar to *Before Breakfast*, in which the pictured person explains what is happening. In one class, for example, many of the girls chose a picture of a young woman holding a baby standing outside an apartment building. Some imagined that she is an unmarried mother, while others determined that she is homeless. They wrote soliloquies in which the woman lamented about her situation.

After the revision process, the students perform their monologues for their classmates, standing next to the pictures that inspired them. While I do not require students to perform this assignment from memory, I encourage those with the best monologues to expand them (since they are usually about a page in length) and perform them in forensics competitions or auditions.

Students frequently write very convincing monologues for this project. In the following examples, one does not even need to see the picture to understand what is being discussed:

> Damn oil spill—one little spark and I'm dead. I should be at home relaxing but I'm out here fixing this damn leak. I want to leave so badly, but that check is coming in two days and I have kids to feed. This oil is everywhere; those other idiots that don't know how to fix things probably screwed this one up.
>
> I can just imagine what that one little spark would do. An inferno for miles. I hope the other guys are alright back there— that seemed to be a pretty big blast. I gotta find another line of work. I'm completely covered with oil. I know that once I go home the shower is going to be mine for three hours.
>
> —*Mariano Lloret*

> I'm fifteen years old, homeless, and with a baby. I don't know what to do. I sell myself to earn a living, and now I'm infected with the worst sickness a person could ever have—AIDS. What's going to happen to me in a year? What's going to happen to my baby? All I have to offer her is a cardboard box with one blanket on the steps of a church. I can't go to my parents because they wouldn't understand. They would never accept the fact that I have a child. They would tell me that I'm a bad example for my siblings.
>
> I only have one thing to do and that is just to leave her . . . because if I were to kill the child I'd be a murderer.
>
> —*Priscilla Adames*

Unit 2: *Abortion* and *The Sniper*

The next two plays we read deal with topics that have connections with current events. *Abortion* deals with a topic that is as controversial now as it was in O'Neill's time. For the playwright it was especially pertinent, as his mother aborted several fetuses prior to having him, and he always thought it could have prevented him from being born. *The Sniper* deals with civilians in wartime. In addition to reading and seeing similar stories in the news, many students at Grover Cleveland came to the United States to escape wars in other parts of the world, and so, to them, it is a tale with personal connections.

Both of these plays are well-constructed, and students have no trouble acting and understanding them.

Abortion—synopsis

Jack Townsend has just pitched the winning championship game at his university. His family and fiancée, Evelyn, are now awaiting the triumphal parade to celebrate the playoffs. Jack manages to get his mother, his sister, and Evelyn out of his dorm room so he can talk privately with his father. He thanks his father for providing the $200 to pay for an abortion for Nellie, a young stenographer he has gotten pregnant. He tells his father Nellie lives with her widowed mother and several siblings, whom she helps support. Although he has not heard from her since the day of the operation a week ago, at that time she said everything had gone well. After his father leaves, a young man—Joe Murray—arrives at Jack's room, identifies himself as Nellie's brother, and accuses Jack of killing her. First, he threatens to shoot Jack, then explains that he will simply expose Jack's part in his sister's death. Jack begs him to reconsider, for the sake of his (Jack's) mother and fiancée. Joe leaves in disgust, leaving his revolver behind. In desperation, Jack shoots himself in the head. Just before the curtain falls, Evelyn returns, sees what has happened, and faints.

After reading *Abortion*, I instruct students to write newspaper articles, pretending that they are reporters arriving at the dormitory. While some students have taken journalism classes or have experience writing for the school newspaper, I find it useful to begin by reviewing the structure of a newspaper article, making sure they know to include the who, what, where, when, why and how in the opening paragraph. Supporting details should be included in subsequent paragraphs.[1]

Here is one student's response:

Star pitcher for Eastern University, Jack Townsend, 22, committed suicide before the parade for the University's victory. He was found by his fiancée, Evelyn, in his dormitory with a revolver in his hand. The cause of this terrible incident was due to another woman named Nellie.

Jack had dated Nellie while his fiancée, Evelyn, was back in his hometown with his family. Nellie got pregnant and Jack arranged for her to have an abortion. She got very sick from it and died. Jack never knew until Nellie's brother, Joe Murray, came to the university and told Jack that his sister died.

Murray then wanted to go to the police and tell them the story so Jack would get arrested. Jack pleaded and told Murray that he would give him anything if he didn't. Murray left to tell the police. Murray left his revolver with Jack, who shot himself in the temple. He then instantly dropped and was dead.

—*Jade Velasquez*

The Sniper—synopsis

In a Belgian village during World War I, a peasant, Rougon, examines the rubble of his farmhouse. After having sent his wife away that morning with the family of his son's fiancée, Louise, he hid himself in a well and watched the morning's battle, in which he saw his son killed. While Rougon is telling the village priest these details, a German officer arrives and tells the priest to be sure to notify his parishioners that any civilians found with weapons will be shot. A young boy, Jean, arrives with the news that the convoy of people trying to escape the village was attacked on the road—Rougon's wife, Louise, and her family are all dead. Rougon, incensed, takes his rifle out of its hiding place and fires at a group of German soldiers. He is overtaken and executed in front of the priest, whose prayers he spurns.

The assignment for *The Sniper* requires that the students become dramaturgs—the theatrical equivalent of an editor. Dramaturgs are usually on the staff of theater companies and work with playwrights on making their creations more stageworthy. For this project, I have the students imagine that O'Neill submitted this play to a theater company, whose artistic director does not like the conclusion. They have to come up with a different ending to the play, which can be either narrative or dialogue, and can start at any point they want in O'Neill's play.

Some students give the play a happy ending—the Belgians are able to hide or the U. S. Army enters to save the day. More than one "dramaturg" has had Rougon's family survive. Others remove the execution and have Rougon die in a blaze of gunfire as he shoots back, or have him commit suicide so he is not taken by the Germans.

Unit 3: Movie Treatments Inspired by O'Neill's *Titanic* plays

Whether because of hubris, heroism, or the unavoidable specter of fate, the story behind the sinking of the RMS *Titanic* never fails to interest the public at large—it remains a stimulus for books, theater, and movies. At Grover Cleveland there is also a more personal connection, inasmuch as one of the shipwreck's survivors was a faculty member for 36 years, and some students' parents or grandparents had him as a teacher.

At the time of *Titanic*'s sinking, authors as respected and diverse as Thomas Hardy, George Bernard Shaw, and Arthur Conan Doyle wrote about the disaster.[2] O'Neill used the tragedy as the inspiration for two of his early plays—*Warnings* (1913) and *Fog* (1914).[3]

Warnings—synopsis

Scene 1. In the Bronx dining room of James Knapp, the wireless operator of the SS *Empress*, his family's problems are obvious. His wife is struggling to raise five children, including one baby, on an inadequate income, while their two adolescents are inadequately supervised because their father is away at sea for months at a time. Additionally, Knapp has been having trouble hearing the wireless signal and has gone to an ear specialist for advice. He arrives home and informs his wife that he is going deaf and that he feels he should quit his job. The specialist has told him that it will probably happen gradually, but that a sudden shock could cause it to happen immediately. His wife rages at him that he is too old to get another job and that their finances are precarious as it is. He agrees to go on one more sea voyage and not to tell his employer about his condition

Scene 2. The *Empress* has hit a derelict ship and is sinking. The captain continually comes into the radio room to ask Knapp if he has made contact with other ships. His only answer is "I haven't heard a thing yet, sir." The captain and his mate first ascribe Knapp's bizarre behavior to fear, but it soon becomes obvious to all that Knapp is deaf. The captain remembers that there is another wireless operator on board who is returning home on vacation. When this second wireless operator arrives on the scene, he tells them that another ship is on the way, and that this ship had previously wired the position of the derelict vessel to the *Empress*. The captain has all this communicated to Knapp in writing, then gives the order to abandon ship. Left alone, Knapp pulls out a revolver and shoots himself.

Warnings is not a very sophisticated play, and parts of it rely too heavily on coincidence for it to be taken seriously as a tragedy. As theater, its realistic depiction of a poor family in the first scene is its best asset. *Fog*, on the other hand, is a poetic and mysterious rhapsody, and a good introduction to surrealism for students.

Fog—synopsis

Three passengers from a ship that sank off the coast of Newfoundland are stranded in a lifeboat. Two of them, the Poet and the Business Man, discuss what has happened—their ship hit a derelict vessel and they were able get into the lifeboat, which has no oars but is stocked with food. They have been drifting in the fog for two days. They relate how the third passenger—a Polish Woman—cried when her child died. She is now sleeping, clutching her child, in the back of the boat. The two men feel a sudden drop in temperature, and realize they have drifted against an iceberg. They hear a ship's whistle. The Business Man wants to signal to the ship, but the Poet is concerned that the steamer will strike the iceberg. They fight, and the Poet keeps the Business Man from crying for help. Then they hear the sound of a small boat being rowed nearby. It is a tender from the steamer. The officer in charge wonders why no one shouted for help and says that the only way they found the lifeboat was by following a child's cries. The two stranded passengers are confused; they are sure the child died the previous day. When they try to rouse the Polish Woman, they realize that she, too, is dead.

Because *Warnings* requires an elaborate slanted set and *Fog* calls for two boats and an iceberg, the two plays are more cinematic than theatrical. At this stage in his career O'Neill was in fact working on movie ideas, which he thought he could sell to Hollywood. None were ever accepted.

The writing assignment for this unit involves writing a movie treatment. A treatment is a proposal for a film that contains a plot summary and descriptions of any notable shots.[4] Treatments can range from a one-page synopsis to a forty-page document that outlines the character development and explains the required camera angles. Once a treatment is accepted, the author then goes on to write the script.

Before they begin writing, I show students part of a documentary about *Titanic* films,[5] which includes newsreels of the maiden voyage as well as early silent and sound movies. While most students are familiar with James Cameron's Academy Award-winning film, they have usually not seen *A Night to Remember*, the 1958 movie considered the most accurate rendering of the ship's tragic voyage.

The students' assignment is to write a treatment (usually two to four pages) about the *Titanic* or another shipwreck. Since most high school students have considerable movie-watching experience, it is easy for them to think cinematically. Writing a successful treatment requires inventing an entire plot and summarizing it. Often students do so very creatively: some place themselves on the *Titanic*, others update the disaster to the present day. Some do not use the *Titanic* at all, but create their own shipwreck fantasies, including fishermen being attacked by a giant octopus, a cruise ship attacked by the Cuban army, and boats being swamped by giant storms or waves.

One student made the *Titanic* an American ship:

> It is the Fourth of July and the ship leaves to a beautiful fireworks display out of Sheepshead Bay in Brooklyn, N.Y. There are four main characters—Captain McLaughlin, a young, wealthy couple named Mr. and Mrs. Johnson, and a ship's engineer named James Wilson.
>
> Mrs. Johnson has begun to be attracted to Captain McLaughlin. They begin having and affair and, at the time the when the vessel hits the iceberg, Captain McLaughlin is busy with Mrs. Johnson. The rescue efforts begin and engineer James Wilson risks his life to do his best to keep the vessel afloat.
>
> —*Harry McLaughlin*

Hollywood has certainly not produced its last *Titanic* movie—the next one may have its origins in this exercise.

Unit 4: Letters from the SS *Glencairn*

Between 1915 and 1917, O'Neill wrote four one-act plays set on and around a tramp steamer, the SS *Glencairn*. Although not originally written as a quartet, the four plays share some of the same characters and a similar setting. In 1924 they were first performed together, and have successfully been revived as such many times. O'Neill based many of the characters on men he got to know on his several trips as a merchant seaman. In 1911, he shipped on the British steamer *Ikala*—the model for the *Glencairn*—from Buenos Aires to New York, and later that year he also worked on two passenger liners, the *New York* and the *Philadelphia*.

These four plays are the best of his early one-act dramas. The characters and situations are both believable and engaging. High school students are quick to understand the hierarchy of life on board ships and the inevitable outcome of the characters' actions.

Moon of the Caribbees—synopsis
The tramp steamer SS *Glencairn* is at anchor off the coast of a Caribbean port. Driscoll, one of the sailors, has arranged for a group of bumboat women to come on board. Along with the fruit and other items the bumboat women are permitted to sell, they will smuggle forbidden alcohol in their baskets. After some of the men get drunk, a fight starts that engulfs the entire crew. One of the seamen gets stabbed. The captain and his mate break up the fight and send the women to shore without paying them.

Bound East for Cardiff—synopsis
Onboard the SS *Glencairn*, Yank, one of the crew members, is severely injured falling down an open hatch. Carried to his bunk, his shipmates recognize how precarious his situation is. When most of the seamen have to go on watch, Yank's friend Driscoll remains with him. They reminisce about the years they have been together at sea. Yank realizes he is dying and asks Driscoll to take care of distributing his pay and effects. Just before he dies, Yank sees "a pretty lady dressed in black."

In the Zone—synopsis
The SS *Glencairn* is carrying ammunition during World War I. Blackout conditions are strictly enforced, and the crew is worried about the ship's position being betrayed by spies. They are especially wary about Smitty, a crew member who came on board in South Africa. He is not like the rest of them—educated and antisocial, he has a secret locked box that he hides under his mattress. The crew is convinced that he is a spy. They tie him up, take his keys and open the black metal box. Inside are letters from his former fiancée, who abandoned him because he could not stay away from alcohol.

The Long Voyage Home—synopsis
The SS *Glencairn* has docked in England, and one of its long-time crew members, Olsen, has decided to return home to Sweden. His friends are determined that he not get drunk, yet they want to celebrate. They enter a seedy waterfront pub, but only allow Ollie, as he is called, to drink ginger beer. While his friends are in another room, Ollie gets friendly with a young woman, Freda, at the bar. When Freda finds out he is not drinking alcohol, she slips a drug into his drink. When he passes out, several men carry him out. The proprietor tells them to take him to the *Amindra*, a ship known for its poor conditions, which is in need of crew members. He steals the two years' pay from Ollie's jacket and tells the thugs to be sure and get his first month's pay from the captain of the *Amindra*. When his friends come back, the proprietor tells them Ollie has gone out with Freda.

I introduce these plays to students with John Ford's 1940 movie *The Long Voyage Home*. Based on the four plays, the film features a young John Wayne as the Swedish sailor Olsen, replete with Swedish accent. Unlike some of his static later plays, the sailor life O'Neill depicts in these four contains a lot of action, which lends itself well to cinematography. O'Neill considered the Ford film the best Hollywood adaptation of any of his work.[6] Ford followed O'Neill's texts closely, although he did make some changes, shortening the expositions and updating the action to World War II. He also added shots of the ship at sea, which could never be introduced into a stage production.

The movie is useful in the classroom for several reasons. It provides a visual reference for the cramped living quarters and shows firsthand the gulf between officers and seamen. It also helps students hear O'Neill's written dialects. Whereas other playwrights would write in standard English and explain in the stage directions about characters' accents, O'Neill wrote out the dialects phonetically, which can be difficult for students to get used to. Additionally, the movie script removes the racial references in O'Neill's original.

Over several days, I show the first section of the movie, *The Moon of the Caribbees*, then have the students act out *Bound East for Cardiff* and *In the Zone*, and then do both with *The Long Voyage Home*. We focus on analyzing the characters in preparation for students to write their own plays. I ask students to imagine they are one of O'Neill's characters, and then to write letters to their families and friends about life on board ship.

Here are some sample letters:

Dear Sister Julie,
It has been such a long journey. I would do anything to be away from here and be with you. Nothing compares to being home. However, being a sailor is not so bad, it is just that right now we are in a war zone and I'm very scared that any minute they may sink the boat. Therefore, I try to keep calm—if it is God's will that I must die, then let it be. So, many miles away from home, I just wish I was near Julie. I would just swim—ha, ha. Dear one, I'm so scared, but happy. I became a sailor—something I always wanted to be since I was a child—but I'm scared of death. I will be writing soon. Let Mama and Papa know I love them. Goodbye Julie. . . .
    —Angel

    —*Angelica Rivera*

Dear Maria,
Life is tough on the SS *Glencairn*. People around here are edgy because of the war. Dave said three ships following our route have been sunk. I am scared.

One night, during a blackout, we could hear a nearby ship being destroyed by a German U-boat. They hadn't turned all their lights off. We could hear the screams and explosion from our location. Luckily, we were far enough away that the explosion's light didn't give us away.

I would love to be eating in a little café in New York City with you right now. I love you very much. Adieu. . . .

—*Dennis Sitarevich*

Dear Victor,

I'm just writing to tell you the news that happened on the SS *Glencairn* today.

Well, a couple of sailors thought that one sailor by the name of Smitty was a spy and that he had a bomb to blow up the ship. Jack, Davis, Cocky, and Scotty all thought that it was a bomb in the black box until they opened it and found out that it was letters from his girlfriend ending their relationship. While they were looking through these letters, they tied Smitty up. All the sailors felt stupid and had to let Smitty go. All the guys felt bad and said that they were sorry. I'll write again with more stupid things that the sailors do on the SS *Glencairn*.

—*Stacy Cortes*

Unit V: Writing One-Act Plays

Now that the students have read and responded to a number of O'Neill's one-act plays, they are ready to write their own. I begin this component by having students go back and analyze the plays we have just read, using Freytag's Pyramid. Gustav Freytag, a nineteenth-century German literary scholar, devised a graphic means of depicting the action in drama, basing his work mainly on Greek tragedy and the plays of Shakespeare. Since O'Neill was strongly influenced by both Shakespeare (his father worshiped the Bard) and the Greeks (his oldest son became a classics professor), Freytag's guidelines provide a particularly good means of examining O'Neill's plays. Freytag depicted dramatic structure as a triangle (not really a pyramid), with the climax of the play at the apex. The elements of the drama are as follows:[7]

> 1. *Exposition*: tells the audience what happened before the play began.
> 2. *Complication*: the part of a plot in which the entanglement caused by the conflict of opposing forces is developed; also called the rising action.
> 3. *Climax*: the turning point in the action, the crisis at which the rising action turns and becomes the falling action. In a five-act tragedy, this usually occurs at the end of the third act.
> 4. *Falling Action or Resolution*: the various plot lines begin to come together.
> 5. *Denouement*: the unraveling of the plot of the play.

These can be indicated graphically:

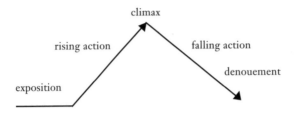

In most of O'Neill's early plays, these elements are easy to find. The one exception is *Bound East for Cardiff*, in which the climax (Yank's death) occurs just before the end of the play, allowing for very little denouement. After we analyze one play together, I have the students work in groups, assigning each group a different play and telling them to apply Freytag's pyramid to it. Each group then reports their findings back to the class.

After this, students are ready to write their own one-act plays. I use the following framework to guide them, having them begin with the middle of the play, after which they write the end and then the beginning. Before beginning the dialogue, I have them write detailed scenarios—this is a technique O'Neill learned from his teacher, George Pierce Baker.[8] The other thing that needs to be pointed out to students is how to weave the elements of the exposition into the dialogue. Many students include narrators in their first drafts; this must be avoided.

Handout: Writing a One-Act Play

1. Invent a character.
2. Make two lists—one of the character's physical characteristics (tall, blue-eyes, etc.), the other of mental characteristics (happy, mean, sly, etc.).
3. Figure out the conflict—will it be a conflict with another character, a conflict with nature, a conflict with society?
4. Figure out the climax of the story.
5. Plot out the events leading up to the climax.
6. Figure out the denouement.
7. Figure out what has to be included in the exposition.
8. Write a scenario (outline) of everything that happens. Make it as specific as possible, as the more work you do here, the easier it will be to write the dialogue.
9. Write the dialogue.
10. Go back and insert stage directions and any other necessary data.
11. Make a list of the characters and other necessary information.
12. Hold a reading to make sure your play works as theater.
13. Revise where necessary.

In my experience, once students understand the procedure for writing a play, they have little trouble actually doing it. Doing it extremely well, however, is another matter; historically, the first efforts of even the most successful dramatists have been problematic. However, all playwrights need to begin somewhere, and high school is an excellent place to start. There they can work under the guidance of a teacher and have access to a pool of willing actors to try out their efforts.[9] Many of my students have written plays based, like O'Neill's, on their own lives. With such an intimate connection with the subject matter, they can create passionate drama.

Unit VI: "Life Doesn't Give Us Happy Endings"

Around the time O'Neill was writing his early one-act plays, his landlady, Helen Rippin, asked him why he always gave his plays such depressing conclusions. He replied, "Life doesn't give us happy endings."[10]

As the final project of their study of O'Neill, I ask students to react to this quotation. While some choose to write a "traditional" literary essay, others decide to respond creatively, writing poems or playlets. One student even tried his hand at rhyme:

Everywhere I turn,
Everything I see,
I feel I'm being spurned,
Because death is stalking me.

If you were forced to kill someone,
In the heat of battle or the glare of the day by the sun,
You have chosen to force his life gone,
But you, my friend, have not won.

One can never see where life is going
In the endless, surreal fog.
You can go in any direction without knowing
That you are stuck in a bog.

When you know your life no longer can bear,
And your soul and will are bending,
You know it is because despair is everywhere
And life doesn't give us happy endings.

—*Dennis Sitarevich*

Bibliography

Achity, Kenneth, with Chi-Li Wong. *Writing Treatments That Sell.* New York: Henry Holt, 1997.
Baker, George Pierce. *Dramatic Technique.* New York: Da Capo Press, 1919; reprinted 1976.
Bernardi, Philip. *Improvisation Starters.* Cincinnati, Ohio: Betterway Books, 1992.
Biel, Steven. *Titanica.* New York: Norton, 1998.
Black, Stephen. *Eugene O'Neill: Beyond Mourning and Tragedy.* New Haven, Conn.: Yale University Press, 1999.
Floyd, Virginia. *Eugene O'Neill at Work.* New York: Frederick Ungar, 1981.
Freytag, Gustav. *Technique of the Drama.* Translated by Elias J. MacEwan. Chicago: Scott, Foresman, 1904.
Gelb, Arthur, and Barbara Gelb. *O'Neill: Life with Monte Cristo.* New York: Applause Books, 2000.
Manheim, Michael, editor. *The Cambridge Companion to Eugene O'Neill.* Cambridge, England: Cambridge University Press, 1998.
Muschla, Gary. *Writing Workshop Survival Kit.* West Nyack, N.Y.: Center for Applied Research in Education, 1993.
O'Neill, Eugene. *Complete Plays.* Three volumes. New York: The Library of America, 1988.
Schaeffer, Louis. *O'Neill: Son & Playwright.* New York: Paragon House, 1968.

Videography

Hughie. RKO Home Video, 1994.
The Long Voyage Home. Warner Home Video, 1968, 35076.
Titanic: End of an Era. Madacy Entertainment Group, Inc., 1998, TTC-3-8362-2.

Notes

1. There is an excellent mini-lesson, with handouts, on teaching journalistic style in Gary Muschla, *Writing Workshop Survival Kit*, pp. 108–110.
2. Their writings can be found in Biel's *Titanica.*

3. O'Neill wrote another play dealing with a shipwreck, *Thirst*. However, its tropical setting gives it less in common with the *Titanic* disaster than the other two.

4. Samples of treatments can be found in Kenneth Atchity, *Writing Treatments That Sell*.

5. *Titanic: End of an Era*.

6. See Kurt Eisen, "O'Neill on Screen," in *The Cambridge Companion to Eugene O'Neill*, pp. 116–134, for a discussion of movies based on O'Neill's plays.

7. These elements are discussed at length in Gustav Freytag, *Technique of the Drama*.

8. Baker devotes a chapter to writing scenarios in his book *Dramatic Technique*. Examples of O'Neill's scenarios can be found in Virginia Floyd, *Eugene O'Neill at Work*.

9. There are many contests for student dramatists, the most prominent being that conducted by Young Playwrights, Inc., an organization founded by Stephen Sondheim to encourage school-age authors. Contact www.youngplaywrights.org for more information.

10. Printed in Stephen Black, *Eugene O'Neill: Beyond Mourning and Tragedy*, p. 154.

Zora Neale Hurston

Catherine Barnett

Square Toes and Icy Arms
Zora Neale Hurston and Personification

"Is anger a man or a woman?" I asked a student in class last week. The young woman—she is sixteen and has a one-year-old son—thought for a long moment, about to give up. "Tell me what Anger looks like," I asked, "where he or she lives. Close your eyes and tell me everything you know about this character." I roamed around the classroom, and when I made it back to her desk, she had written:

> Anger's hands are hammers. His teeth are two-edged swords. His head is made of stone. Anger has no face, just two beady little eyes. His eyebrows always hang low. Anger tastes bitter.

This exchange took place during one of my favorite exercises. The student's writing owes its energy and power to passages from Zora Neale Hurston's autobiography, *Dust Tracks on a Road*, and her novel *Their Eyes Were Watching God*. Throughout these works, Hurston personifies both the fictional and real worlds, turning philosophical concepts (like time and fate), life passages (like death), and even the weather into active characters.

In *Their Eyes*, she uses an unusual personification to describe the damage wrought by a flood: "Havoc was there with her mouth wide open." The overflowing lake itself takes on human characteristics: thunder "woke up old Okechobee and the monster began to roll in his bed. Began to roll and complain like a peevish world on a grumble. . . . The people felt uncomfortable but safe because there were the seawalls to chain the senseless monster in his bed." Hurston gives the sun a distinct personality throughout the novel. Janie, the main character, goes to bed one night filled with doubt about her new husband, Tea-Cake, who had disappeared with her money. It is the sun who first reassures her:

> Janie dozed off to sleep but she woke up in time to see the sun sending up spies ahead of him to mark out the road through the dark. He peeped up over the door sill of the world and made a little foolishness with red. But

pretty soon, he laid all that aside and went about his business dressed all in white.

Night, too, takes on human characteristics in Hurston's Florida: "Night was striding across nothingness with the whole round world in his hands."

In *Dust Tracks on a Road*, Hurston writes that "fate was watching us and laughing," and that Hurston herself has "been in Sorrow's kitchen and licked out all the pots." In an unpublished chapter, Hurston personifies Time, calling him "hungry" as he "squats" and "waits." She sees his footprints, and gazes into his reflections:

> His frame was made out of emptiness, and his mouth set wide for prey. Mystery is his oldest son, and power is his portion. For it was said on the day of first sayings that Time should speak backward over his shoulder, and none should see his face. . . .

Death makes a dramatic appearance in both Hurston's novel and in her autobiography. In *Their Eyes*, Janie encounters Death as she watches her husband grow weak:

> So Janie began to think of Death. Death, that strange being with the huge square toes who lived way in the West. The great one who lived in a straight house like a platform without sides to it, and without a roof. What need has Death for a cover, and what winds can blow against him? He stands in his high house that overlooks the world. Stands watchful and motionless all day with his sword drawn back, waiting for the messenger to bid him come. Been standing there before there was a where or a when or a then. She was liable to find a feather from his wings lying in her yard any day now. . . .

In a deft 100 words, Hurston manages to give the idea of death a home, gestures, a history, feathers, and flesh.

Those eerie square toes reappear in her autobiography as she describes the day her mother died. Hurston was nine years old and no match against "that two-headed spirit that rules the beginning and end of things called Death."

> The Master-Maker in His making had made Old Death. Made him with big, soft feet and square toes. Made him with a face that reflects the face of all things, but neither changes itself, nor is mirrored anywhere. Made the body of Death out of infinite hunger. Made a weapon for his hand to satisfy his needs. . . . Death had no home and he knew it at once. . . . He was already old when he was made... . Death finished his prowling through the house on his padded feet and entered the room. He bowed to Mama. . . .

Try reading either of these passages aloud—several times over—to a class of students and see how the room quiets. I've read Hurston's work to fourth, fifth, and sixth graders, and to a group of teen mothers. Something about those square toes and that feather—you can see it sailing slowly to the inevitable ground—stops chatter and commands attention.

I like to give the students examples of personification from other writers, if time allows. A poem titled "Go Down Death," by James Weldon Johnson (who with his brother composed "Lift Every Voice and Sing," a song once known as the Negro national anthem), complements Hurston's prose. Death appears in the third stanza of Johnson's poem:

> And that tall, bright angel cried in a voice
> That broke like a clap of thunder:
> Call Death!—Call Death!
> And the echo sounded down the streets of heaven
> Till it reached away back to that shadowy place,
> Where Death waits with his pale, white horses.
>
> And Death heard the summons,
> And he leaped on his fastest horse,
> Pale as a sheet in the moonlight.
> Up the golden street Death galloped,
> And the hoof of his horse struck fire from the gold,
> But they didn't make no sound

Later in the poem, Johnson writes that Death "didn't say a word, / But he loosed the reins on his pale, white horse / And he clamped the spurs to his bloodless sides. . . . And the foam from his horse was like a comet in the sky." At the end of this poem, Death cradles a smiling woman in his "icy arms."

The contrasts between Hurston's and Johnson's personifications help students realize that there is no "right" way to treat something that is as universal as death. And the simple fact that both writers end up with such peculiar and striking images—that Death can take such different guises, unique to each writer's vision—leads the class naturally to an all-important discussion of clichés and how to avoid them. The best way to get around clichés, I tell students (and myself), is to be as specific as possible. Two fifth graders' efforts with this exercise provide good examples of how to dig beneath the surface of clichés. One girl began with a stereotype, defining "courage" rather than personifying it. "Courage," she wrote, "is a brave person who is not afraid of anything." But as she worked she began to discover more about her character:

Courage is a man of human size. He wears a white t-shirt and tight blue jeans and has a beautiful voice. He is nineteen years old. He's 100 times stronger than any man. He can lift up the Empire State Building.

Imagining herself as Courage, another girl worked her way from the general—"I am invisible"—to the very specific:

I can only be seen in the dark. I sneak in people's houses when they are afraid. I calm them down by putting their hands on my heart. . . . I like to drink rain and eat five feet of clouds a day for breakfast, lunch, and dinner. I sleep underground where the ants live.

Along with my plea—this prayer! this push!—for specificity and detail comes another, equally essential to this (and every) exercise: include the five senses. Johnson's poem illustrates the power of sensory detail: his Death has those "icy arms," his horse is silent as it gallops down the gold street.

By now some students may be getting confused. Two Deaths, five senses, a dozen details—what's going on? If so, a brief discussion of personification is in order. "How and why give human traits to something as seemingly abstract as death?" I ask them. I encourage the students to name some other abstractions they might want to personify.

I often make this same mistake: at the mention of "abstract," faces go blank, so I simply ask the students for words they hear over and over— words they've heard so often they've lost their meaning. Words like death, love, happiness. What others? As a class, we create a list. Even though these words are universal, the lists reflect the make-up and concerns of each class. At a school in uptown Manhattan, for example, fifth graders thought of Trouble, Fear, Racism, Greed, and Courage. A class of teen mothers came up with Depression, Fatigue, and Ambition.

It is often a good idea to start by writing a group description. This loosens everybody up, and creates a mood for writing. The students choose which word they want to transform into a character; a group of teen mothers, for example, chose "Pain." I usually ask a few leading questions, borrowing heavily from Hurston and Johnson and encouraging students to bring the senses into their descriptions. With the teen mothers, responses came fast. "Pain," they said (as I wrote their words on the blackboard),

wears dirty sneakers and a black sweatshirt. He lives on the corner of your block, an unwanted visitor. He has gold teeth, an afro, dirty fingernails. He never uses condoms. His voice is rusty, scratchy, screechy. He says, "I love you, I love you, I love you. Hi Baby. Suffer. You look good." He tastes like lime and hot sweat. His face feels like alligator skin. He has calluses all over his feet. He's afraid of losing honor.

Soon I ask each student to choose his or her own word from the long list of words on the board and to create a living, breathing character out of it.

"You never hear Fatigue," wrote one fifteen-year-old mother who had given birth six weeks earlier. "He is so quiet and smooth. He comes to you like thirst and leaves like wind. He touches the weakest part of your body, which is your eyes. He lives anywhere he wants to live. . . ." Her friend, also the mother of a young boy, discovered a very different Fatigue:

> Fatigue drags her feet all day. Her shoes make a scraping sound against the ground and whenever she passes by someone they yawn. She carries a pillow and blanket in a shopping cart, along with a clown. When she pulls the clown's chord it plays "Rock-A-Bye Baby" and that soothes her. . . .
>
> Her voice is gentle and she is soft spoken. Her mellow voice will hypnotize you and make you sleepy. She always says Relax, don't work so hard, there's always tomorrow. . . .

Another young mother wrote a brief sketch of Ambition, a woman who "walks with her head high":

> She wears yellow. When you look at her she slows and dazzles in front of your eyes. Her hair and nails are always neatly done. . . . She carries a crystal rock in her pocket. She always says believe in yourself and you can do anything.

A fourth grader with learning disabilities described Fear as someone who "brings a warrant made out of fire." Peace, wrote one of his classmates, "is a lady with love written all over her." Love is always a popular figure in this exercise, and appears in many guises. One defiant fifth grade boy surprised his classmates with his portrait of Love as a man who carries a suitcase:

> He smells like apples. He wears black pants, a white t-shirt, white shiny shoes. . . . In his suitcase he carries presents for his wife and love poems. He has friends who say, "We care about you." He gives everyone presents and sometimes says "I love you." Every day he goes to church and prays.

Two third grade girls came up with very different pictures of Love. "Love is when the sky turns blue," wrote one shy girl. "She comes knocking on my door quietly. Then she calls my name five times. And I say, 'Who is it? Who is it? Who is it?'" Her classmate saw Love as a boy.

"When I hug him," she wrote, "it feels like his eye has heaven in it." At a neighboring desk, a boy wrote about "Anger, a man with a black robe":

> His eyes are strange. One of them is black and one of them is brown. When he touches the ground it cracks. He goes down into the ground and says, "Come, Michael, Come." And I follow him to the underground. I see angry faces. I was saying, "It can't be true. It can't be true. It can't be true." And everything in the underground faded and he said, "Please don't leave me. Please, Please."

Happiness, wrote another third grader, "looks like my grandmother. She is wearing black pants and a black shirt. She is carrying presents. She lights candles."

After reading aloud the Hurston or Johnson excerpt (or both), you might choose a few of the following personification sketches by third, fourth, and fifth grade students to demonstrate how others have transformed words like Wealth, Jealousy, and Sadness into characters of their own.

> Wealth is somebody who is dressed in a polka-dot suit. I call him when me and my sister need some cash in our stash. When he comes to give us money he drops a gold coin on the ground. And then he throws a sack of money to each of us. His teeth are yellow and his face is green and his eyes are blue, and his ears are flat but oval shaped. All the time in his pockets he has gold coins. Real gold coins. And he never spends his money. He saves it up all the time.

> Jealousy goes around looking at things that other people have that he wants. He is always jealous of the clothes they wear, the things they carry out. He mumbles to himself, "I wish I had that," with a frown on his face. I always see him at the bakery buying a muffin. When he sees me he says, "Get out of my way, kid, you bother me!" I don't know what he has in his suitcase, but people say he carries a dead bird in there. I think he keeps it for good luck.

> Sadness has sad, big, blue eyes and skinny lips. He smells like the breeze in the sun. He has a deep low voice. He is never happy and he carries a broken heart in his hand. You can see him in the alleys at night. He is very skinny and has little toes. He wears only a worn-out suit.

> Joy looks like an elf. He wears a green overcoat and green tight pants. He carries many, many presents. His voice is very high and screechy. He has white hair and a long beard. You can find him on special occasions.

> Sadness just came to my house. All she did was ask for sugar, but she looked so sad her eyes were watery. . . . She told me her daughter just died. She got hit by a car. And she could remember when she held her in her arms when

she was born. The old lady has bags on her eyes. She has a cane. She was leaning on me crying.

This exercise acquaints students with Hurston's work and with the technique of personification, and it can also lead them to their best writing. The pleasure of reading Hurston's prose aloud is soon matched by that of listening to the students read their own. Their images are often so strong that their descriptions—like Hurston's—approach the intensity and lyricism of prose poems.

Bibliography

Hurston, Zora Neale. *Folklore, Memoirs, and Other Writings.* New York: The Library of America, 1995.

———. *Novels and Stories.* New York: The Library of America, 1995.

Johnson, James Weldon. "Go Down Death." In *American Negro Poetry.* Edited by Arna Bontemps. New York: HarperCollins, 1996.

Jean Toomer

Julie Patton

Cane in the Classroom

Teaching Jean Toomer

SOME TEXTS RESONATE so deeply within us that we never forget their
haunting spaces. So we read them again and again, to ourselves and to
others. This is what I do with Jean Toomer's *Cane*. Published in 1923,
Cane is a seed-book at the root of modern American poetics, memorable
for its striking language and rich, sensual imagery, and its alternation of
prose vignettes and poems.

> Oracular.
> Redolent of fermenting syrup,
> Purple of the dusk,
> Deep-rooted cane.

These lines from *Cane* describe the close connection between a people and their environment, people the color of *caramel, oak leaves on young
trees, gold glowing,* and *dark purple ripened plums,* immersed in their environment in a manner reminiscent of Brueghel's peasants. This in-
termingling of ground and figure in *Cane* invites us to explore the
relationship between humans and their environment, between language
and place. Sugar cane forms the background of Toomer's text. His characters are steeped in cane, their lives tied to the slow-motion grind of it,
and rage at the boiling point:

> The scent of cane came from the copper pan and drenched the forest and
> the hill that sloped to the factory town, beneath its fragrance. It drenched
> the men in circle seated around the stove. Some of them chewed at the white
> stalks, but there was no need for them to, if all they wanted was to taste the
> cane.

Everyone breathes this air; it colors the speech, thickens the tongue,
and extends the southern drawl.

Toomer's lush stream of consciousness pulls us into a particular time
and place that surge with the rhythm of a people trying to get a foothold.
In this sense, *Cane* echoes the African diaspora: "The dixie pike has grown

from a goat path in Africa." But Toomer focuses on another mass odyssey, that of black people to the big cities of the north. The reader is awash in this critical moment, the south-to-north migration of a group so held in limbo that contemporary African-American literature still holds this pattern between its teeth. The seasons and internal rhythms of the agrarian past comes through in the work of Toni Morrison, Alice Walker, Zora Neale Hurston, and Jamaica Kincaid. On the other hand, James Baldwin, Ishmael Reed, Paul Beatty, Richard Wright, Walter Mosley, and Ann Petry seem to be the gate-keepers of the urban. *Cane* mirrors the same dichotomy. The north frames a largely male domain, while the American south is associated with nature and the fecundity of women:

> And when the wind is in the south, soil of my homeland falls like a fertile shower upon the lean streets of the city.

In *Cane*, city and country, male and female, dawn and dusk, and black and white are a space apart, but Toomer makes it clear that each informs or resonates in the other. Some of my Harlem and South Bronx students trace a similarly alternating pattern. I can tell which ones hopscotch between South Carolina and Manhattan, Mexico or Puerto Rico and the Bronx: traces of these places show up in their vocabularies.

I read *Cane* to my students to provoke the creative writing impulse in them, but I have another motive as well. Like Toomer, I view writing as a potential nature preserve for endangered voices. Toomer wanted to articulate a future for a world facing extinction. Decrying the devastation of the pastoral world and the folk culture that was tied to it, he scored his memories of them into *Cane* as if its pages were another kind of earth, a field of view for preserving that world. Yet *Cane* is not a nostalgic lament for the segregated, sharecropper South, with its painfully oppressive conditions; it is an affirmation of the historical, cultural, and spiritual significance of a nation at a pivotal point in its history, faced with escalating industrialization.

> Red soil and sweet-gum tree
> So scant of grass
> So profligate of pines
> Now just before an epoch's sun declines.

In the Toomer poem "Song of the Son," the "son of the soil" returns to remind "a song-lit race of slaves" about the roots he fears they'll lose in city streets:

Though late, O soil, it is not too late yet
To catch thy plaintive soul, leaving soon gone . . .

Cane's characters live in close contact with the land because they are tied to it, yoked to the earth they sweat over and till. The enforced cutting of cane in the sharecropper South left a deep mark, another incision branding the skin of the so-called children of Cain. In this book, plum-dark women hold forth against a blood-burning moon, people and earth re-figure themselves, change shapes in the dark. Life in *Cane* is not romantic or idealized. It is often oppressive, violent, and terrifying. People disappear under the cover of a darkness Toomer refuses to cloak his own identity in, as he insists on blurring the color lines, or "passing" in a world that *Cane*'s dusk-colored Karintha would never be allowed access to: "Her skin is like dusk on the eastern horizon."

The blurring of borders in *Cane* echoes the dreamy edges that all poetry encourages: a migration of meaning, as in this poem by Michael Spann, a Harlem fourth grader, written in response to hearing passages from *Cane*:

I find the chains of my ancestors and the underground railroad
a stair of broken wood-stack of stairs.
this is how they got out.
A big clear hot sky. There is no moon or stars. It is black out.
We light candles. As you come from the doctor it gets dark.
It's time to go home.
You sing and count plump sheep to go to sleep and have a red wobbled
    dream.

Like Elegba, the Yoruba trickster god, Toomer is always at a crossroads. He is the writer as nomad, searching for a deeper, more oneiric place of being, outside the identifying labels attached to an uprooted people. He is hell-bent on making a place out of a non-place, enclosing a space to be. He backtracks over the same words, the same scenes, as if digging deeper to make a receptive space for others to live in, as well.

*   *   *

People tend to read black literature for its sociological content and ignore its aesthetic achievement. Experts argue about which texts are most relevant to the black experience, which ones constitute an "authentic black experience" for children, and which authors should represent African America and which should not. Entire legacies are oversimplified, homogenized into sound bites everyone can chew on. (One such "expert" once informed me that the writing of many of my Harlem students wasn't "black enough.") I wrote about some related concerns in my teaching diary:

> *Hic sunt leones* ("Here there are lions") was the designation used by Renaissance cartographers to indicate unknown, unexplored, and unmapped corners of the world—the vanishing point they directed their imaginations toward. The contemporary "inner city" conjures up a similarly forbidding terrain, with high walls and monsters sitting at the portals. The graffiti on the walls are the disembodied voice of a culture, echoing the fragmentation and dissolution of a community. I know firsthand how language can carve up the city streets, dismember and disembody the civitas. I can recall when another designation first skirted the edges of the place I called home. The word *ghetto* hovered about our heads for years before finally settling down on them. I remember asking my mother what they called the turf she inhabited as a youth. She said, "Oh, they just called it 'neighborhood.'"

But language can enable children to re-site themselves, to renew and enrich our civitas. In many ways, imaginative writing gives students the tools to root their lives in a different landscape of meaning and address, tools to challenge and complicate language.

In the classroom, I do not shy away from bringing in literature that is "above" or "beyond" my students, provided that it is charged and evocative. I read aloud to them, walking around the classroom, bearing down on specific words to instill a dreamy and sometimes mysterious atmosphere, going on Gaston Bachelard's assumption that "the best training for poets is achieved through reverie, which puts us in sympathy with words and with substances."

> O R A T O R S. Born one an I'll die one . . . Been shapin words t fit my soul. Never told y that before, did I? Thought I couldnt talk. I'll tell y. I've been shapin words; ah, but sometimes theyre beautiful and golden an have a taste that makes them fine t roll over with y tongue.

I read parts of *Cane* to my elementary school students for a variety of reasons: to steep them in listening, to call attention to Toomer's imaginative use of language, or simply to fill the room with startling images. Of course I skip over the earthier passages, but it doesn't matter, since I am not emphasizing narrative.

I jump-start one imaginative writing exercise by using my voice to highlight a vocabulary that will sensitize my students to their surroundings, seizing details in the passage that emphasize the fact that the city (in our case, New York) is also land:

Through the cement floor her strong roots sink down. They spread under the asphalt streets. Dreaming, the streets roll over on their bellies, and suck their glossy health from them. Her strong roots sink down and spread under the river and disappear in blood lines that waver south. Her roots shoot down.

In reading *Cane* aloud, I project certain words the way a painter dabs on color. *Boll weevils, dew, knolls, dusk, cotton-stalks,* and *pines* dot the landscape. *Cane* is perfectly scored for the ear, and I read it as a background text before giving an imaginative writing exercise that simply focuses on the associations and meaning inherent in the sounds of single words. We start with the familiar *clouds, flower, rain, tree, pigeon,* etc., then move on to *mountain, forest, river* (things that are absent from the city). I don't explain much, I simply urge my students to *listen* to each word, to *see* what it is trying to tell them through the sounds, and to *notice* the shape and feel of the word in their mouths. Some words have a music, an inner mystery or depth that attracts the students, and they fall into the mysterious words, spend a long time contemplating them. I also emphasize the idea that the world speaks and inscribes itself in myriad ways. The children count the ways—trees "tell us" the seasons, deer and birds leave tracks we can trace, rivers babble, and rain rains.

Contemplating a certain word as both noun and verb introduces students to the idea that houses *house* us, clouds *cloud*, and rain definitely *rains*, and this prepares them for a writing process that underscores the idea of movement in a particular word's journey; otherwise students often end up with static poems instead of complex, shifting ones. Because Toomer's characters are elusive, I read *Cane* beforehand to establish the groundwork for this sense of movement. In any case, the students approach the assignment with the imperative of listening to a given word and thinking about what it does or about its impact on their lives. *Cloud, dusk, fern, rose,* or *snow.*

When I was a child, the "doing" words in my reader, *Skip Along*, were particularly inspiring. *Run, skip, hop.* There was something compelling about the fact that we were bombarded with "doing" words while anchored to our seats. *Come here . . . See my . . . Look up* always pointed to the outside world. The interplay between those commands and my own imagination made me leap, and I eagerly anticipated going outside to do all the thrilling things watercolor children and lithographed animals were engaged in all day long. But, as a visiting writer, I don't bring in childhood readers, I bring in the literature that tumbles from my own shelves, even grown-ups' books such as *Cane.* I trust that the hop, skip, and jump of my students' minds can help span the distance. The following poems by third graders at Harlem's P.S. 30 are proof of their ability to do this:

A Herd of Stars

I am a star
I have talked to the sky
I've shaken hands with the sun
But I only come out at night
I shine through the windows of planes that fly by
I shine on the birds that flap their wings at night
How do I see such things?
I work my way through by shining
But how do I shine?
I am mixed in a herd of stars
At night
I see the rain or snow fall
I do not speak
But if you listen very closely
you will hear my mind
I can see through the moon when it passes through the sky
I don't see everything, I just remember

I can hear the balloon float in the air from a child's hand
I can hear the rain come across the soft clouds
I can hear the groundhog fighting its shadow
I can hear the deep sea waving
I can hear the cries when I am reading a poem

I can hear the worm wriggle across the ground
waiting for a chick to come and eat it
I can hear the snowflakes tugging on a tree
I can hear tiny creatures trying to find a home
I can hear the silence

   —*Leonor Moody*

Listen to the Mystery
Listen to
The voice of water when
The water splashes
        to put out a fire
Listen
to a loud roar of water putting out fire
Listen to the mystery
   that hasn't been solved yet
Listen
        to the voice of the river crying

because it is in the palm of my right hand
Listen to the voice of water
    crying because it is hot and on fire
Listen to the voice of a
pencil when it is losing its head for you
    to write on
When
the point of your pencil breaks
It tells you,
"Use another pencil,
I'm tired."

    —*Jamal Johnson*

Silent World

When I am dreaming
I hear darkness switching to daylight
I can't see the wind but I can hear it

I hear the sun rattling in the day and the
moon shining at night time
I can hear my bed when I am jumping on it

I can hear chalk writing on a chalkboard
I can hear the trees shake

I can hear the flag saying hello to me
I can hear the other countries get together
and chatter

I can hear God singing in the blue sky He doesn't scream

He sings in a nice low voice just so that I can hear him.

    —*Jamal Johnson*

The Baby's Heart

Remember the shadows
of the sky
Think of the wonderful
things that happen to you
Listen to the cradle that rocks the baby's heart
Hold the soul
of the baby's cries
Recall all the things
that happen to you

Romantic evenings, suffering, pain,
sorrow and death
Listen to the call of the trees
when it rocks your heart to sleep
The cradle that is still
rocking in the baby's heart
Listen, listen
closely to the baby's cries
Hear the wind speaking to the sun
saying sun, sun
Shine harder so I can melt but I am not really dead
But sun, O sun, keep on shining
so you and I can hear the melting sounds of me
Listen to the winds that blow
Melt the baby's
heart away
He will cry, I will cry
But the sorrow never ends

So, wind, blow, O wind, blow
so softly that we can hear the baby's
heart melt away
So wind, wind,
Dear old wind,
blow that baby's heart away

   —Robert Yates

Why do you
come out

At night
You're yellow

and bumpy
at night

You, like
glass in the sky

Why do you come
down

You, like
part of the sun

Part and grow

a wishing star

Wish your way
home

Go your way the dark
bark moon

   —*José Sullivan*

The Rain Is Falling

Hear me
the earth

Hear me
and the rain

A star
that's talking

the rain
falling

and jumping
Stars

are combing
their hair

in light
and going
to sleep

I talk to the rain
and stars

The rain crashing
and singing

The earth moving and the sky
darkening.

   —*Guillermo Colon*

*   *   *

I often use *Cane* in conjunction with another poet's work or to explore a
particular theme. The dictionary defines *cane* as a "thin reed used for

wickerwork or baskets," a perfect companion for Chilean poet Cecilia Vicuña's investigation into the weave as a metaphor for writing and the connections between things, which she highlights by interweaving her poems with photographs. Children are fascinated by Vicuña's sense of permission and fantasy. Her poetry is often about the connections between humans and nature, but her images resonate further than the usual sloganeering that children might encounter on Earth Day, because her images are drawn from everyday life. Like Toomer, Vicuña implies that nature has the potential to lead us back into a fuller communication with the world.

In Vicuña's *Unravelling Words and the Weaving of Water* there is an arresting image of clay snakes on a New York City water hydrant that point the way back to the sea. Students are also intrigued by Vicuña's image of trees filled with white yarn. Yoking, tying, binding, stitching, darning, knotting, and weaving are all related to the very ins and outs of writing, the loop-ti-loops children go through as they explore the links between themselves and the world, so that a ball in their hands suggests the sun and other round things, and eyes resemble stars.

My lifeless controller keys
keep me intact to my
big-headed man, the sky.

—*David Kaczynski, seventh grade*

I sprinkle the blackboard with the above-mentioned "weaving" words that proliferate in Vicuña's text, as well as other words that suggest the process of binding. Eventually we get to *glue*, *tape*, and *staples*, as is evident in the following poem:

I'm sticking to my mother like strange
glue. I love my mother like
hearts flying in the sky. Shiny
sky. Beautiful flower. You can guess
the most beautiful world.

The most beautiful people. Black
white, it's nothing. The color gray it's
a beautiful color. I'm looking for a
beautiful world.

I grow crazy weaves in my hair. Hair, hair,
no hair, hair looks like string I keep combining and

attaching. Sew new world, night
tie yellow rope looping along jump up yokes

—*Brenda Villot, fourth grade*

Poetry such as Vicuña's leaves an impression that things touch and fuse in strange conjunctions, as Ta'Donna Nagle, a fourth grader, in Harlem spelled out:

I will attach my legs
to a rooster
so it will know
it becomes morning
I will combine
a piece of
the world to a head
See if you can
find the difference
of the most
needed
I can attach a
needle into
the live skin of a
goat see
if it will run
jump stop
and cry or
be crammed
if I jump from
Earth to Venus
and sew
them together
one will fly
one will
be forced by
gravity

This poem emphasizes acts of will, empowerment, and possibility that underscore the very roots of the word *poesis* ("to make"). Ta'Donna repeatedly states *I will* while exploring connections we don't usually assume in everyday life. Suddenly we have worlds that didn't exist before, heaven and earth bound and unbound through transcendent leaps of the imagination. Ta'Donna's classmate Sabrina Valcarel, a child with a bent for challenging boundaries and edges throughout the normal classroom day, uses words associated with sewing, in a way that makes things seem totally integrated:

There it was
a girl
named Ta'Donna And she was
wearing a
woven shirt
my sister
has stitched
her head to
the bedspring in my garden

the leaves are grown, hide them
in a kite
my mother sewed my head to
the wall
because I
was very bad
I had attached
my friend's heart to my soul so
She won't
go nowhere

Seventh grader Brandon Pittman wrote this poem:

A Battle with Trees

My eyes
connecting to the beautiful sight
of the young woman before me
My hair
Woven together like a wool
Sweater
As tall as I am
I stand a battle with trees

In poetry, one can situate one unlikely thing next to another. Art accomodates the deviating paths, twists, and turns real life can't. The analogical curves and spirals of poetry counter the linear thinking that rules the classroom. In this sense, language is both a way of creating space and extending its margins.

Obviously, writing and reading go hand in hand, just as listening and spinning once did. I go from classroom to classroom just as the ancient storyteller went from village to village. In my imaginative writing workshops, I observe the same relationship between work rhythms and stories. The students spin their own "yarns" before or after my delivery of *Cane*. Walter Benjamin said that storytelling was never a job for the voice alone, that hands pick up the rhythm, and lace, thread, or pound it into the work. To me, writing is often about a recovery of lost human gestures. In my urban classrooms, the rhythm of the sewing needle is replaced by the rhythm of the pen, and "when the rhythm of work has seized [them], [they] listen to the tales in such a way that the gift of retelling them comes to [them] all by itself" (Benjamin).

The joy of reading *Cane* to children is ultimately about the art of repeating stories. Call and response—the dialogue continues as contemporary urban culture bears witness and testifies to the intimacy of the human voice and human gestures. Thousands of schoolchildren have opened their ears to the fresh cadence of writers in the schools such as June Jordan, Kurt Lamkin, Victor Hernández Cruz, Bernadette Mayer, Ron Padgett, Pedro Pietri, Grace Paley, Abiodun Oyewole, Wayne Providence, Janice Lowe, and others performing work that shores up distant voices in a new landscape of meaning. In *Cane*, many of my students hear speech rhythms that are akin to their own. Somewhere, inside the words, there's a pine-torched night punctuated by cries, yells, and whimpers that recall the voices of holy rollers or a wailing blues song. My reading of *Cane* emphasizes this sense of echo.

> Their voices rise . . . the pine trees are guitars,
> Strumming, pine needles fall like sheets of rain . . .
> Their voices rise . . . the chorus of cane

The alternation of prose and poetry and the persistent references to pine knots in *Cane* echo the culture of harvesting rituals:

> O Negro slaves, dark purple ripened plums
> Squeezed and bursting in the pine-wood air
>
> Pour O pour that parting soul in song,
> O pour it in the sawdust glow of night,
> Into the velvet pine-smoke air to night
> And let the valley carry it along

The lyrical patterns of *Cane* still reverberate in African-American music and poetry. In it we still hear the chant connecting distant bodies and continents, the relationship between body and speech in African work rhythms. And today's percussion-based rap is the banished talking drum beating an ancient meter and rhythm into a new language.

Bibliography

American Poetry: The Twentieth Century. Volume Two: E. E. Cummings to May Swenson. New York: The Library of America, 2000.

Bachelard, Gaston. *The Poetics of Space.* Translated by Maria Jolas. Boston: Beacon, 1969.

Benjamin, Walter. *Illuminations.* Translated by Harry Zahn. New York: Schocken, 1969.

Toomer, Jean. *Cane.* New York: Liveright, 1975.

Vicuña, Cecilia. *Unravelling Words and the Weaving of Water.* Translated by Eliot Weinberger. Minneapolis: Greywolf, 1991.

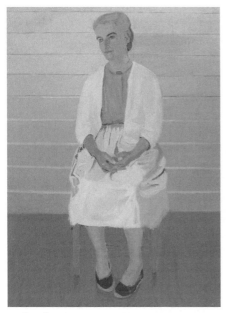

Anne Porter

Lorine Niedecker

Elizabeth Bishop

Mark Statman

Beauty, Urgency, Surprise

Teaching Poems by Anne Porter, Lorine Niedecker, and Elizabeth Bishop

FOR A NUMBER OF YEARS I've had a good time teaching the poems of Anne Porter, Lorine Niedecker, and Elizabeth Bishop. The three poets are rarely thought of together, and yet they seem linked to me by a striking kind of aesthetic independence. Anne Porter's literary connections are mainly with poets of the New York School. Yet Porter, born in 1911, married to the painter Fairfield Porter, is best known as a religious poet, displaying a kind of expression not usually associated with those writers. Niedecker (1903–1970), despite early associations with the Objectivists, especially Louis Zukofsky and Cid Corman, spent most of her life living in Wisconsin in a rural isolation that echoed her own disinterest in any single school of poetry. Bishop (1911–1979), whose friendships with poets Robert Lowell and Marianne Moore clearly influenced her writing, seems to have been equally, if not more, influenced by the many places she lived—Nova Scotia, New York City, Brazil, Key West—than by any kind of literary ethos.

What makes these three writers so interesting to teach is their common attentiveness to their immediate worlds. It is this sense of invitation and anticipation that makes these three poets so inspiring to bring into the classroom. Their poems challenge students to think and think hard. Their meditations on beauty, faith and God, the meaning of one's life, and the meaning of knowledge itself, demand rigorous thinking about poetry and the writing of poetry.

I.

> *My heart grows light*
> *As light as if the world*
> *Had never fallen.*
>
> —Anne Porter, "Listening to the Crows"

I am always struck by the depth and range of emotions and ideas that Anne Porter's poems provoke in my students. In a poetry that for all its artfulness is extraordinarily clear, Porter pays attention to the things of her world: family, place, memory, nature, and religion. In doing so, she shows us how to pay similar attention to our own worlds.

Porter's poems are blessedly simple to teach; I've had success teaching them to both elementary school students and college students. Before we read "In Childhood," for example, I begin with a class discussion of beauty. I ask my students, regardless of age, "Have you ever seen anything beautiful?" Younger students respond easily and enthusiastically: stars, moon, clouds, my mother's garden, the mountains, a New York City sunset, the glittering city at night. With my college students, my question is often met with the question, "What do you mean by 'beauty'?" These students are aware of the problems that come with the idea of beauty—for one, the skewed public perceptions that arise from media exposure. After some discussion, often intensely observant and personal, I ask them if there is any kind of consensus they think we can come to on this. Some students are happy to agree we all have own ideas about what beauty is, that beauty is something we recognize when we see it. I relate to them John Keats's closing lines to the "Ode on a Grecian Urn":

> 'Beauty is truth, truth beauty,'—that is all
> Ye know on earth, and all ye need to know.

If the class doesn't agree on this, I'll ask students to think about what beauty does for us. And here there is much more of a consensus. Beauty makes us see and feel things differently. The experience of beauty *changes us.*

I take the discussion one step further. "Has anyone ever shown you something beautiful?" "Of course." I ask them then to think about the difference between being shown beauty and finding it for themselves. Younger students talk about a time when they stumbled on something—in the park, at a museum, in their backyards—or a special moment shared with an older family member. Older students will talk about how sharing a beautiful moment creates a bond, how a shared experience deepens a relationship, in the present and for the future.

Then we read Porter's "In Childhood."

In Childhood

The first time
I saw the morning star
I was a small child
Two years old or three
I woke up sobbing

My mother came to me
Gathered me in her arms
And took me to the window
Look she said
There's the morning star

I soon gave over crying
For there it was alone
In the dawn sky
Bright and very beautiful
As beautiful as my mother.

This poem is about beauty, but also about memory and time. It's a classic Porter poem in its descriptions of a world filled with disparate things—night, sleeplessness, a child crying, the morning star, a mother—that become intimately and unexpectedly connected by the end of the poem. Students see in this poem a quality of beauty we haven't yet covered: that, while it can often remind us of the sadness of this world, it can also take away that sadness, if only for a short time.

The closing lines in particular intrigue my students. Often, when poets describe something beautiful, they use images from nature. Here, the star's beauty is reflected by the mother's beauty, a terrific reversal.

When I ask my students to write their own poems about beauty—either as something shared or something discovered solo—I tell them not to feel that their poems need to be about what beauty is or what they find beautiful. I remind them that starting with an idea often leads poets to unexpected places and that this is one of the most fun things about writing.

Here are three poems from young students:

The Sun

The sun sings to me
In the voices of the sky, trees birds and seas
The whales jump and play

The birds fly away
The monkeys jumping
Branch to branch
The lions roar after they get up
The grass swaying in a single

breeze

— *Kevin Collins, fourth grade*

The flowers start in the
beginning of spring.
Every flower grows with
joy.
The colorful flowers,
they are everywhere.
The flowers love to be happy.
Open it over the best.

— *Justin Flores, second grade*

The Growing Times

The puppies are growing in
the summer.
The caterpillars are turning
into cocoons and then into
butterflies.
The cubs are turning into
lions.
The eggs are going to tadpoles
then to frogs
The kids go to the goats.
The kittens are growing into cats.
I'm growing big like animals
in the forest.

— *Jordan Pacheco, second grade*

Two other Porter poems I like to teach, primarily with younger students, are "Getting Up Early" and "Looking at the Sky." They go well together with "In Childhood," as all three focus on the different appearances and effects that night can have on those who pay attention. To

Porter, knowledge of the world is something we must actively seek—we cannot be passive. In order to see the moon—to know this moon that is "gold in the grey of morning" and yet without life—we have to get up early.

Getting Up Early

Just as the night was fading
Into the dusk of morning
When the air was cool as water
When the town was quiet
And I could hear the sea

I caught sight of the moon
No higher than the roof-tops
Our neighbor the moon

An hour before the sunrise
She glowed with her own sunrise
Gold in the grey of morning

World without town or forest
Without wars or sorrows
She paused between two trees

And it was as if in secret
Not wanting to be seen
She chose to visit us
So early in the morning.

In "Looking at the Sky" that importance takes on a sense of urgency: we must act because there isn't enough time to do all the things in the world we wish we could.

Looking at the Sky

I never will have time
I never will have time enough
To say
How beautiful it is
The way the moon
Floats in the air
As easily
And lightly as a bird
Although she is a world
Made all of stone.

I never will have time enough
To praise
The way the stars
Hang glittering in the dark
Of steepest heaven
Their dewy sparks
Their brimming drops of light
So fresh so clear
That when you look at them
It quenches thirst.

This poem always interests my students with its unusual juxtapositions: here the stone moon is a floating thing, light as a bird. Unwritten, though clear, is the idea that moon and bird are of equal size as well. The stars, actually fiery hot, are fresh drops of light that quench thirst. But Porter's quiet urgency is what attracts students. I ask them about how that urgency figures in *their* lives. They respond by talking about time passing. Occasionally they bring up the cliché about time and how quickly it passes when you're having fun.

"Why do people say that?" I ask.

"Because when you're doing what you want, you aren't paying attention to anything else," they answer. "You're too busy because you're paying attention to what matters."

I ask them to think about this when they're writing. I ask them to write a poem about what *really* matters. With the line "I never will have time enough," Porter reminds us that, no matter how long the poet lives, she still sees her time as limited and precious. This calls to mind Mary Oliver (a poet whose sensibilities in many ways are close to Porter and whom I often teach prior to teaching Porter) and her question from "The Summer Day": "Tell me, what is it you plan to do / with your one wild and precious life?"

Looking at the Sky

Sky beautiful
like the shiny rainbows ,
the Milky Way pours milk on the moon,
it looks so neat
maybe my teacher could teach us about it.
My family would want to know about it.
Looking at the sky is so beautiful at night
because I never have other time to look at it.
The sky is so beautiful because of the stars.
The stars hang in the sky with their glittering smiles

and steepest heavy and dewy sparks
so fresh
so clear
because when you look at them
it makes
you think
how beautiful the sky is.

—*Rebecca Ortiz, fifth grade*

This is the day in spring
when flowers grow and
they get watered. And
they are very
good because they
stay watered and so does
the soil and seeds.
And when it is summer they
go away and in the
spring they come
back and people
plant more and
more and they
get bigger and they
will be dead and
trees grow because
people put seeds
and they get a little
big and then they
grow leaves and they
are a tree and
then they get
old but they live
forever and they
have somebody to cut
them down.

—*Drake Garner, second grade*

I never will
have time
to see
all the things
that are

beautiful

Like
the colorful rainbows and
flowers some standing tall & red
the white gassy stars and
the blue morning and evening dark sky

I never will
have time
to praise
all the beautiful
things
that are part
of my
life.

—Francisco Valencia, fifth grade

Porter's "A Child at the Circus," as her work so often does, has a concise description of a particular setting that, as it unfolds, surprises the reader. Reminiscent of Elizabeth Bishop's "First Death in Nova Scotia," where the poet describes with unusual clarity the kinds of things a child would find at a funeral (the admonition to say good-bye to her little cousin Arthur, the way Arthur looked in his coffin, incomplete, the wondering about how Arthur would be able to join the King, Queen, and courtiers with the snow so high and the royals so far away), "A Child at the Circus" combines the sophistication of the mature poet with the perspective of youth: its grown-up voice using grown-up words describes what a child sees and knows.

A Child at the Circus

When you're a traveller and the evening air turns golden
Every house you pass begins to look like home
Because it's supper-time, it's time to be at home.
But there's another stormier light that's golden-green
With the chemical green beauty of green beans soaked in soda
Or the false gold light on the false green trees of the theater.

When I see this kind of light I remember being a small child
at the theater
When the curtain came up on a banquet of wonder and belief.
Scene One: A wood.
The princess came on stage with her waist-length hair
And the regal flash of her sequins broke into the play

Like taxi-horns in the street when they clash with a concert.
I believed that the princess was a princess in real life,
Everything was real life.
I had no unbelief,
Everything was equally believable because nothing made sense,
The entire world was one big surprise,
Even a shock.
Whether it was the man in the play with the donkey head
Or the raisin-spotted pudding at my grandmother's, when it
    burst into flames
And I dove under the table,
Or that morning when there was white stuff all over the grass
And I asked if it was sugar and my big sisters laughed,
Whether it was the leaves of the columbine turning to silver
    under water
As my mother showed me,
Or the black and orange turtle who hissed at me
    in the strawberry-patch,
Or the sparrow singing beet greens, beet greens
    as if he could talk like us,
Or the wet bloody kittens coming out of my cat's belly,
It was all brand-new and none of it made sense
And I didn't expect it to make sense.

The circus was like the rest of the world, only more so.
It was always our grandfather who took us there.
Since he was a doctor, which is a grown-up of grown-ups,
And even a psychiatrist on top of that,
He had to do without a certain kind of wonder,
But he wanted to give it to us.

In the circus were all the colors of the rainbow,
There was glitter and whirling and jumping and coarse music,
There were shuffling, swaying elephants, rippling their skins,
Shifting from foot to foot,
Always in motion like the sea.
There was a dancing pony with chalk-white wings
That I believed were real
Until my grandfather said they were artificial.
That was a grown-up's word, but I knew he was saying
There's something not quite right about wings on a pony.
It was a bit disappointing.

The entertainment I liked the best of all

Was to sit out on the back steps with my brother
Enjoying the company of our father's coachman
Michael Grady
And his rich rolling stories.
He sat between us,
And while he was telling the stories I peered at his greenish eyes
In which there were little brown threads
    as wonderful as the stories.

Reading "A Child at the Circus" is a challenge, especially for younger students. The image that surprises them most is that of the green beans cooking in soda. Few will have read *A Midsummer-Night's Dream* (though I was pleasantly surprised by one group of fifth graders who had!). Even the idea of a coachman takes time to explain. But the poem's sense of how children understand the world—the idea that children and grown-ups in fact understand it differently—is not difficult for any of them to understand. I remember one fourth grader's excitement over the idea that "Everything was equally believable because nothing made sense." He felt exactly that way, he said. He noted, approvingly, that Porter must be an interesting person to know, a grown-up who takes very seriously her experiences from childhood.

After reading "A Child at the Circus," I ask my students to write poems about being surprised. I tell them to try to remember *why* they were surprised and how the element of surprise changed things. I also ask them to think about what Porter means by "real life."

What is in the World You Don't Realize

Many times I wonder what is in the world, but I know there's cool breezing air, enormous trees, silent lakes, noisy cars, chirping birds, straight houses, fast animals, slow animals, daytime and night, big, small, and average size, lonely and friendly will soon realize that they weren't the ones chosen to inherit the earth because animals were made to inherit this small world not to be endangered the world wasn't made for danger but it was made for life to be everlasting. The world needs natural and unnatural things to be moving. We were born to live in a world made up by atoms from the big bang.

    —Pierre Percy, fifth grade

Life is full of surprises
too many to be told of
some surprises are very natural
but some are very queer
as if ghouls and demons are real

When the daffodils bloom in the winter
surprises are sure to come
as tiny surprises come
humongous surprises also do
as like when a giant wave
swallows a tiny boat
as when the giant eagle
when the pen is thrown in the air
either it is caught or it lands somewhere
or the bird flies and grabs it away

   —*John Cheng, fifth grade*

Porter is also a great poet of the spirit, and her deeply held religious beliefs are a fundamental part of her poetry. Although I don't dwell on those aspects of her work with my younger students, poems such as "For My Son Johnny," a moving elegy for her dead son, and "The Ticket," a stunningly brave meditation on her own eventual death, have inspired my college students into thinking about life and death, into examining their own understanding of religion and of the spirit. For many of my students, conversations about faith and religion are often difficult to have. Many are skeptical about organized religions in general, associating them (often mistakenly) with dogmatic teachings that seem to them politically conservative and unimaginative. Those students with deeply held beliefs are often reluctant to speak, fearing that, in announcing their beliefs, they will be considered (again, often mistakenly) as such by their classmates. But Porter's directness, the absence of any kind of proselytizing, her consideration of her religious faith as simply *her own* often provide a meeting point for the skeptical and the faithful. The following poem by Porter has been particularly inspiring to them:

Four Poems in One

At six o'clock this morning
I saw the rising sun
Resting on the ground like a boulder
In the thicket back of the school
A single great ember
About the height of a man.

*   *   *

Night has gone like a sickness,
The sky is pure and whole.
Our Lady of Poland spire

Is rosy with first light,
Starlings above it shatter their dark flock.
Notes of the Angelus
Leave their great iron cup
And slowly, three by three
Visit the Polish gardens round about,
Dahlias shaggy with frost
Sheds with their leaning tools
Rosebushes wrapped in burlap
Skiff upside down on trestles
Like dishes after supper.

*   *   *

These are the poems I'd show you
But you're no longer alive.
The cables creaked and shook
Lowering the heavy box.
The rented artificial grass
Still left exposed
That gritty gash of earth
Yellow and mixed with stones
Taking your body
That never in this world
Will we see again, or touch.

*   *   *

We know little
We can tell less
But one thing I know
One thing I can tell
I will see you again in Jerusalem
Which is of such beauty
No matter what country you come from
You will be more at home there
Than ever with father or mother
Than even with lover or friend
And once we're within her borders
Death will hunt us in vain.

Along with the specificity we expect from Porter—the fiery sunrise, the "pure and whole sky" and the flowers of morning, the earth as her husband's coffin is lowered into the ground—what attracts my students to this poem is Porter's certainty in her faith that there is a sacred place where even Death cannot overtake love. Here are two poems by college students:

The Song "All is full of love" wasn't written yet, but we knew it.

And where were we anyway?
The light didn't ferociously radiate.
There was pillow talk, hug therapy; we made each other whole.
The fuzz on our earlobes, breathing gently, lying side by side

We became air as our thought patterns joined hands
I licked an eyelash from his blushing cheek
Elastic halos illuminated the world between us
It made such sense.

   —*Cat Goncalves*

A place exhausted
of possibilities
or, we were sure, simply immune
to the impossible.

A quiet place, not so
fragmented as this—
Words that come in strings
now stutter and disintegrate halfway.

"in memory of" not a thing
I could possibly say, or stop remembering.

I'd like to ask you how it felt
that I sat in the back of the church
never learned the location
of your grave.

I'd like to ask you if that was wrong,
and do you think value lies in standing there—

a highway,
thin tombstone,
yellow grass.

It took eighteen years
but you exhausted this place
committed the impossible

(the obvious)

you taught me it is possible to drown.

　　—*Tracy Thompson*

　　　II.

　　　　　　Along the river
　　　　　　　　wild sunflowers
　　　　　over my head
　　　　　　　the dead
　　　　who gave me life
　　　　　　　give me this

　　　　　　—Lorine Niedecker,
　　　　　　　　from "Along the river"

　　　　　Oh, must we dream our dreams
　　　　　And have them, too?

　　　　　　—Elizabeth Bishop,
　　　　　　　　from "Questions of Travel"

Like Porter's poems, those of Lorine Niedecker and Elizabeth Bishop invite us to experience what we may have missed, not because we meant to but because we were hurrying ourselves along on the lines of our lives. Niedecker and Bishop remind us how too often we forget to slow down, to remember, to see. Here is Niedecker's "My Life by Water":

My Life by Water

My life
　by water—
　　　Hear

spring's
　first frog
　　　or board

out on the cold
　ground
　　　giving

Muskrats
　gnawing
　　　doors

to wild green
  arts and letters
      Rabbits

raided
  my lettuce
      One boat

two—
  pointed toward
      my shore

thru birdstart
  wingdrip
      weed-drift

of the soft
  and serious—
      Water

Like many of Porter's, this poem is one that particularly resonates with my younger students. Before we begin reading the poem, I often ask them to think about a place that means something to them, a place they feel closely connected to and with which they might identify. Usually I ask them to think about this as a place they would go to be alone, a place to be able to think and wonder, undisturbed by others.

Some students go even further, suggesting that their own heads, their thoughts, their imaginations, their dreams, are "the places" they like to go. As one fifth grader observed, "It's something you can do anywhere and then not have to think about or be where you are."

The students often comment on the swiftness of "My Life by Water" —the short, haiku-like lines, rapid verses—and the way that creates a dramatic tension with the idea that this quickness can somehow describe one's life. They also note the further tension of this life being described as a series of small moments in early spring. They also like the poem's descriptive qualities—the way Niedecker invites them to hear the frogs, the sound of the board sinking into the mud as someone steps on it. There's always someone who likes to demonstrate the sucking vacuum sound that might make. They're interested, too, in how the speaker lives in balance with nature. The muskrats are chewing at her doors; rather than rail against them, she simply observes how much the results remind her of a kind of (accidental) creativity.

The eighth verse, with its coinages, is one I'm particularly fond of. It shows Niedecker's attentiveness not only to what our senses reveal to us of the world, but to the possibilities for language.

I have students look closely at those words: *birdstart, wing-drip, weed-drift*. At first, the students are confused. "What is 'birdstart'?" I ask. Puzzled expressions all around. Someone ventures: "The place where birds start from?"

"And where do Niedecker's birds start?"

They go back to the poem. I suggest they look at the title.

"The water?"

"And so?"

And so, they get it. *Birdstart* is Niedecker's ways of naming water, a name derived directly from how it works in her life. The same is true with *wingdrip*, the water that comes off the bird's wings as they fly. *Weed-drift*, they discover, is water, too, because it's where the weeds move slowly back and forth.

I have students come up with a few of their own coined words. I start by writing *treefall* on the board. "Leaves," someone calls out. I write: *daystart*. "The sun!" says another voice. Someone suggests *schoolsit*. "Tables and chairs." *Darkout* is nighttime. *Rockmound* is a mountain. After just a few more minutes students really have a feel for it, how many possibilities there are in language.

Then I ask the students to think about their special places again, about what those places are, what they look like. "What does this place mean to you?" I ask. I ask them to begin their poems the same way Niedecker does: by inviting the reader to hear and see in new ways.

Dreams

Floating away—on a cloud—
see the bird glide through the
sky
The sun shines brightly on
your face
You feel the wind push
you and blow you
away in your dreams
you hear birds chirping
leaves rustle above you far
away in your dreams
you swing with the wind

behind you and your passion
before you
raindrops twinkle on the leaves like stars
applebuilders, flowerstarters,
away in your dreams
bees buzz, flowers buzz
apples taste like your heart
feels
    away in your dreams

   —*Brittany Harwood, fourth grade*

My Life by the Beach

hear the waves crash against the
shore

out on the sticky sand

jelly-fish at noon

sand castles knocked down by the
soft water

see surfers fall into the water

see fishermen catch different
fish

see boat sailing across the water

feel the hard rocks hit your feet

large swimming pool

sanddock

wavespark

   —*Andrew Maria, fourth grade*

*   *   *

When I teach Elizabeth Bishop's poetry (mainly to my college students), one of the observations students often make is that Bishop doesn't seem interested in calling attention to herself. They contrast this with Porter and with another poet we read, Frank O'Hara. In his poems, O'Hara is keenly interested in writing about himself, his friends and lovers, the world he lives in. He sees the world as an extension of himself, and his poetry reflects this idea of the "I"—all things point to the poet.

Conversely, Bishop seems to be pointing away from herself in her poems; rather than seeing the world as an extension of her personality, she seems intent on not making herself the subject. In those moments when Bishop does appear in her poems, it is usually by way of describing someone or something else. In "At the Fishhouses," for example, she connects place and time by describing the fisherman as a "friend of my grandfather." Describing a particular seal, she gives him a kind of good-humored intelligence by noting, "He was curious about me."

At the Fishhouses

Although it is a cold evening,
down by one of the fishhouses
an old man sits netting,
his net, in the gloaming almost invisible
a dark purple-brown,
and his shuttle worn and polished.
The air smells so strong of codfish
it makes one's nose run and one's eyes water.
The five fishhouses have steeply peaked roofs
and narrow, cleated gangplanks slant up
to storerooms in the gables
for the wheelbarrows to be pushed up and down on.
All is silver: the heavy surface of the sea,
swelling slowly as if considering spilling over,
is opaque, but the silver of the benches,
the lobster pots, and masts, scattered
among the wild jagged rocks,
is of an apparent translucence
like the small old buildings with an emerald moss
growing on their shoreward walls.
The big fish tubs are completely lined
with layers of beautiful herring scales
and the wheelbarrows are similarly plastered
with creamy iridescent coats of mail,
with small iridescent flies crawling on them.
Up on the little slope behind the houses,
set in the sparse bright sprinkle of grass
is an ancient wooden capstan,
cracked, with two long bleached handles
and some melancholy stains, like dried blood,
where the ironwork has rusted.

The old man accepts a Lucky Strike.
He was a friend of my grandfather.
We talk of the decline in the population
and of codfish and herring
while he waits for a herring boat to come in.
There are sequins on his vest and on his thumb.
He has scraped the scales, the principal beauty,
from unnumbered fish with that black old knife,
the blade of which is almost worn away.

Down at the water's edge, at the place
where they haul up the boats, up the long ramp
descending into the water, thin silver
tree trunks are laid horizontally
across the gray stones, down and down,
at intervals of four or five feet.

Cold dark deep and absolutely clear,
element bearable to no mortal,
to fish and to seals . . . One seal particularly
I have seen here evening after evening.
He was curious about me. He was interested in music;
like me a believer in total immersion,
so I used to sing him Baptist hymns.
I also sang "A Mighty Fortress is Our God."
He stood up in the water and regarded me
steadily, moving his head a little.
Then he would disappear, then suddenly emerge
almost in the same spot, with a sort of shrug
as if it were against his better judgment.
Cold dark deep and absolutely clear,
the clear gray ice water . . . Back, behind us,
the dignified tall firs begin.
Bluish, associating with their shadows,
a million Christmas trees stand
waiting for Christmas. The water seems suspended
above the rounded gray and blue-gray stones.
I have seen it over and over, the same sea, the same,
slightly, indifferently swinging above the stones,
icily free above the stones,
above the stones and then the world.
If you should dip your hand in,
your wrist would ache immediately,
your bones would begin to ache and your hand would burn
as if the water were a transmutation of fire

that feeds on stones and burns with a dark gray flame.
If you tasted it, it would first taste bitter,
then briny, then surely burn your tongue.
It is like what we imagine knowledge to be:
dark, salt, clear, moving, utterly free,
drawn from the cold hard mouth
of the world, derived from the rocky breasts
forever, flowing and drawn, and since
our knowledge is historical, flowing, and flown.

Though "At the Fishhouses" provokes strong reactions from my students, many feel like they don't quite understand it. They feel overwhelmed by the absence of the poet, by the seemingly unemotional descriptions. The movement of the poem, from the specific descriptions of scales and knife, of colors and smells, to its widening vision, the endless trees, ocean, night, and the growing coldness of the poem, leaves them longing for Bishop to bring the poem back to the specific place of the fishhouses. When she does, though, the "if" of the water—what it would feel like, what it would taste like—is hard for them. They are unsure of the connection of the experience of the water to knowledge.

Bishop is, in fact, pointing out how in the grand scheme of things our knowledge is just that: *ours*. It is knowledge that is historical, that comes out of experience. It is something we can pass on, write about, and communicate. But knowledge for Bishop is *not* subjective. In fact, it is *larger than us*. Despite the many similarities in their work, it is this that separates her from Porter and Niedecker. There is a faith for the latter two that what we know of the world—intellectually, emotionally, spiritually—is intrinsically important *to the world*. This is not true for Bishop. There is the knowledge we have, which is like the water we can touch and taste, like the trees we can see immediately around us. But there are trees we can't see, and the fact that we can't see them doesn't mean they aren't there. There is also much more water than we will ever know.

When teaching "At the Fishhouses," I always ask students to consider this idea. Few of them have ever actually thought about knowledge this way, but that's not surprising. I ask them to think about how important *they* think *they* are *themselves*. Then I ask them to write poems that reflect on these complex and strange questions. Here are a few responses:

Halloween and Going Home

The party was how parties are,
beer, and green, and white,
people dressed as—

pregnant nun, as
baptist preacher, as
other.
And me dressed as—
mustache, as
hair slicked back, as
more of me.
    Every day I feel like salmon,
    like driving the wrong way
    down a one-way street.
    Everyone else trying to get out,
    when I'm still trying to get in.
Then I see the wings and sparkle
of her in the corner,
eyes eating the twenty feet between us.
She says: come home.
Kissing on the subway and I
hear some man yell dyke at me
pretending to throw up
on the floor.
I think—we could get killed for this,
and the thought makes the
metal of her hands heat and
cool as bullet fingers to
tear open. But that is wrong.
Wrong because it was him who had
sharp, mean hands, and after
that sick in my own head there's
nothing to do but fuck. Fuck till
there are no more bullets,
only hands and wanting, and
the way all people want hands.

—Nora Oberman

days when

I see you, sometimes

my heart falls endlessly off a cliff inside you   that suddenly stops like a

bicycle wheel,   and my brain becomes beautiful in your mouth

and other times you feel
    still in me

> like water in books about King Arthur,
> water with no edge for miles,

which makes me think I don't want you

I am not here now to love you

but then I see myself
as hollow, and search
for your water and your cliffs,

we end up nowhere completely musical
>>> And I can't find you.

—*Luc Schloss*

Bibliography

American Poetry: The Twentieth Century. Volume Two: E. E. Cummings to May Swenson. New York: The Library of America, 2000.

Bishop, Elizabeth. *The Complete Poems.* New York: Farrar, Straus, and Giroux, 1969.

Niedecker, Lorine. *The Granite Pail: The Selected Poems of Lorine Niedecker.* Edited by Cid Corman. San Francisco: North Point Press, 1985.

O'Hara, Frank. *The Poems of Frank O'Hara.* Edited by Donald Allen. Berkeley: University of California Press, 1995.

Oliver, Mary. *House of Light.* Boston: Beacon Press, 1990.

Porter, Anne. *An Altogether Different Language: Poems 1934–1994.* Cambridge, Mass.: Zoland Books, 1994.

Edward R. Murrow

Kristin Prevallet

Writing through War

Using History to Teach Imaginative Writing

WARS, UNFORTUNATELY, are the focal point of history as it is taught in most schools today. When I arrived at Manhattan's P.S. 116 to do a curriculum-specific World War II writing residency, the students (fifth graders) had already studied the Revolutionary War, the Civil War, and World War I. Both of the classroom teachers, Andrea La Rocca and Elspeth McCusker, had presented these wars through a variety of sources, from history books written for children to oral histories and newspaper accounts. The students understood that the people who study wars and write history books are usually different from the people who actually lived through them. In our first discussion together, I asked the students about the distinctions between oral histories and history books: "Oral history is more emotional and sad," said one student. "You see how war makes people feel, which is different from just studying the facts."

Many of the students had family members who had served in at least one of the Twentieth century's wars. One boy related how his father had once shared a few stories about his experiences in Vietnam, and then never wanted to talk about them again. Students came to understand that the experience of war is very personal, and for those who witnessed it, the immediacy with which it remains in their memories does not dissipate just because their stories are part of a larger history.

World War II in particular was a devastating war—it affected every continent in the world and killed at least 30 million people. It is often studied from a distance, as a series of strategies, battles, and new weaponry. But as Paul Fussell describes in his book *Wartime*, such representations of World War II rarely convey the day-to-day psychological and intellectual toll that the war took on all the people who lived through it. By focusing on the perspectives of individuals, whether they be soldiers or civilians, students are more likely to remember the historical details of war; by recounting it as a human drama that affects and changes the routines and personal lives of ordinary people like them, they begin to see how history is a lived experience, something that is happening around them all the time, not simply facts memorized from a textbook. As Margot Fortunato Galt writes in her book *The Story in History*, "Students usually gain by studying their own memories and family histories before those of the more distant past. . . . Such exercises make us aware that public events become personal milestones . . ." (*The Story in History*, p. 6)

I began the residency telling the students that history and memory are interrelated. History may seem like the required subject studied between science and gym, but it is in fact living, right now, in the memories of countless individuals whose experience, knowledge, and emotional lives were altered by historically imposed events that occurred beyond their control. As Elaine Scarry theorizes in her book *The Body in Pain*, "a record of war survives in the bodies, both alive and buried, of the people who were hurt there." There is always, "the grandfather whose distorted feet permanently memorialize the location and landing site of a piece of shrapnel in France, the feet to which there will always cling the narration of a difficult walk over fields and corn stubble; . . . a cousin whose damaged hip and permanent limp announce in each step the inflection of the word 'Vietnam'"(*The Body in Pain*, p. 113). One girl decided to interview her grandfather, a 77-year-old World War II veteran, whom we later invited to talk with the class. "Not a day has gone by in the last 56 years that I haven't thought about all that I saw and lived through during the war," he said. "No one who lived through it has been able to forget it." The students, even though they may not have fully comprehended the weight of his stories, now will have an image of him when they study war in the future. Attaching a living human being to history makes history come alive. And when students are attached to their subject, the space of writing is opened.

To begin writing about memory, we read an excerpt from Joe Brainard's long poem *I Remember*. Then we brainstormed our own list of memories. Brainard's poem uses the phrase "I remember" as the catalyst for hundreds of sentences that evoke, in their overall effect, moments when the individual's memories are his own, and moments when they are part of a larger cultural consciousness.

> I remember in very scary movies, and in very sad movies, having to
>   keep reminding myself that "it's only a movie."
> [. . .]
> I remember Marilyn Monroe in fuchsia satin, as reflected in many
>   mirrors.
> [. . .]

I remember that Rock Hudson "is still waiting for the right girl to come along."

[. . .]

I remember the mostly unique to childhood problem of losing things through a hole in your pocket.

[. . .]

I remember, out walking in the rain, people scurrying by with their faces all crunched up.

[. . .]

I remember a brief period of "bad breath" concern: the product of a health class at school.

[. . .]

I remember sneezing into my hand, out in public, and then the problem of what to "do" with it.

[. . .]

I remember walking down the street, trying not to step on cracks.

After discussing the excerpt, we discussed which lines refer to Brainard's own memories and which refer to shared cultural memories. I then asked the students to write their own "I remember" lines, with a particular focus on how their memories related to the larger memories of the outside world: references to TV, movies, observations of the city, newspaper headlines, and lessons learned in school. Then I introduced the two books I was using for the residency: excerpts from Studs Terkel's *The Good War* and The Library of America's *Reporting World War II: American Journalism 1944–1946*. Terkel's book is a collection of "oral histories," and *Reporting World War II* is a collection of articles and essays written by journalists that appeared in American newspapers and magazines during the war. We discussed the two genres, and over the course of the residency students gradually became aware of the differences—in style, agenda, content, and audience—between oral history and journalism.

I found these two books to be very helpful in inspiring students to write, because they present eyewitness accounts of the war through texts that are descriptive, poetic, and filled with vivid detail. For each session, I brought in a page-long excerpt that served as the springboard for the writing exercise. After reading excerpts from these books, I found that the students were able to mimic the language and syntax in their own writing; this gave them a model for how to think and write with passion and conviction. Equally important, using excerpts from journalism and oral history provided a comprehensive study of these two different modes of writing. As we read through the different excerpts, I asked the students to tell me who was speaking or writing in the texts. By the time the residency was completed, they had gotten a thorough lesson on point of view and could relay with certainty the difference between a writer who was writing someone else's story and a writer who was telling his or her own story. This proved to be useful when it came time for the students to think about their own processes as writers, and the multiple points of view they can use.

Given the material covered in the two books, I organized the course around certain key events: the Siege of Leningrad, the Siege of St. Malo, the Holocaust, and the bombings of Hiroshima and Nagasaki. I began each session with the historical facts that pertained to the text we were about to read. *Reporting World War II* is useful for this since it includes a comprehensive month-to-month chronology of the war from an international perspective.

The first exercise I did was inspired by Studs Terkel's retelling of the Siege of Leningrad as remembered by Oleg Tsakumov (*The Good War,* p. 234). Tsakumov remembers how on the morning of June 22, 1941, the sky was clear, and everyone strolled in the streets in their holiday dresses and white pants. Everything suddenly came to a halt. Hitler's surprise attack was announced over loudspeakers. Only seven years old during the 900-day siege, Tsakumov recalls how he read a poem over the Russian radio because "it was important for the soldiers at the front to know that the children of Leningrad were still alive." From his perspective as a little boy, walking through the snowy streets looking for food was like walking through "snow mountains." Tsakumov describes how silent the city was, except when explosions would suddenly erupt out of the blue. We made a list of all of the people present in Tsakumov's account. The exercise was to write a story from the point of view of one of these people. I told the students that they should use details from the text in writing their stories.

> It was 5 A.M. on a Sunday morning when it began to get hot. A boy walking on a road saw a soldier and he said, "You were the boy who was on the radio." There were a lot of mountains with snow on them. He couldn't even walk up the mountains there was so much snow on them. And it felt like he was wearing boots and walking up the big mountain. The boy was so tired he couldn't even walk so he rested for a day and then continued to walk. He got where he needed to go.
>
> The snow started to melt and the sun started to come out and he kept on walking. Then he heard someone yell, "Move out of the way!"
>
> —*Melissa Carbonell*

Like many of the exercises used in this residency, this experiment with point of view works well with any text—from a historical narrative to a poem—and with any grade level. It is a staple exercise in my college freshman composition courses as well.

I then handed out two pages from an article by French *Vogue* correspondent and surrealist-affiliated photographer Lee Miller, "The Siege of St. Malo" (*Reporting World War II* , p. 236). The excerpt is stylistically interesting and dramatic, but not too complicated for younger students to understand. There were, of course, vocabulary words that had to be discussed (*stricken, sordid, ramparts, conjured*), but I have found that young students really enjoy deciphering big words. (Note: the ellipses are part of the paragraph.)

> Stricken lonely cats prowled. A swollen horse had not provided adequate shelter for the dead American behind it . . . flower-pots stood in roomless windows. Flies and wasps made tours in and out of underground vaults which stank with death and sour misery. Gunfire brought more stone blocks down into the street . . . I sheltered in a kraut dugout, squatting under the ramparts. My heel ground into a dead detached hand . . . and I cursed the Germans for the sordid ugly destruction they had conjured up in this once beautiful town. I wondered where my friends were . . . that I'd known here before the war . . . how many had been forced into disloyalty and degradation . . . how many had been shot, starved, or what.

In using this text, I did not attempt to gloss over the brutal details of war. And although her derogatory reference to the "Krauts" may seem antithetical to ethical standards students learn in school, it made for a brief but productive discussion of name-calling. (For older students, try presenting some of the examples in Paul Fussell's chapter on the "fresh idioms" [what he calls the "poetry of war"] that were invented by the servicemen and women to undercut, satirize, humorize, and ironize their bleak situation, and to "evoke the cant of horse-age military supply." Toilet paper, for example, became "blank," "bumf," or "bum-fodder" [*Wartime*, pp. 255–256].)

Using the Miller excerpt, I presented the students with a strategy for writing that I call "movie reading"—an active reading strategy that teaches students to use their imaginations to see into the text by creating a visual image of it as they read. Most of them had seen movies about war—including *The Thin Red Line* and *Saving Private Ryan* (movies I would have thought much too graphically violent for children)—and already had images in their imaginations that they could access when reading these relatively difficult texts. I told them that it is an excellent trick when reading to fill in the blanks with images and facts that you already know—a lesson I myself have found useful when attempting to remember what I read. Because the average class session was only 45 minutes, I read the texts to the students and asked them to read along silently. As I read, I consciously dramatized the text as much as possible. After I finished reading, I asked them to relay what they had "seen" while I was reading.

Based on what they "saw" in their imaginations, I then asked them to write sentences beginning with "I see. . . ." A few had trouble, so I worked with these students individually, helping them to re-read portions of the text and asking them to tell me what they thought the writer was trying to convey. Once they could say it, they were able to write it. Here are two examples:

> I see men falling with pain to the muddy ground which is covered by layers and layers of smoke from the many guns that shot out big black bullets one by one.
>
> I see flies and wasps making their way around the bloody area of where there are only doors left of the houses.
>
> I see cats walking through the pass trying to stay in a shelter but unable to find any.
>
> I hear the shots of the machine guns killing everyone they can get to, killing everybody in their way.
>
> I see a dark sky filled with madness, filled with smoke and memories of what was once a beautiful place but now is so covered with the sight of dead bodies and dirt.
>
> —*Ryan Mellinger*

As in this example, most of the students were able to pick up on the flow of Miller's language, and the urgency with which she attempts to allow her readers to see the horror of the death and destruction she witnessed. As an exercise in both reading and writing, the "I See" exercise is very effective. I was glad that I introduced it at the beginning of the residency, because the students were able to use the "I see . . . " structure whenever they were stuck.

Another text from *Reporting World War II* that worked well was "Atomic Bombing of Nagasaki Told by Flight Member" by William Laurence, a *New York Times* journalist on board a plane following behind the one that dropped the atomic bomb on Nagasaki on August 9, 1945. In the story, Laurence describes the colors of the explosion as they evolved from purple, to brown, white, orange, and then blue. He describes it as "a living thing, a new species of being . . . a creature in the act of breaking the bonds that held it down" (*Reporting World War II*, p. 771). This text provided a particularly useful way to teach personification, and resulted in some of the most powerful writing from the students. As with many of the wartime accounts written for American newspapers and magazines, this text lacks the perspective of the fact that 80,000 people were killed three days earlier in Hiroshima, and that 35,000 were killed when the bomb dropped on Nagasaki. Alerting students to these facts, and showing them pictures of the leveled city of Nagasaki, enabled them to read the article with a more balanced perspective.

I asked the students to personify the bomb by turning it into a creature. The students immediately understood what they were supposed to do. Personification also enabled them to re-imagine the bomb in their minds, using their own powers of description and imagination. Ms. McCusker commented on the fact that we had not shown them a photograph of the atomic bomb before they read the account; this was important in enabling them to "see" it in their heads using the Laurence passage, and prevented them from depicting the bomb using the overused "mushroom" description.

The Bomb

As we let it go, it looked like a bear taking a deep breath about to roar. A bear about 20 feet high with big red eyes and the size of a house. He was milk color. He had nails the color of smut. He sounded like he was getting beaten. Blood poured from his body. Tears rolled from his eyes.

—*Jessyca Ross-Williams*

The Furry Beast

I imagine the atom bomb as a furry beast. He has bloodshot red eyes that will frighten anyone who dares to stare straight at him. White, creamy foam is seeping out at the corner of his mouth as he searches for prey. He reeks the smell of fresh blood. He lurks around the cemetery at night looking for a decent meal. He is lonely and cruel with no mate of the same species in sight. He drinks the blood of the innocent and steals the soul of the cruel. This creature of being is disgusting and intensely ugly. His scaly prune-like body will raise the hair on your arms. His roar will freeze a town. There is not one speck of kindness in his body.

—*Kimberly Laughman*

As with the other exercises I used, this exercise in personification enabled the students to engage emotionally with the material—and then convey their reactions through writing. One of the most valuable lessons that I learned from doing this residency was that when students are presented material that is well-written and even "above" them in terms of references and sentence structure, they will absorb whatever they can, at their own pace. I taught these exercises to two classes on seemingly different "levels"—one was the more "gifted" class, the other the more "average." Although the "average" class did not write as extensively as the "gifted" one, the quality of their work and the depth with which both classes approached the subject in their writing was the same.

The following week I brought in American journalists' photographs from World War II and asked the students to "read" them the way they would read a book—writing down everything they saw, no matter how small, unrecognizable, or seemingly unimportant. Given the proliferation of books on World War II, finding the photographs was simply a matter of going to my local used bookstore and purchasing a single book for seven dollars. I then cut the book up and pasted the photographs on construction paper. I gave each child one photograph to work with. Working with photographs is a staple exercise fo many writers-in-the-schools. Bill Zavatsky, in his article "Writing through Photographs," outlines an excellent approach: "Most of the things in the world have no mouths, and cannot talk the way we do, but tell us things all the same," he writes. "I asked them to be the poets of their photographs, to lend their voices so that the photograph could tell its story" (*The Whole Word Catalogue 2*, p. 118). Since World War II photographs are mostly black and white, I asked the students to "tell the photograph's story" by adding color to the images and then filling in the weather and descriptions of the landscape. After they had finished listing all that they saw in the photograph, I asked them to think about the fact that these photos were shot by journalists. The writing exercise was to write from the point of view of a journalist, describing the story of the photograph to a reader who was not at the scene. The example below is from a Polish-American boy whose struggle with speaking and reading English caused him to have some trouble grasping the "movie reading" exercises—but he did a good job of "seeing" into the photograph.

(List)
I see five soldiers who won in Iwo Jima raising the flag of the United States. They are standing the flag in rocks. I see the destroyed homes. The sky is white with two black clouds.

(Story)
One day the war started in Iwo Jima. One night all the people thought the war was over. In an afternoon in 1945 the war was over and the United States won, so the flag is raised. Five soldiers are standing because only five sol-

diers are alive. This is half the army and these five soldiers are trying to stand up the flag, and they are crying because they won. The sky is white and there are two black clouds.

—*Przemek Galus*

One instruction that helped the students to write about the photographs—and was also useful for the texts—was to find one detail and compare or contrast it with another. For example, in a photograph of two prisoners of war, a student named Gabriella didn't know what to write except, "I see skinny men." I asked her to look at their faces and describe them. She said she thought they looked confident. Then I asked her to look at their bodies, and to compare them to their faces.

> I took a photograph of two men struggling to stay alive with no food and barely any clothing. They have such confident smiles but not such confident bodies. Their ribs are showing due to being starved, their arms are long and their skin is hanging off. The area that they are in is very dried up and dead, and there is barely any food for anyone. Their lives are coming to an end and they are struggling to keep moving. Their lives are coming to an end but they will try to keep moving on.
>
> —*Gabriella Chibbaro*

We concluded the residency by going to the Museum of Jewish Heritage, where museum docents explained how Jewish children in Germany led normal lives in the early 1930s—going to school, playing in their backyards, celebrating their religious traditions, and spending time with their families who had been rooted there for many generations. Suddenly it was as if time stopped, and they were no longer able to go to school, play on teams with non-Jewish children, or participate in the everyday activities of their cities. The final exercise we did—which relates to the first "I Remember" exercise, thus bringing the residency full circle—was inspired by Frank O'Hara's well-known poem "The Day Lady Died." (See Margot Fortunato Galt's chapter "The Glare of the Historical Moment" in *The Story in History*.) We read the poem and discussed it as an onslaught of everyday details that come to a halt when a newspaper headline announcing Billie Holliday's death triggers O'Hara's memory. I asked the students to write about their daily routines, giving as many boring details as possible before "time stops."

> It is 7:30 in the morning.
> I wake up. I see my brother leaving and going to school. I go to brush my teeth. I live on the 6th floor so I run down and come up. I do that 15 times for exercise. I take a bath, eat breakfast, change clothes, and walk to

school. Today we have a math test. I'm nervous. When I reach school I take the test.

I hope I did well. I take my book and do my math work. I do social studies. I walk home. When I rang the buzzer nobody answered. I had to wait for my brother. When I came home I saw Grandpa lying down. I tried to wake him but he wouldn't move. Then I realize he is dead.

—*Tenzing Mingmar*

Recalling Tsakumov's narrative, another student used the O'Hara exercise to imagine what it might be like to live in a war zone:

I wake up at 10:30 A.M.
I am three years old and the year
is 1991. I eat oatmeal for breakfast
and turn on the news.
There is a war a few blocks away.
My grandma tells me to stay
in the house where it is safe and
I go play with my Legos and I start
hearing gunshots. There must be a
riot outside and I try to
act normal but it's hard.
I feel like they'll come in and
kill us and time seems to stop.

—*Tim Novikov*

Before and after our trip to the museum, Andrea and Elspeth (the two classroom teachers) had been preparing the students with films, discussions, and lessons on the Holocaust. I supplemented their lessons with two excerpts from *Reporting World War II*: "Dachau: May 1945" by Martha Gellhorn and "Nazi Mass Killing Laid Bare in [Maidanek] Camp" by W. H. Lawrence. These journalists' accounts of witnessing the evidence of genocide are both emotionally and descriptively powerful. Gellhorn contrasts the piles of clothing neatly stacked behind the crematoria with the piles of bodies that were "dumped like garbage rotting in the sun." She also describes the hothouses where prisoners were forced to grow flowers and vegetables that they were prohibited from eating. Lawrence describes the vegetable gardens behind the crematoriums that were fertilized with human ashes, and contrasts this to the thousands of shoes "spread like grain in a half-filled elevator." Both Gelhorn and Lawrence use precise examples that provide powerful contrasts. As with the photographs, the students made a list of all the details that they "saw" in the text.

But just "seeing" isn't enough. Teachers are rightly concerned that students not just know the facts, but truly empathize and comprehend the effects that this massive genocide had on future generations. Students watch films that graphically portray the death camps and the mass graves. But when students are asked to write about their emotional experience in trying to comprehend the material, often they freeze, or resort to flat sentimentality. One exercise (suggested by Margot Fortunato Galt) that works well with any sensitive, violent topic (or any troubling episode in history) is to write from the perspective of an animal who innocently happened to witness human barbarism. What inevitably comes through is the innocent perspective of the child. Writing from the perspective of an animal allows students to project these feelings onto another creature— thus avoiding superficial sentimentality and cliché. Almost all of the students were very excited by this exercise, and most wanted to take it home to finish as homework. Here are two examples:

> I am a stray chicken. I live in a farm near a camp. This camp has people in it who are shouting and screaming all around. People are coming out and coming in. There are these people called Nazis and they have these people that grow food for them. How skinny they were, but they couldn't eat. I see all this everyday because I live in a nearby farm. If the Nazis see the people eating, they get beaten. Then I wandered off somewhere and I never saw anything like it. It was a red river that used to be bluish green and now it's red. It was blood from all the dead people that died. There were heads of people in the river. I went in the camp and saw a lot of clothes and dead bodies.
>
> —*Dewi Rani*

> As I fly over a large building I see people with no feathers on their heads, or what humans call hair. I see smoke coming from a building so thick it chokes me as I fly down to land. Now I can walk around. Then I hear loud mean words and when I get on the ground I'm chased around by a large tall man with a suit on. When I look down I see happiness in that man's face, as though he was born to be fierce and mean.
>
> —*Jasmina Sidberry*

The media may saturate children with terrifying images of violence and destruction, but the writing my students at P.S. 116 produced proved to me that they are anything but emotionally apathetic. Their writing was extremely revealing, because it showed their own very particular ways of coping with death, violence, and sadness. All 60 of the students managed to write their way through this difficult material with thoughtfulness and intensity. I was very surprised and proud of the way they were able to show respect for the material that they were given—understanding that when you attempt to write from another person's point of view, you owe it to them to be sincere and genuine. On the final day we wrote a collaborative poem inspired by William Blake's poem "The Tyger" in *The Songs of Experience*. We picked an animal and then asked it all the questions about war that we didn't understand. This collaborative poem is a powerful summation of the way the students absorbed the illogical, bloody, and, as one student put it, "emotionally tragic" repercussions of war.

Owl, Owl
Sleeping tight
in the forests of the night.
Why do wars start?
What amount of anger do humans contain?
Who created evil?
Why did they suffer?
How many died?
Can people be so cruel yet so blind?
What happens to the corpses?
What is the military?
How do you feel about people getting killed?
Why do people want war?
Does war bring us good?
Why do people suffer for what they didn't do?
Did the person who created guns make this war?
Why did the person who started this war feel this way?
How many deaths must it take for the war to end?
How many graves will it take to fill a graveyard?
How many eyes must a man have to see what he did was wrong?
Why must someone feel the pain for someone else's anger?
Owl, Owl
awake at night
answer our questions
before it's bright.

　　—*Ms. McCusker's fifth grade class*

Although probably not making war any easier to understand, using history to write creatively gives students a "way into" the past, and allows them to participate in it as empathetic human beings with their own unique sets of eyes. It also makes history become a part of their memories, an experience of reading and writing that they can take with them beyond the classroom.

Bibliography

Blake, William. *Songs of Experience*. In *The Complete Poetry and Prose of William Blake*. Edited by David Erdman. New York: Anchor Books, 1988.

Brainard, Joe. *I Remember.* New York: Penguin Books, 1995.

Fussell, Paul. *Wartime*. New York: Oxford University Press, 1989.

Galt, Margot Fortunato. *The Story in History: Writing Your Way into the American Experience*. New York: Teachers & Writers Collaborative, 1992.

O'Hara, Frank. *The Selected Poems of Frank O'Hara*. Edited by Donald Allen. New York: Vintage Books, 1974.

Padgett, Ron and Bill Zavatsky, editors. *The Whole Word Catalogue 2*. New York: Teachers & Writers Collaborative, 1977.

Reporting World War II: American Journalism 1944–1946. New York: The Library of America, 1995.

Scarry, Elaine. *The Body in Pain*. New York: Oxford University Press, 1985.

Terkel, Studs. *The Good War: An Oral History of World War Two*. New York: The New Press, 1997.

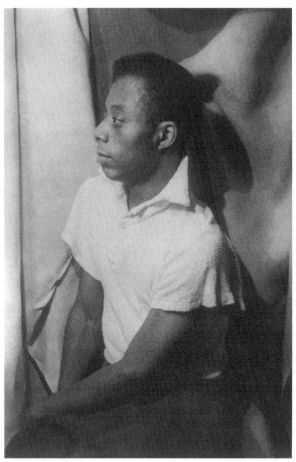

James Baldwin

Phillip Lopate

Teaching James Baldwin

WHENEVER I have used personal essays to motivate students to write their own, I have relied on James Baldwin's work, because I know that he will get high school and college kids engaged and excited. The resistances they show to Lamb, Hazlitt, Montaigne, and all those other "old-timey writers" seem to melt away under Jimmy's fiery gaze. It is Baldwin to the rescue, in part because his honesty and passion are very attractive to young people; but also because Baldwin dramatized adolescence again and again as his own particular crucible of selfhood—boy preacher, loss of faith, yearnings to write, father's death, foregoing college, struggles over racial anger and sexual preference—and sympathized so warmly with the efforts of all youth to forge an identity.

In an essay entitled "They Can't Turn Back," on the desegregation of the schools in the South, he writes, parenthetically and characteristically, about the "really agonizing privacy of the very young. They are only beginning to realize that the world is difficult and dangerous, that they are, themselves, tormentingly complex and that the years that stretch before them promise to be more dangerous than the years that are behind. And they always seem to be wrestling, in a private chamber to which no grownup has access, with monumental decisions. Everyone laughs at himself once he has come through this storm, but it is borne in on me, suddenly, that it *is* a storm, a storm, moreover, that not everyone survives and through which no one comes unscathed. Decisions made at this time always seem—and, in fact, nearly always turn out to be—decisions that determine the course and quality of a life. I wonder for the first time what it can be like to be making, in the adolescent dark, such decisions as this generation of students has made."

This is catnip to the young.

I am being a bit ironic because, while I love Baldwin's writing, I sometimes feel that I have to exert counter-pressure to pry students from its appeal and exercise a little critical intelligence. Once they fall under the spell of his voice, they tend to buy into his whole analysis of race, politics, America—the bombastically prophetic, wrongheaded parts as well as the sensible. What they really buy into is his presentation of self as a wounded being: there can be no doubt that, in a talk-show culture that enshrines victimhood, Baldwin plays exceedingly well.

*   *   *

When I teach Baldwin I focus on his essays, because I think he is a great essayist—indeed, the most important American one since the end of World War II—and only a so-so fiction writer. His long novels, *Another Country* and *Just above My Head*, now seem windy and unfocused; *Giovanni's Room*, precious. When there is enough time, I have occasionally assigned *Go Tell It on the Mountain*, which many consider his best, just to show how the same material (a Harlem adolescence) may be treated via both fiction and non-fiction. To my mind, this first novel of Baldwin's, atmospheric but clotted, cannot hold a candle to his infinitely more expressive personal essay, "Notes of a Native Son."

A twenty-page miracle, a masterpiece of compression, "Notes of a Native Son" seems to pour out in a white-heat of emotional prose, though it is everywhere artfully shaped. The portrait of his father, David Baldwin (whom he later learned was actually his stepfather), is a model of unsentimental ambivalence. Many students, encountering it for the first time, are shocked to see that one can actually tell such tales out of school. Baldwin's ferocious and fastidious candor liberates them to begin writing about the meanings of their parents' lives.

I generally focus on the following amazing paragraph:

> He was, I think, very handsome. I gather this from photographs and from my own memories of him, dressed in his Sunday best and on his way to preach a sermon somewhere, when I was little. Handsome, proud, and ingrown, "like a toenail," somebody said. But he looked to me, as I grew older, like pictures I had seen of African tribal chieftains: he really should have been naked, with warpaint on and barbaric mementos, standing among spears. He could be chilling in the pulpit and indescribably cruel in his personal life and he was certainly the most bitter man I have ever met; yet it must be said that there was something else in him, buried in him, which lent him his tremendous power and, even, a rather crushing charm. It had something to do with his blackness, I think—he was very black—with his blackness and his beauty, and with the fact that he knew that he was black but did not know that he was beautiful. He claimed to be proud of his blackness but it had also been the cause of much humiliation and it had fixed bleak boundaries to his life. He was not a young man when we were growing up and he had already suffered many kinds of ruin; in his outrageously demanding and protective way he loved his children, who were black and menaced, like him; and all these things sometimes showed in his face when he tried, never to my knowledge with any success, to establish contact with any of us. When he took one of his children on his knee to play, the child always became fretful and began to cry; when he tried to help one of us with our homework the

absolutely unabating tension which emanated from him caused our minds and our tongues to become paralyzed, so that he, scarcely knowing why, flew into a rage and the child, not knowing why, was punished. If it ever entered his head to bring a surprise home for his children, it was, almost unfailingly, the wrong surprise and even the big watermelons he often brought home on his back in the summertime led to the most appalling scenes. I do not remember, in all those years, that one of his children was ever glad to see him come home. From what I was able to gather of his early life, it seemed that this inability to establish contact with other people had always marked him and had been one of the things which had driven him out of New Orleans. There was something in him, therefore, groping and tentative, which was never expressed and which was buried with him. One saw it most clearly when he was facing new people and hoping to impress them. But he never did, not for long. We went from church to smaller and more improbable church, he found himself in less and less demand as a minister, and by the time he died none of his friends had come to see him in a long time. He had lived and died in an intolerable bitterness of spirit and it frightened me, as we drove him to the graveyard through these unquiet, ruined streets, to see how powerful and overflowing this bitterness could be and to realize this bitterness now was mine.

It's all there, in this paragraph, but it requires some unpacking: Baldwin's sheer love of language; his intoxication with adjectives and adverbs, at a time when others avoided them; his Biblical rhythms, oral-sermon repetitions and series syntax ("and . . . and"); his oxymorons ("crushing charm"); his witheringly undercutting use of subordinate clauses ("never to my knowledge with any success"); his anglicisms ("rather" or the impersonal pronoun "one"); his verbal arrows and pointers ("yet it must be said that," "therefore"); his ability to sustain an extremely long sentence without wearying or confusing the reader; his willingness to pull back from a specific detail and make a broader generalization; his balance between rejection and tenderness, between rage and forgiveness; his ennoblings and deflations, often in the same sentence; his detachment and grim humor; and finally, his generous move to identify with, show complicity with, the sin ("this bitterness") he had seemed to be indicting.

Baldwin's prose is a carefully crafted, highly mannered (in the best sense) performance, and some of what I do when I teach him is to draw attention to his techniques. Students tend to inhale powerful prose in an undifferentiated rush, and I want to slow them down. Of course I don't wish to dilute their human feeling for this person who has suffered and witnessed great suffering; but I want them to understand the mastery of language that Baldwin accomplished, because this is part of the positive side of the ledger that helped him survive—and may help them survive.

I ask them to write a portrait of their mother or father, and to reflect on how we take on the traits of our parents, for better or for worse. Or I ask them to write about some incidents in which anger got the better of them, or to consider in an essay the nature of bitterness. Or just write about their growing up. By the time they have finished reading "Notes of a Native Son," they have often gotten the point—the challenge to be as honest and personal as possible on the page—and don't need much specific prodding to be off and running.

I follow it with as many Baldwin essays as I can, because I find that he is one of those writers whom students are willing to be saturated by. The more they read him, the more comfortable they become with his strategic moves and range of interests, and the more he seems a friend. Ideally, I can assign as a text the fat, collected book of Baldwin non-fiction, *The Price of the Ticket*, though one can also get by in a pinch with the earlier, paperback collections such as *Nobody Knows My Name* and *The Fire Next Time*, which are still in print. I ask them to read such gems as "Equal in Paris" (a narrative vignette about his getting arrested), "Stranger in the Village" (a meditation on otherness and the expatriate experience), "The Harlem Ghetto" (just to show how fully formed a stylist he was at twenty), "Alas, Poor Richard" (a searching double portrait of Baldwin and his patriarchal mentor/rival, Richard Wright), "Sweet Lorraine" (about the playwright Lorraine Hansberry), and, of course, "The Fire Next Time."

This last, full-length essay has portions as great as anything Baldwin ever wrote. You may have to supply a certain amount of historical context for students (the mood of the Sixties, the Civil Rights movement, the Black Muslims, etc.), though I have found, on the whole, that they get it. A bigger problem is the one I alluded to earlier: when this ambitious conglomeration of an essay begins to fall apart, the rhetorical smoothness of Baldwin's writing may fool students into not even questioning his apocalyptic overkill (such as that if America doesn't support revolutions abroad and at home, it will be burned to the ground).

The full-length essays that Baldwin continued to write, such as "No Name in the Street" or "The Devil Finds Work," are fascinating to teach—partly because they have such wonders in them and partly because they don't really hold together. (It's salutary, I think, for students to realize that the structural problems of essay writing may be so daunting when the ante is raised that even a master of the form can get bogged down.) In one sense the long, long essay *was* Baldwin's form: it brought out relaxed, self-surprising passages in him that nothing else did. But in another sense, he never figured out how to pull it off artistically, how to tie up the loose ends or give it an inevitable shape. This may have as much to do with the essay form today as with any inadequacies on Baldwin's part.

There are lessons anyone attempting to write personal essays can learn from Baldwin. How to dramatize oneself, for instance. Most personal essays misfire because of the blandness of the narrative persona, but this was never a problem for James Baldwin: he could always project himself on paper as in the midst of some burning conflict or dire strait. He was a bit of an actor, which an essayist needs to be—willing and able to take on one mask or another.

Another of his admirable qualities was a self-reflective insight that let us into his thinking process. Six pages into "Alas, Poor Richard," we encounter this passage:

> I was far from imagining, when I agreed to write this memoir, that it should prove to be such a painful and difficult task. What, after all, can I really say about Richard . . . ? Everything founders in the sea of what might have been. We might have been friends, for example, but I cannot honestly say that we were. There might have been some way of avoiding our quarrel, our rupture; I can only say that I failed to find it. The quarrel having occurred, perhaps there might have been a way to have become reconciled. I think, in fact, that I counted on this coming about in some mysterious, irrevocable way, the way a child dreams of winning, by means of some dazzling exploit, the love of his parents.

I began by implying that James Baldwin had in some ways been fixated on his adolescent crisis and had over-acted the part of the racial victim. But we see from this passage how incomplete my assessment was; for it demonstrates the worldy, sorrowful realism and willingness to take responsibility for one's fate that makes Baldwin, at his best, a hero of American maturity. Perhaps what finally makes him so attractive to young people is the way he epitomizes the process of becoming a man, without losing touch with, or falsifying, the part of himself that remains a very vulnerable boy.

Bibliography

Baldwin, James. Collected Essays. New York: The Library of America, 1998.

————. *Early Novels & Stories*. New York: The Library of America, 1998.

Selected Bibliography

I. Books about American Literature

Ashbery, John. *Other Traditions*. Cambridge, Mass.: Harvard University Press, 2000. Includes essays on American poets John Wheelwright, Laura Riding, and David Schubert.

Auchincloss, Louis. *Pioneer Caretakers: A Study of American Women Novelists*. Minneapolis, Minn.: University of Minnesota Press, 1965. Biographical studies of Sarah Orne Jewett, Edith Wharton, Willa Cather, Jean Stafford, Carson McCullers, Mary McCarthy, Katherine Anne Porter, Elizabeth Madox Roberts, and Ellen Glasgow.

Brooks, Van Wyck. *The Dream of Arcadia: American Writers and Artists in Italy, 1760–1915*. New York: Dutton, 1958.

———.*The Flowering of New England, 1815–1865*. New York: Dutton, 1936.

———. *The Times of Melville and Whitman*. New York: Dutton, 1953.

Callahan, John F. *In the African-American Grain: The Pursuit of Voice in Twentieth-Century Black Fiction*. Urbana and Chicago: University of Illinois Press, 1988. Traces the influence of African and African-American oral storytelling techniques in the work of Jean Toomer, Zora Neale Hurston, Ralph Ellison, Alice Walker, and others.

Cowley, Malcolm. *The Flower and the Leaf: A Contemporary Record of American Writing Since 1941*. New York: Viking Penguin, 1985.

Cowley, Malcolm. *New England Writers and Writing*. Edited by Donald W. Faulkner. Hanover, N.H. University Press of New England, 1996.

Creeley, Robert. *The Collected Essays*. Berkeley: University of California Press, 1989. Extraordinary essays on Whitman, Hart Crane, and American poets of the mid-twentieth century.

Fiedler, Leslie A. *Love and Death in the American Novel*. New York: Stein and Day, 1966.

Fisher, Philip. *Still the New World: American Literature in a Culture of Creative Destruction*. Cambridge, Mass.: Harvard University Press, 1999. Provocative capitalist reading of Emerson, Whitman, Melville, Twain, Henry James, and others.

Fishkin, Shelley Fisher. *From Fact to Fiction: Journalism and Imaginative Writing in America*. Baltimore, Md.: The Johns Hopkins Press, 1985. Study of the journalistic careers of Whitman, Twain, Dreiser, Hemingway, and Dos Passos.

Fuller, Margaret. *The Portable Margaret Fuller.* Edited by Mary Kelley. Penguin, 1994.

Gates, Henry Louis, Jr. *Loose Canons: Notes on the Culture Wars.* New York: Oxford University Press, 1992.

―――. *The Signifying Monkey: A Theory of Afro-American Literary Criticism.* New York: Oxford University Press, 1988.

Gates, Henry Louis, Jr., and Nellie McKay, editors. *The Norton Anthology of African American Literature.* New York: Norton, 1997.

Ginsberg, Allen. *Deliberate Prose: Selected Essays, 1952–1995.* Edited by Bill Morgan. New York: HarperCollins, 2000. Scholarly and tender essays on Whitman, William Carlos Williams, and the Beats.

Howe, Irving. *Selected Writings, 1950–1990.* New York: Harvest Books, 1992.

―――. *The American Newness: Culture and Politics in the Age of Emerson.* Cambridge, Mass.: Harvard University Press, 1986.

Howe, Susan. *The Birth-mark: Unsettling the Wilderness in American Literary History.* Hanover, N.H.: University Press of New England, 1993. Inspired view of marginalia and variants that offers alternatives and complements to more traditional histories.

―――. *My Emily Dickinson.* Berkeley, Calif.: North Atlantic Books, 1985. Where is Emily Dickinson in American literary history, and is that her?

Kazin, Alfred. *An American Procession: The Major American Novelists from 1830 to 1930, The Crucial Century.* New York: Knopf, 1984.

―――. *On Native Grounds: An Interpretation of Modern American Prose Literature.* New York: Harcourt Brace Jovanovich, 1995.

Kenner, Hugh. *A Homemade World: The American Modernist Writers.* New York: Knopf, 1975.

Lawrence, D. H. *Studies in Classic American Literature.* New York: Penguin Putnam, 1977. An historic confrontation with Franklin, Cooper, Poe, Hawthorne, Melville, and Whitman.

Matthiessen, F. O. *American Renaissance: Art and Expression in the Age of Emerson and Whitman.* N.Y.: Oxford University Press, 1941.

―――. *The James Family: Including Selections from the Writings of Henry James, Sr., William, Henry & Alice James.* New York: Knopf, 1947.

Morrison, Toni. *Playing in the Dark: Whiteness and the Literary Imagination.* New York: Random House, 1992. Discusses the "Africanist"presence in Poe, Melville, Cather, and Hemingway.

Nelson, Cary. *Repression and Recovery: Modern American Poetry and the Politics of Cultural Memory.* Madison: University of Wisconsin Press, 1989.

North, Charles. *No Other Way: Selected Prose*. Brooklyn, N.Y.: Hanging Loose Press, 1998. Illuminating essays on Elizabeth Bishop, John Ashbery, and other poets.

Pizer, Donald, editor. *Documents of American Realism and Naturalism*. Carbondale, Ill.: Southern Illinois Press, 1998. Includes essays by Henry James, William Dean Howells, Clarence Darrow, Frank Norris, Theodore Dreiser, Lionel Trilling, Malcolm Cowley, Alfred Kazin, and contemporary scholars.

Poirier, Richard. *Poetry and Pragmatism*. Cambridge, Mass.: Harvard U. Press, 1992. A look at twentieth-century American poetry in light of Emerson and William James.

Rideout, Walter. *The Radical Novel in the United States, 1900–1954: Some Interrelationships of Literature and Society*. New York: Columbia University Press, 1992.

Sherman, Joan. *Invisible Poets: Afro-Americans of the Nineteenth Century*. Urbana: University of Illinois Press, 1974.

Stegner, Wallace, editor. *The American Novel from James Fenimore Cooper to William Faulkner*. New York: Basic Books, 1965. A collection of pithy, accessible essays by Irving Howe, John Berryman, and others, designed for presentation over the Voice of America.

Stepto, Robert B. *From Behind the Veil: A Study of African-American Narrative*. Urbana: University of Illinois Press, 1991.

Thomas, Lorenzo. *Extraordinary Measures: Afrocentric Modernism and Twentieth-Century American Poetry*. Tuscaloosa: University of Alabama Press, 2000. Excellent essays on Margaret Walker, Melvin Tolson, Amiri Baraka, and others.

Trilling, Lionel. *The Liberal Imagination*. New York: Harcourt Brace Jovanovich, 1978.

———. *The Moral Obligation to Be Intelligent*. New York: Farrar, Straus and Giroux, 2000. Includes Trilling's well-known essays on Dos Passos, Hemingway, James, Twain, and others.

Van Doren, Carl. *The American Novel 1789–1939*. New York: Macmillan, 1968. A classic survey.

Vendler, Helen. *Voices and Visions: The Poet in America*. New York: Random House, 1987. Accompanies a series of thirteen hour-long videos about American poets from Whitman and Dickinson through Elizabeth Bishop.

Walker, Cheryl. *Indian Nation: Native American Literature and Nineteenth-Century Nationalisms*. Durham, N.C.: Duke University Press, 1997.

Whitehead, Kim. *The Feminist Poetry Movement*. Jackson: University Press of Mississippi, 1996. Supplements those "Lives of the Poets" which might be more accurately titled "Lives of Male Poets."

Williams, William Carlos. *In the American Grain*. New Directions, 1956. Williams's look at American history includes incisive readings of Franklin and Poe.

———. *Collected Essays*. New Directions, 1969.

Wilson, Edmund. *Patriotic Gore: Studies in the Literature of the American Civil War*. New York: Oxford University Press, 1962.

———. *The Shock of Recognition*. New York: Farrar, Straus and Cudahy, 1955. Essential documents of American literary history, with pertinent introductions by Wilson.

Wright, Nathalia. *American Novelists in Italy*. Philadelphia: University of Pennsylvania Press, 1965. An intriguing study of nineteenth-century Americans abroad, including Washington Irving, James Fenimore Cooper, Nathaniel Hawthorne, William Dean Howells, and Henry James.

II. Titles Available from The Library of America

Adams, Henry. *Novels, Mont Saint-Michel, The Education*.

———. *History of the United States During the Administrations of Thomas Jefferson and James Madison*. 2 vols.

American Poetry: The Nineteenth Century. Volume I: Freneau to Whitman.

American Poetry: The Nineteenth Century. Volume II: Melville to Stickney; American Indian Poetry; Folk Songs and Spirtuals.

American Poetry: The Twentieth Century. Volume I: Henry Adams to Dorothy Parker.

American Poetry. The Twentieth Century. Volume II: E. E. Cummings to May Swenson.

American Sermons: The Pilgrims to Martin Luther King Jr.

Audubon, John James. *Writings and Drawings*.

Baldwin, James. *Early Novels and Stories*.

———. *Collected Essays*.

Bartram, William. *Travels and Other Writings*.

Brown, Charles Brockden. *Three Gothic Novels*.

Cather, Willa. *Early Novels and Stories*.

———. *Later Novels*.

———. *Stories, Poems, and Other Writings*.

Chandler, Raymond. *Stories and Early Novels.*
———. *Later Novels and Other Writings.*
Cooper, James Fenimore. *The Leatherstocking Tales.*
———. *Sea Tales: The Pilot and The Red Rover.*
Crane, Stephen. *Prose & Poetry.*
Crime Novels: American Noir of the 1930s and '40s.
Crime Novels: American Noir of the 1950s.
The Debate on the Constitution: Federalist and Antifederalist Speeches, Articles, and Letters During the Struggle Over Ratification. 2 vols.
Dos Passos, John. *U.S.A.*
Douglas, Frederick. *Autobiographies.*
Dreiser, Theodore. *Sister Carrie, Jennie Gerhardt, Twelve Men.*
Du Bois, W.E.B. *Writings.*
Emerson, Ralph Waldo. *Essays and Lectures.*
———. *Collected Poems and Translations.*
Faulkner, William. *Novels 1930–1935.*
———. *Novels 1936–1940.*
———. *Novels 1942–1954.*
———. *Novels 1957–1962.*
Fitzgerald, F. Scott. *Novels and Stories 1920–1922.*
Franklin, Benjamin. *Writings.*
Frost, Robert. *Collected Poems, Prose, and Plays.*
Grant, Ulysses S. *Memoirs and Selected Letters.*
Hamilton, Alexander. *Writings.*
Hammett, Dashiell. *Complete Novels.*
———. *Crime Stories and Other Writings.*
Hawthorne, Nathaniel. *Tales and Sketches.*
———. *Collected Novels.*
Howells, William Dean. *Novels 1875–1886.*
———. *Novels 1886–1888.*
Hurston, Zora Neale. *Novels and Stories.*
———. *Folklore, Memoirs, and Other Writings.*
Irving, Washington. *History, Tales and Sketches.*
———. *Brackbridge Hall, Tales of a Traveller, The Alhambra.*
James, Henry. *Novels 1871–1880.*
———. *Novels 1881–1886.*
———. *Novels 1886–1890.*
———. *Literary Criticism. Volume I: American and English Writers.*
———. *Literary Criticism. Volume II: European Writers; Prefaces.*
———. *Collected Travel Writings.* 2 vols.
———. *Complete Stories 1864–1874.*

————. *Complete Stories 1874–1884.*
————. *Complete Stories 1884–1891.*
————. *Complete Stories 1892–1898.*
————. *Complete Stories 1898–1910.*
James, William. *Writings 1878–1899.*
————. *Writings 1902–1910.*
Jefferson, Thomas. *Writings.*
Jewett, Sarah Orne. *Novels and Stories.*
Lewis, Sinclair. *Main Street and Babbitt.*
Lincoln, Abraham. *Speeches and Writings. Volume I: 1832–1858.*
————. *Speeches and Writings. Volume II: 1859–1865.*
London, Jack. *Novels and Stories.*
————. *Novels and Social Writings.*
Longfellow, Henry Wadsworth. *Poems and Other Writings.*
McCullers, Carson. *Complete Novels.*
Madison, James. *Writings.*
Melville, Herman. *Typee, Omoo, Mardi.*
————. *Redburn, White-Jacket, Moby-Dick.*
————. *Pierre, Israel Potter, The Confidence-Man, Tales, Billy Budd.*
Muir, John. *Nature Writings.*
Nabokov, Vladimir. *Novels and Memoirs 1941–1951.*
————. *Novels. 1955–1962.*
————. *Novels. 1969–1974.*
Norris, Frank. *Novels and Essays.*
O'Connor, Flannery. *Collected Works.*
O'Neill, Eugene. *Complete Plays.* 3 vols.
Paine, Thomas. *Collected Writings.*
Parkman, Francis. *France and England in North America.* Vol. I.
————. *France and England in North America.* Vol. II.
————. *The Oregon Trail and The Conspiracy of Pontiac.*
Poe, Edgar Allan. *Poetry and Tales.*
————. *Essays and Reviews.*
Powell, Dawn. *Novels 1930–1942.*
————. *Novels 1944–1962.*
Reporting Vietnam. Part One: American Journalism 1959–1969.
Reporting Vietnam. Part Two: American Journalism 1969–1975.
Reporting World War II. Part One: American Journalism 1938–1944.
Reporting World War II. Part Two: American Journalism 1944–1946.
Sherman, William Tecumseh. *Memoirs.*
Slave Narratives.
Stein, Gertrude. *Writings 1903–1932.*

———. *Writings 1932–1946.*
Steinbeck, John. *Novels and Stories 1932–1937.*
———. *The Grapes of Wrath and Other Writings 1936–1941.*
Stevens, Wallace. *Collected Poetry and Prose.*
Stowe, Harriet Beecher. *Three Novels.*
The American Revolution: Writings from the War of Independence.
Thoreau, Henry David. *A Week on the Concord and Merrimack Rivers, Walden, The Maine Woods, Cape Cod.*
———. *Collected Essays and Poems.*
Thurber, James. *Writings and Drawings.*
Twain, Mark. *Mississippi Writings.*
———. *The Innocents Abroad and Roughing It.*
———. *Historical Romances.*
———. *Collected Tales, Sketches, Speeches, and Essays.* 2 vols.
Washington, George. *Writings.*
Welty, Eudora. *Complete Novels.*
———. *Collected Stories 1891–1910.*
———. *Collected Stories 1911–1937.*
———. *Stories, Essays, and Memoir.*
West, Nathanael. *Novels & Other Writings.*
Wharton, Edith. *Novels.*
———. *Novellas and Other Writings.*
Whitman, Walt. *Poetry and Prose.*
Williams, Tennessee. *Plays 1937–1980.*
———. *Plays 1957–1980.*
Wright, Richard. *Early Works.*
———. *Later Works.*

Notes on Contributors

CATHERINE BARNETT teaches writing with Teachers & Writers Collaborative, at New York University, and at the Children's Museum of Manhattan. Her essays, interviews, and reviews have been published widely. She has an M.F.A. from Warren Wilson College.

A former Detroit public school teacher, TERRY BLACKHAWK now directs InsideOut, a Detroit-based writers-in-schools program that she founded in 1995. She has served as Michigan Council for the Arts writer-in-residence at a Detroit high school and has conducted poetry workshops for the Michigan Youth Arts Festival, the Detroit Institute of Arts, Cranbrook Writers' Retreat, and the Michigan Department of Education summer program for gifted and talented students. She is the author of two collections of poetry—a chapbook, *Trio: Voices from the Myths* (Ridgeway Press, 1998) and *Body and Field* (Michigan State University Press, 1999). She has read her work at the Geraldine R. Dodge Poetry Festival and she received the 2000 Governors' Arts in Education Award from ArtServe Michigan.

BOB BLAISDELL edited and introduced *Tolstoy as Teacher: Leo Tolstoy's Writings on Education* and contributed essays to *The T&W Guide to William Carlos Williams* and *Classics in the Classroom*. He is the editor of *Thoreau: A Book of Quotations* (Dover), the forthcoming *Classic Tales and Fables for Children* by Leo Tolstoy (Prometheus), and several other literary anthologies. He teaches English at Kingsborough Community College in Brooklyn and has written about his teaching experiences in *The Chronicle of Higher Education*, *Academe*, *Spectrum*, *Radical Teacher*, *The New York Times*, and *Teaching Tolerance*.

BOB BOONE directs Young Chicago Authors, a creative writing program for inner-city students. He has written more than 60 articles for the *Chicago Reader*, the *Chicago Tribune*, *Writing!*, and other publications. Currently, he is writing a book about his experiences as a teacher.

JORDAN CLARY grew up in Ohio and for the past 25 years has lived in various locations around the western United States. She currently resides in southern California. She recently completed a novel and also wrote the text for a coffee-table book on murals in rural California. She has worked as a writer-in-residence at both elementary and high schools. For several years, as a contract artist through the William James Association, she taught writing and literature at two California state prisons. She has published poetry and fiction with a number of small and literary presses, and essays in two other T&W anthologies—*Classics in the Classroom* and *The Alphabet of the Trees*. Clary has received grants from the California Arts Council and the Ludwig Volgestien Foundation.

JEFF S. DAILEY was the Assistant Principal, Supervision, in charge of English, Music, Art, and Library at Grover Cleveland High School in Ridgewood, Queens, New York City, when he wrote this article. He is now the Director of Fine and Performing Arts for the Deer Park School District in Suffolk County, New York. His article "Dealing with Dragons," on teaching *Beowulf*, appears in T&W's *Classics in the Classroom*.

CHRISTOPHER EDGAR's poems have recently appeared in *Boston Review*, *Sal Mimeo*, *Best American Poetry 2000*, and *Best American Poetry 2001*. He has co-edited a number of books on education, including *Educating the Imagination, Volumes 1 & 2*, and is the translator of *Tolstoy as Teacher: Leo Tolstoy's Writings on Education*. He is Publications Director of Teachers & Writers Collaborative.

PENNY HARTER has published fifteen books of poems—five since 1994: *Shadow Play: Night Haiku*, *Stages and Views*, *Grandmother's Milk*, *Turtle Blessing*, and *Lizard Light: Poems from the Earth*. A new collection, *Buried in the Sky*, will be published by La Alameda Press in late summer of 2001. Her work appears in numerous anthologies and magazines worldwide, and her autobiographical essay appears in the 1999 edition of *Contemporary Authors, Volume 172*. She has won awards from the New Jersey State Council on the Arts, the Geraldine R. Dodge Foundation, and the Poetry Society of America, and she has just been named the first recipient of the William O. Douglas Nature Writing Award (best in the book) by John Murray, editor of the forthcoming *American Nature Writing 2002* (Fulcrum Publishers). She lives in Santa Fe, New Mexico, and teaches at Santa Fe Preparatory School.

DANIEL KANE has poems published in *The Hat*, *The Denver Quarterly*, *TriQuarterly*, and other magazines. He is an Assistant Professor of English at Kingsborough Community College in Sheepshead Bay. His book on the poetic community of the Lower East Side in the 1960s will be published by the University of California Press in 2002. He is often melancholy.

GARY LENHART is the author of five collections of poetry, including *Father and Son Night* and *Light Heart* (both Hanging Loose Press). He has contributed poems, essays, and reviews to many magazines and anthologies, and was an editor of the magazines *Mag City* and *Transfer*. He was also an editor of *Clinch: Selected Poems of Michael Scholnick* (Coffee House) and *The T&W Guide to William Carlos Williams* (Teachers & Writers Collaborative). He teaches writing at Dartmouth College.

PHILLIP LOPATE is the author of ten books, including *Being with Children, Portrait of My Body*, and *The Rug Merchant*, and is the editor of *The Art of the Personal Essay*. He teaches at Hofstra University.

ANGE MLINKO is author of *Matinées* (Zoland Books), a book of poems, and is editor of *The Poetry Project Newsletter*.

YVONNE MURPHY is Assistant Professor of Cultural Studies at SUNY Empire State College on Long Island.

CHARLES NORTH's books of poems include *New & Selected Poems* (Sun & Moon) and *The Nearness of the Way You Look Tonight* (Adventures in Poetry). His *No Other Way: Selected Prose* was published by Hanging Loose Press. He received an NEA Creative Writing Fellowship for 2001.

JULIE PATTON is a poet, visual artist, and vocalist. Her most recent work can be found in *The Hat 2, Moving Borders: Three Decades of Innovative Writing by Women* (Talisman), and *Experimentation and Innovation in African American Literature* (Tripwire). A third collection of her poetry, *Typographical Topographies*, is forthcoming from Tender Buttons. Patton tours and performs with Uri Caine, Don Byron, and Barnaby McAll. She has taught at Case Western Reserve University, New York University, the Naropa Institute, and for Teachers & Writers Collaborative.

KRISTIN PREVALLET is a poet and writer whose essays have appeared in *Poets & Writers, The Chicago Review, Boxkite*, and *Jacket*. She has been a writer-in-residence with Teachers & Writers Collaboorative for three years, and also teaches at Pratt Institute in Brooklyn. She is the author of one book of poetry, *Perturbation, My Sister* (First Intensity Press).

JULIE MOULDS RYBICKI has a M.F.A. in Creative Writing and has published one volume of poems, *The Woman with a Cubed Head* (New Issues Press, 1998). She taught Writing for Elementary Teachers and Children's Literature for seven years at Western Michigan University. She is currently writing a series of sonnets inspired by Edward Lear's limericks.

MARK STATMAN's poetry, fiction, and essays have appeared in numerous journals and collections, including *Tin House, conduit, The Village Voice*, and *The Nation*, and, among others, *Luna, Luna: Creative Writing Ideas from Spanish, Latino, and Latin American Literature; Sing the Sun Up: Creative Writing Ideas from African-American Literature;* and *World Poets.* He is the author of *Listener in the Snow* and co-edited, with Christian McEwen, *The Alphabet of the Trees: A Guide to Nature Writing.* A recipient of fellowships from the National Endowment for the Arts and the National Writers Project, he was awarded the Gold Key in 1991 and the Jubilee Award in 2000 by the Columbia Scholastic Press Association. Since 1985, Statman has taught writing for Teachers & Writers Collaborative and at Eugene Lang College of New School University. He lives in Brooklyn with his wife and son.

One of SAM SWOPE's children's books, *The Arboolies of Liberty Street*, is being made into an opera. He has taught writing for Teachers & Writers Collaborative since 1988. Swope acknowledges the Spencer Foundation, the Overbrook Foundation, and the Thomas Phillips and Jane Morre Johnson Foundation for their support of his work.

LORENZO THOMAS is Professor of English at University of Houston-Downtown. He is a widely published poet whose books include *The Bathers, Chances Are Few*, and *Es Gibt Zeugen/There Are Witnesses* (OBEMA Series, Editions Klaus Isele, 1996). He is also editor of *Sing the Sun Up: Creative Writing Ideas from African American Poetry* and author of the critical study *Extraordinary Measures: Afrocentric Modernism and 20th-Century American Poetry* (University of Alabama Press).

LEWIS WARSH is the author of two novels, *Agnes & Sally* and *A Free Man*; two volumes of stories, *Money Under the Table* and *Touch of the Whip*; and numerous books of poems, including *Avenue of Escape* and *The Origin of the World* . He is co-editor, with Anne Waldman, of *The Angel Hair Anthology*, published by Granary Books in Fall 2001. He has taught at

SUNY Albany, Fairleigh Dickinson, The New School, Naropa University and The Poetry Project. He is presently on the faculty at Long Island University in Brooklyn.

BILL ZAVATSKY has published two books of poems and two books of translations, the last of which, *Earthlight*, poems by André Breton, won the PEN/Book-of-the-Month Club Prize for translation. He taught under the auspices of the Teachers & Writers Collaborative for many years and since 1987 has taught English in New York City at the Trinity School.

OTHER T&W BOOKS YOU MIGHT ENJOY

Handbook of Poetic Forms, edited by Ron Padgett. Seventy-four entries by nineteen teaching poets. "A treasure."—*Kliatt*. "A small wonder."—*Poetry Project Newsletter*. Revised second edition.

The Alphabet of the Trees: A Guide to Nature Writing, edited by Christian McEwen and Mark Statman. A superb collection of essays about teaching all aspects and forms of nature writing, including field journals, poems, fiction, and nonfiction.

The Dictionary of Wordplay by Dave Morice. Over 1500 endlessly fascinating entries covering all the myriad forms of wordplay. "The most ingenious publication of the new millennium."—*Times Literary Supplement*.

The Teachers & Writers Guide to Walt Whitman, edited by Ron Padgett. Fifteen poets offer practical ideas for fresh ways to read Whitman and to write poetry and prose inspired by him. "A lively, fun, illuminating book."—Ed Folsom, University of Iowa, editor of *The Walt Whitman Quarterly Review*.

The Teachers & Writers Guide to William Carlos Williams, edited by Gary Lenhart. Seventeen practical and innovative essays on using Williams's short poems, fiction, nonfiction, and long poem *Paterson*. "Wonderful—such a thorough and fine job."—Robert Coles.

The Teachers & Writers Guide to Frederick Douglass, edited by Wesley Brown. "An impressive collection [of essays on teaching Douglass' *Narrative*], well-written . . . very usable . . . particularly inspiring."—*Contemporary Education*.

Luna, Luna: Creative Writing Ideas from Spanish, Latin American, & Latino Literature, edited by Julio Marzán. In 21 lively and practical essays, poets, fiction writers, and teachers tell how they use the work of García Lorca, Neruda, Cisneros, and others to inspire students to write imaginatively. "Succeeds brilliantly."—*Kliatt*.

Sing the Sun Up: Creative Writing Ideas from African American Literature, edited by Lorenzo Thomas. Twenty teaching writers present new and exciting ways to motivate students to write imaginatively, inspired by African American poetry, fiction, essays, and drama. "Especially helpful to language arts teachers on both the elementary and secondary level."—*Kliatt*.

Classics in the Classroom, edited by Christopher Edgar and Ron Padgett. Presents fascinating strategies for using great literature—by Homer, Sappho, Rumi, Ovid, Bashō, Shelley, and others—to inspire imaginative writing. "English teachers at any level will find ideas and approaches that will liven up their classes."—*Kliatt*.

For a free copy of the complete catalogue of T&W books, contact:

Teachers & Writers Collaborative
5 Union Square West, New York, NY 10003-3306
tel. (toll-free) 888-BOOKS-TW
Visit our World Wide Web site at www.twc.org